PRISON ELITE

How Austrian Chancellor Kurt Schuschnigg
Survived Nazi Captivity

After the *Anschluss* (annexation) in 1938, the Nazis forced Austrian
Chancellor Kurt Schuschnigg to resign and kept him imprisoned
for seven years, until his rescue by the Allies in 1945. Schuschnigg's
privileged position within the concentration camp system allowed
him to keep a diary and to write letters which were smuggled out
to family members.

Drawing on these records, *Prison Elite* paints a picture of a little-
known aspect of concentration camp history: the life of a VIP prisoner.
Schuschnigg, who was a devout Catholic, presents his memoirs as
a "confession," expecting absolution for any political missteps and,
more specifically, for his dictatorial regime in the 1930s. As Erika
Rummel reveals in fascinating detail, his autobiographical writings
are frequently unreliable.

Prison Elite describes the strategies Schuschnigg used to survive
his captivity emotionally and intellectually. Religion, memory of
better days, friendship, books and music, and maintaining a sense
of humour allowed him to cope. A comparison with the memoirs
of fellow captives reveals these tactics to be universal.

Studying Schuschnigg's writing in the context of contemporary
prison memoirs, *Prison Elite* provides unique insight into the life of
a VIP prisoner.

ERIKA RUMMEL is a Professor Emerita in the Department of History
at Wilfrid Laurier University.

PRISON ELITE

How Austrian Chancellor
Kurt Schuschnigg Survived
Nazi Captivity

Erika Rummel

UNIVERSITY OF TORONTO PRESS
Toronto Buffalo London

Toronto Buffalo London
utorontopress.com
Printed in the U.S.A.

ISBN 978-1-4875-2757-0 (cloth)   ISBN 978-1-4875-2760-0 (EPUB)
ISBN 978-1-4875-2758-7 (paper)   ISBN 978-1-4875-2759-4 (PDF)

Library and Archives Canada Cataloguing in Publication

Title: Prison elite : how Austrian Chancellor Kurt Schuschnigg survived
    Nazi captivity / Erika Rummel.
Names: Rummel, Erika, 1942– author.
Description: Includes bibliographical references and index.
Identifiers: Canadiana (print) 20210161094 | Canadiana (ebook) 20210161760 |
    ISBN 9781487527570 (cloth) | ISBN 9781487527587 (paper) |
    ISBN 9781487527600 (EPUB) | ISBN 9781487527594 (PDF)
Subjects: LCSH: Schuschnigg, Kurt, 1897–1977. | LCSH: Statesmen –
    Austria – Biography. | LCSH: Statesmen – Austria – Diaries. |
    LCSH: Statesmen – Austria – Correspondence. | LCSH: World War,
    1939–1945 – Prisoners and prisons, German – Biography. |
    LCSH: World War, 1939–1945 – Prisoners and prisons, German – Diaries. |
    LCSH: World War, 1939–1945 – Prisoners and prisons, German –
    Correspondence. | LCSH: World War, 1939–1945 – Concentration camps. |
    LCSH: Sachsenhausen (Concentration camp) | LCGFT: Biographies.
Classification: LCC DB98.S3 R86 2021 | DDC 943.605/12092–dc23

University of Toronto Press acknowledges the financial assistance to its
publishing program of the Canada Council for the Arts and the Ontario
Arts Council, an agency of the Government of Ontario.

Canada Council   Conseil des Arts
for the Arts   du Canada

ONTARIO ARTS COUNCIL
CONSEIL DES ARTS DE L'ONTARIO
an Ontario government agency
un organisme du gouvernement de l'Ontario

Funded by the   Financé par le
Government   gouvernement
of Canada   du Canada

Canadä

Contents

Contents

Acknowledgments

I am grateful to my friends and colleagues Susan Ingram, Karin MacHardy, and Milton Kooistra for their help and advice. Thanks are due also to Karin Holzer, Christoph Mentschl, James Baker, Nancy Lyon, and James King as well as the staff at the Austrian State Archive, the Institut für Zeitgeschichte at the University of Vienna, the Sterling Library at Yale University and the library of the University of Warwick respectively. Finally, I would like to thank the anonymous reviewers of the manuscript for their incisive comments, Anne Laughlin for her sharp-eyed copyediting, and Stephen Shapiro for shepherding this book through the publication process. I am greatly obliged to them for their time and effort on my behalf.

PRISON ELITE

How Austrian Chancellor Kurt Schuschnigg
Survived Nazi Captivity

Introduction

Sachsenhausen, 1942. Our home is quite nice. Outside: wood panelling. Inside: central heating and electric stove. Rooms small but adequate for our needs: 4 full-sized and 2 small rooms, plus kitchen and bath.

Few people in wartime Germany enjoyed the luxury of central heating and a functional electric stove – least of all prisoners in concentration camps. Yes, the cozy wood-panelled cottage described above was located in a concentration camp just north of Berlin, where Kurt Schuschnigg was interned 1941–5. Some 100,000 Jews and political prisoners died in Sachsenhausen. According to the testimony given by Camp Commander Anton Kaindl at his 1947 trial in Berlin: "There was an execution place where prisoners were shot to death, a mobile gallows and a mechanical gallows which was used for hanging 3 or 4 prisoners at a time ... In March 1943, I introduced gas chambers for mass exterminations."[1]

The atrocities committed in concentration camps and the horror of the gas chambers are well documented and widely known. However, the existence of elite or "VIP" sections within the various camps is not common knowledge. No ordinary prisoner ever entered these special areas. Primo Levi writes in *Survival in Auschwitz* that they "were reserved for the *Prominenz*": the famous, the wealthy, the aristocrats.[2] The Nazis segregated prisoners who had powerful connections in the outside world and whose death or disappearance would have raised inconvenient questions for the regime. Toward the end of the war, as defeat became certain, these elite prisoners came to be seen as valuable hostages and were therefore moved to safe places.[3] Kurt Schuschnigg, the last chancellor of Austria before the Anschluss, belonged to that select group, and the description of his home in the concentration camp Sachsenhausen comes from a letter he wrote to his uncle on 15 January 1942.[4] He was assigned a house and, on his insistence, household help. He was permitted to live with his wife and infant daughter. But however privileged his position, Schuschnigg was a prisoner, torn from normal life, incarcerated without due process, and increasingly without hope of release. His writings give evidence of the trauma he suffered as a result of his overnight transformation from leader of a country to a non-person. He was first kept in solitary confinement at Gestapo headquarters in Vienna and Munich (May 1938 to December 1941), and then transported to the concentration camp Sachsenhausen, where he was interned until his liberation by the Allies in May 1945.

Schuschnigg's years of incarceration are the focus of my book. My purpose is to document the material conditions of his imprisonment and to explore, through a critical reading of his diaries and letters, Schuschnigg's management of these conditions and his strategies for psychological and intellectual survival. This approach naturally raises the question how to find the "truth" in first-person accounts based on memory and fraught with unstated intent. Working with this type of source requires of the reader a sensitivity to the problems of subjectivity, psychic blocking, and, since "all telling modifies what is being told," to the rhetorical shaping of the material by the author.[5] I examine these problems in more detail in the section below entitled "Sources,"[6] where I discuss the publication history of Schuschnigg's diaries and the changes introduced in the course of the editing process. Other pitfalls are pointed out in the chapters concerned with Schuschnigg's use of memory as a palliative, where I discuss authorial intent and historization.[7] The political context – Hitler's annexation of Austria, the question whether Schuschnigg made wrong decisions or could have done more to save the autonomy of his country, and more generally, the course of World War II – are subjects I consider only in so far as they are relevant to my chief purpose: examining Schuschnigg's coping strategies.

However important (and frustrating) it is for a historian to sort fact from artificial construct and imagination, my book is not centred on the quest for a historical reconstruction. Rather, to quote Bruno Latour, it is important to move on from "matters of fact" to "matters of concern,"[8] from establishing the factual truth of Schuschnigg's narrative to viewing it as a contribution to the collective memory of the Nazi regime. This in turn will encourage reflection on the lasting implications and relevance of Schuschnigg's experience to our time, in which dehumanization and wrongful imprisonment remain a reality.

Schuschnigg sees his diaries as "bearing witness to the attempt of a man to remain a human being." How to ensure "that something of us, as we once were, still remains," was the crucial problem confronting all Nazi prisoners.[9] A great deal has been written by psychologists about the effects of life in prison, and more specifically in concentration camps – famously by Viktor Frankl and notoriously by Bruno Bettelheim.[10] General research interests have shifted over time, from an emphasis on the intense suffering of prisoners at one end of the scale to the "mental freeze" they supposedly experienced at the other. Recent studies have been more nuanced in their assessment of the effects. They tend to focus on the mental resources and inner strength of the prisoner and the bearing these qualities have on the way individuals cope with imprisonment. As a historian, I do not claim to make a contribution to the subject of psychology. Rather, my study makes use of Schuschnigg's first-person accounts as sources of social history. The aim is to investigate his personal beliefs, habits of mind, and cultural interests, and the role they played in sustaining him during his time of incarceration. Although this is one man's story, it casts light more broadly on the patterns of behaviour of the *Bildungsbürger*, the culturally and intellectually engaged bourgeois, in the first half of the twentieth century. Parallels between Schuschnigg's account and the memoirs of other Nazi prisoners will, moreover, point to common denominators in strategies of survival. This is not to draw a facile equation between the experiences of Schuschnigg and Holocaust survivors. On the contrary, the intent is to reinforce the distinction between them and refine our perception of prison hierarchies by introducing a subject that has so far attracted less attention from historians: the life of elite internees.

Although several studies of life in concentration camps mention elites, they refer to the hierarchy within the general camp population and the privileges enjoyed, for example, by veterans over newcomers, non-Jews over Jews, and political prisoners over criminals.[11] I am aware of only one study dealing specifically with the subject of elite prisoners: Volker Koop's *In Hitler's Hand: Sonder- und Ehrenhäftlinge der SS* (In Hitler's Hand: Special and Honorary Prisoners of the SS). Unlike my book, however, which examines strategies of emotional and intellectual survival, Koop's researches the reasons and circumstances which led to the capture of prominent individuals and focuses on their treatment in Nazi prisons. Indeed, this has been for a long time the general trend in research. In studies describing the lives of prisoners in concentration camps, their thoughts, emotions, cultural expressions, and social engagements often take a back seat to more easily verifiable factual evidence.[12] To a certain extent, this reflects the nature of the sources. The trend to concentrate on the facts is noticeable in many of the autobiographical writings of survivors, perhaps because it is easier to describe the manifestations of cruelty and to let them speak for themselves than to express the feelings and thoughts they evoked.[13] Another reason for the emphasis on external evidence may be the intended function of these first-person accounts. While some inmates wrote for themselves, to allow their minds to rise above the painful reality and to preserve a sense of self,[14] the majority of concentration camp survivors conceived of their accounts as transcending the function of a diary. They were more than records of an individual's experience. They were public documents. The writers regarded their accounts as witness reports attesting to the crimes of the Nazi regime rather than as testimony to their own victimization. Rudolf Wunderlich, a political prisoner at Sachsenhausen, specifically speaks of his duty "to be available as a witness when the hour comes for an accounting before the law." The memoirists also regarded their writings as an important didactic tool since "for young people history is often just so many words. It comes alive only when they learn of the experiences of individuals."[15] It was important for them therefore to focus on the facts, to approximate the language of the courtroom and write in a style "devoid of the frivolity of literature." As Primo Levi explained, "I deliberately assumed the calm sober language of the witness, neither the lamenting tones of the victim nor the irate voice of someone who seeks revenge." Similarly John Lenz, a priest interned in Dachau, stressed that he laid "no claim to literary merit" and that his prime concern was "to present straightforward facts, to give an absolutely truthful account."[16]

Both memoirists and modern researchers had qualms about focusing on the social and cultural aspects of life in concentration camps because they seemed trivial in the face of the enormity of suffering. Harry Naujoks and Arnold Weiss-Rüthel, political prisoners at Sachsenhausen, did describe the cultural events organized by fellow prisoners, but felt obliged to put their accounts into perspective. Weiss-Rüthel wanted to mitigate the bleakness of his memoirs by describing these activities. At the same time, he feared that his "inclination to add the occasional ray of light laid him open to reproaches" because some readers might be misled into thinking conditions in Sachsenhausen "weren't so bad after all." These readers must remember that the purpose of the cultural events was to "wrestle an hour of light from the darkness of our lives." Similarly, Naujoks added almost apologetically that cultural events were not meant purely for entertainment. Lectures were given for the purpose of "political education," and the evenings of skits and music "were primarily aimed at giving the inmates ... a new life impulse." In any case, he says, these efforts reached only about 20 per cent of them. The others were too exhausted to attend. Naujoks felt obliged to offer these explanations because he did "not want to paint a wrong picture" by talking about concerts and plays.[17] Indeed, the social historian Christoph Daxelmüller reports that this was exactly the accusation levelled against him. He was reproached for being insensitive and painting the wrong picture of life in concentration camps by writing about concerts, Christmas celebrations, craftsmanship, and other social and cultural activities.[18]

More recently, however, the trend to focus on the punitive aspects of life in Nazi prisons and concentration camps has been complemented by new work on how prisoners coped with privation and supported each other through cultural activities. The Sachsenhausen Gedenkstätte, for example, now collaborates on the research project "Kultur in nationalsozialistischen Konzentrationslagern – Kultur als Überlebenstechnik" (Culture in Nazi Concentration Camps – Culture as Survival Technique).[19] The new direction of research recognizes that prisoners lost their freedom and their material possessions, but not their social and cultural affiliations. Cultural activities served important functions in retaining a measure of agency, and even constituted a form of resistance in the sense that they were often thwarted by the authorities or pursued secretly.[20] Thus, these activities served a strategic goal and have a place in studies of concentration camps. Maintaining and acting on cultural memories helped preserve the prisoner's humanity in the face of inhuman conditions.[21] They played an important part in the emotional survival of inmates and are therefore also a key element of my study.

It is my intention to outline in this book the role cultural, intellectual, and spiritual pursuits played in Schuschnigg's prison narrative. It is important, however, to contextualize his reminiscences. The following sections will provide the necessary background and introduce readers (1) to the place of Schuschnigg's incarceration, (2) to his life and career, and (3) to the sources used in my research.

1. The Place: Concentration Camp Sachsenhausen

The Gestapo moved Schuschnigg repeatedly, from solitary confinement in Vienna and Munich to the concentration camp in Sachsenhausen, where he spent the longest and final phase of his incarceration. Situated some 30 kilometres north of Berlin on a large plot of land, KZ Sachsenhausen received its first contingent of inmates in the summer of 1936. It was supposed to be a *Vorzeigelager*, a model camp, to demonstrate to visiting government officials that the treatment of prisoners was "hard but fair." The reality was different, however. As one of the prisoners reported, the newcomers were marched through the gate, driven on with sticks. "SS men ranted and waved their pistols, swore at us and uttered threats ... we were not allowed to use the toilets and were left standing all night under glaring searchlights." A number of prisoners died on the transport or overnight. "They were done in by the threats and beatings ... a 63-year-old man begged the commandant to give him the coup de grace and shoot him, but he got only a kick with the boot – he wasn't worth a bullet."[22] Sachsenhausen, then, was primarily a work camp rather than a place of extermination. The authorities dehumanized prisoners through brutality, hard labour, insufficient food, and prolonged psychological assault. In short, Sachsenhausen was a "laboratory of total domination."[23] It would be interesting to know whether Schuschnigg himself realized that the difference between Nazi camps was substantive rather than a matter of degrees of brutality. There is no explicit acknowledgment of this fact in his writings, and I suspect that he, like the majority of his contemporaries, was unaware of the difference, and did not single out the Shoah from the general idea of Nazi atrocities. Indeed, as Michael Rothberg notes, "the perception of the genocide's singularity took decades to emerge" and crystallized only in the 1960s, perhaps under the influence of the testimony given at the Eichmann trial in Jerusalem.[24]

The architectural features of Camp Sachsenhausen were designed to hide the systemic brutality inside and shut it off from public view.[25] The triangular area of the complex was surrounded by a perimeter wall 2½ metres high. An electric fence of barbed wire ran parallel to it on the inside and was reinforced by a second coiled barbed wire fence, called *Spanischer Reiter* (Spanish rider), which kept anyone from even approaching the wall. Guards in eight watchtowers kept machine guns trained on the grounds. Searchlights illuminated the night.[26] Quarters for privileged prisoners were added to the complex on the northeastern edge. A report noted, however, that "the houses were not very favourably situated," meaning not well concealed. "Considering their purpose, they should be located in a more isolated place so that they can't be gawked at (*begafft werden*) by all sorts of people."[27]

Kurt Schuschnigg recorded his first impression on entering the camp in December 1941. He saw a "whole city of shacks and barracks set in a flat, sandy landscape with a few copses of Scotch pine here and there."[28] The region had been celebrated in verse by the poet Theodore Fontane as Schuschnigg noted:

Pine trees dream where ends the wood;
White, fleecy clouds bedeck the sky;
Silence reigns, so deep I hear
The voice of Nature[29]

But Schuschnigg saw only the grey and nameless misery of the camp, the inmates who had been robbed of their individuality and were reduced to ciphers – the numbers tattooed on their arms. He saw "emaciated forms, with ashen faces and flickering eyes, dragging themselves to and fro in absolute silence."[30] At night he heard shots. "The floodlights of the watchtowers moved along the walls and houses. We could hear someone groaning near the barbed-wire fence. So could the guards. A few more shots, a scream, and silence. One of our comrades no longer needs to suffer. Somewhere in this camp a number of five digits has been scratched from the books. It was nothing extraordinary, nothing abnormal." And that was the worst, he writes – it was nothing out of the ordinary.[31] Schuschnigg's shock and dismay mirrors the reaction of other prisoners quartered in the elite section of the camp. The family of Albrecht of Bavaria became Schuschnigg's neighbour in December 1944.[32] Interviewed on Bavarian radio in 2011,[33] the sisters Marie Charlotte and Marie Gabrielle, who were young girls at the time of their incarceration, described the living quarters at Sachsenhausen as *Bungalows* (cottages) separated from each other by walls topped with barbed wire. They recalled their horror when skeletal prisoners were detailed to dig up their garden plot and greedily ate the frozen potatoes left in the ground from the previous year. The sisters acknowledged, "Uns ist es gut gegangen [We were well off]." They did not starve. They received *Wehrmachtsverpflegung* – the same rations as members of the German military. This view is also expressed by Irmingard of Bavaria, another inmate of the special section: "Meals were meagre: a slice of ordinary bread, soup made from roots and cabbage; meat was rare and only in the form of disgusting sausages. Yet, the other inmates of the camp were much worse off. They received less than we, and some of them were brutally abused and tortured."[34]

The section reserved for elite prisoners at Sachsenhausen consisted of four cottages separated from each other, from the outside world, and from the rest of the camp. Next to the wall, on the side that housed the general prison population, was a long, narrow building where pigs were kept and from which emanated a nauseating stench. The Schuschniggs could see the tall stack of the crematorium belching smoke and sometimes raining ashes. One of the guard towers equipped with floodlights was located immediately next to them, overlooking their house. Schuschnigg's neighbours over the period of his imprisonment at Sachsenhausen included the family of the Wittelsbach Prince Albrecht of Bavaria, as well as the family of Crown Prince Rupprecht, the head of the House of Wittelsbach. Rupprecht himself escaped imprisonment, but his wife Antonia was arrested and deported to Sachsenhausen together with her children. Schuschnigg reported their presence in a letter to his uncle in December 1944. He did not identify the family, merely noting that they were aristocracy: "Right next to us – on the other side of the wall, there are no fewer than five children, from a region close to home, though of a higher social rank. Vera [Schuschnigg's wife] knows the parents."[35] Vera was allowed to check in and out of camp and had the opportunity to buy supplies, which she occasionally shared with the Wittelsbach families.[36] Schuschnigg regretted only that Sissy, their little daughter, had no opportunity to play with the neighbouring children – unlike the members of the two Wittelsbach families who lived in adjoining houses. They were able to keep each other company when Commandant Kaindl allowed a hole to be knocked into the wall between the two cottages. Another neighbour of Schuschnigg's was the prominent Socialist Rudolf Breitscheid, "a venerable kindly old man," and his wife.[37] Schuschnigg communicated with them occasionally by wrapping messages around stones and lobbing them over the wall.[38] Breitscheid was later moved to Buchenwald and died there when a bomb struck the camp. "After him came Prince Louis de Bourbon-Parme and his wife, Princess Maria of Savoy, a daughter of the king of Italy, with two charming children," Schuschnigg reports.[39] Another prominent occupant was Lieutenant Colonel John ("Mad Jack") Churchill, a man known for his derring-do. That is when Schuschnigg saw "for the first time in this war a British air force uniform." He also reports that "the French statesmen Paul Reynaud and [Edouard] Daladier were kept [in one of the houses] for a while, but we never had a chance of getting in touch with them, beyond a friendly nod of the head when they were marched past us." The two men had been captured in 1940 when the Nazis invaded France. "Afterwards, their lodgings were occupied by the well-known German industrialist Fritz Thyssen."[40] He and his wife had been transferred to Sachsenhausen in May 1943 after having been interned in a psychiatric clinic for two and a half years.[41]

In 1944 Sachsenhausen became subject to air raids by the Allies.[42] Heavy bombardment in March and April 1945 led to the death of hundreds of prisoners and finally prompted the evacuation of the camp, beginning on the night of 21 April. Some 33,000 prisoners were marched in groups of 500 northwest in the direction of Hamburg. Anyone who was too sick or too weak to go on was shot by the SS. Many prisoners died of starvation or exhaustion before they could be rescued by advancing Allied troops and the International Red Cross. The special prisoners, among them Schuschnigg and his family, were trucked by the Nazis from Sachsenhausen to southern Tyrol by a circuitous route; there they were, finally, liberated by American troops.[43]

2. The Man: Schuschnigg's Life and Career

Kurt von Schuschnigg was born in 1897, the elder of two brothers. The family had roots in Tyrol, a region with a long-standing tradition of engaged patriotism going back to 1809, when farmers in the mountain villages fought a guerrilla war against Napoleon's soldiers. Schuschnigg saw himself as an heir to this tradition. He connected his attempts to preserve Austria's autonomy with "being a Tyrolian by birth." A man of his ancestry, he said, could not allow his country to become "a colony and province of the German Reich."[44]

His habits of mind were shaped not only by Tyrolian history but also by the traditions of the Catholic church. He received his education at the Jesuit boarding school Stella Matutina and throughout his life demonstrated a strong allegiance to the church. The school, as he noted, "exercised a decisive influence on my career and outlook ... and the older I get, the more conscious I am of it." There he was taught that "loyalty to the state and loyalty to the nationality ought to supplement each other."[45] Schuschnigg's father was a career soldier. It was the practice in army circles, he writes, to send their children to boarding school at an early age since "they would inherit nothing except a good education."[46] Immediately after his high school graduation in 1915, Schuschnigg enlisted and served as a lieutenant during World War I. After the war, he studied law in Innsbruck. Credited for his years of military service, he obtained his degree in two years and began practising as a lawyer.

Schuschnigg dances around the question of his career choice in his autobiographical account, *Ein Requiem in Rot-Weiss-Rot*. Was he motivated by patriotism or practical considerations? Returning home from the war at the age of twenty, he was torn – "at a crossroads," as he put it. Interestingly, he speaks of himself in the third person, as if he wanted to distance himself from his account: "Feelings and reason pointed in different directions. After a brief inner conflict, he decided to follow the path of feelings. And so he remained first and foremost an Austrian" – meaning presumably that it was typical of an Austrian to follow his feelings. This analysis does not quite fit the first-person account given in the next paragraph: "To follow my heart, I would have liked to study literature and the history of art as well as general history, but I had no choice." For financial reasons, "I could only go for the shortest and therefore most economical solution to the question." The devaluation of the Austrian currency after the war had reduced his savings to a pittance. The pension of his father "was almost below the poverty level."[47] Similarly, he declares (using the third person again) that "on this path there was no politics in sight. He rejected politics because he found it fruitless and could not relate to its representatives." Switching to the first person, he writes that he became a member of a Catholic fraternity "so as not to become a loner and lose all contact." But fraternities did have strong political associations in those days, and he admits that he was soon involved in *hochschulpolitischen Funktionen* – political functions at the university.[48] A few years later, he entered politics and in 1927 was elected to the national assembly as a representative of the right-wing Christian Social Party.

The burning question in the years after World War I, which had led to the defeat and dissolution of the Austrian empire, was, Should Austria join Germany, and what form should such a union take? The Christian Social Party, under the leadership of Ignaz Seipel, a priest and theologian, was generally seen as nostalgic for the monarchy, but there was some ambivalence among members and considerable differences in opinion about the question of a union with Germany. Seipel himself was hard to read. He left his options open, or as he put it, he wasn't sure "whether the good Lord wanted to have us become German Austrians."[49] Although Schuschnigg suggested that Seipel was deliberately vague, adopting the motto "always talk about it, never think of doing it," the Christian Social Party did in fact draw up a programmatic document, the so-called Sylvester Programm (31 December 1926), in which they expressed a will to maintain Austria's autonomy but, ominously, combined this statement with antisemitic sentiments. The party would fight "the destructive Jewish influence in the intellectual and economic realm." They welcomed a closer relationship with the German empire "on the basis of the right to self-determination." Seipel himself feared that Austria would become a mere province of Germany in the case of an Anschluss: "Under the leadership of Prussia, God has no further use for us."[50]

The political scene changed with Hitler's accession to power in January 1933. Seipel's successor, Engelbert Dollfuss, had to reckon not only with militant Marxists, but also with the growing Austrian branch of Hitler's party. He chose a radical solution to the economic and political problems that plagued Austria and had brought the country to the verge of civil war. He eliminated parliament and established a corporate state, or, rather, "an improvised dictatorship."[51]

Schuschnigg, who served under Dollfuss as minister of justice (1932) and minister of culture (1933), fully endorsed the chancellor's action. As he saw it, "the general atmosphere was poisoned," and Dollfuss had no option but to proclaim martial law. There was danger "that the radical wings of the left and right might, for the sake of temporary convenience, join forces against the government." To avoid this, "there was only one thing to do: to localize the conflagration at all costs, and if necessary with the harshest means."[52] As it was, the Nazis acted on their own and staged a coup d'état in July 1934. The attempt was unsuccessful, but Dollfuss was shot and killed by an assassin. Schuschnigg succeeded him as chancellor.

The times required a visionary. Schuschnigg was merely an experienced bureaucrat when he took the helm of the state. The American journalist Dorothy Thompson gave a shrewd assessment of him in 1938: "A dry man, rather stiff; formal and intellectual, with the precise and subtle mind of one trained by the Jesuits. He had been a soldier in his youth; a lawyer; a politician without the politician's facile urbanity. Ungifted, one would say, for public life."[53]

The émigré Hans Kohn, then teaching at Smith College in Massachusetts, characterized the chancellor in similar terms. Reviewing Schuschnigg's book *Dreimal Österreich*, which appeared in 1938, Kohn contrasted him with "the dictators in neighboring countries" (that is, Hitler and Mussolini). Schuschnigg "argues and reasons quietly, there is no appeal to mass emotions or violence in his words. The book is written in as restrained and reasonable a way as a book by any Western statesman. The author does not strike the reader as an especially forceful person, but as clever and, within the traditional bounds of his upbringing, well-meaning and intelligent."[54]

The years following Schuschnigg's appointment as chancellor brought not only political turmoil but also personal difficulties for him. In 1935 his wife, Herma, died in a car accident, leaving Schuschnigg with sole responsibility for the upbringing of his nine-year-old son.[55] A year later, he became involved with Vera Czernin, an attractive and vivacious divorcée.[56] In his own words, "they found each other ... two people who were no longer romantic youngsters, who had been taught a stern lesson in the school of life." Because of Schuschnigg's prominent position, the couple was in the limelight. Then, as now, the affairs of celebrities were of titillating interest to the public, especially in a society that still regarded divorce as scandalous and did not sanction cohabitation. "Everybody had his own version, his own mixture of truth and fiction, his own spicy details to add to the stories that appeared in the papers," Schuschnigg wrote. Paparazzi hounded the couple, gossip columnists discussed their relationship. At the time of Schuschnigg's arrest by the Gestapo in 1938, Vera was staying with him at his official residence in Belvedere Palace. The press was informed that he had been taken "to the Hotel Metropole [Gestapo headquarters] because we had to make an end of the scandalous concubinage which existed in his own house." Schuschnigg resented these aspersions on his relationship and felt obliged to clarify the situation in his memoirs. "Our intention was marriage. Both of us are convinced Catholics and we regarded ourselves as strictly bound by the laws of the church governing marriage. My fiancée had been free for several years, and I had been a widower for about one year ... The first marriage of my fiancée had been – quite independently of our case – annulled in a regular canonic process by the unanimous verdict of the Ecclesiastical Court at Vienna."[57] The annulment was confirmed by the papal court. Schuschnigg denied that he had called in any special favours to obtain the annulment, although his son Kurt notes in his memoirs that Schuschnigg "had developed a close bond" with Pope Pius XII.[58] Waiting for the annulment had presumably delayed Schuschnigg's marriage plans. He felt that as chancellor he could not afford even a shadow of doubt about his private life, but resignation was not an option. "My resignation for personal reasons would have been akin to treason in the minds of those who believed in my policy."[59]

The political situation Schuschnigg confronted on his appointment as chancellor was complex. He saw himself as the "executor of Dollfuss' political testament,"[60] but rejected the label

"Austrofascism" to characterize the regime. It is a fact, however, that he concentrated executive power in his own hands. His tenure is therefore rightly characterized as a *Kanzlerdiktatur* (chancellorial dictatorship).[61] Schuschnigg furthermore declined proposals to legitimize the autocratic constitution introduced by Dollfuss in 1934 by holding a plebiscite or an election. Democracy was not an option at the time, he declared. "The Austrian government could not afford to hold elections [since they] would not have been managed by our government from Vienna, but by Hitler from Berlin and Munich."[62]

Indeed, Schuschnigg was facing a precarious situation in the aftermath of Dollfuss' assassination. During a brief respite in which Hitler pulled back, dissociating himself from the failed coup, Schuschnigg attempted to shore up Austria's defences. He looked for support in the West, but with little success. So far, Italy had been Austria's main guarantee against German aggression. By 1937, however, Mussolini was aligning himself with Hitler, and it became imperative for Schuschnigg to take independent action. No doubt, he made political mistakes and tactical errors in not attempting a rapprochement with the left,[63] but in the face of Germany's mounting aggression, the rise of Italian fascism, and the politics of appeasement pursued by the Western powers, his efforts were doomed. An agreement signed between Germany and Austria in July 1936 and a personal meeting between Schuschnigg and Hitler in Berchtesgaden in February 1938 settled nothing and only underlined Austria's weak position, which forced Schuschnigg to make significant concessions. In Berchtesgaden, Hitler flouted all diplomatic courtesy and treated the Austrian chancellor with marked contempt, keeping him waiting, forbidding him to smoke in his presence, and shouting at him. He made it clear, moreover, that Schuschnigg could not count on help from the outside world to fend off a German invasion. According to Schuschnigg, Hitler told him bluntly: "Don't think for one moment that anybody on earth is going to thwart my decisions. Italy? I see eye to eye with Mussolini ... And England? England will not move one finger for Austria ... And France? Well three years ago we marched on the Rhineland with a handful of battalions, that was the time I risked everything. If France had stopped us then, we would have had to retreat ... but now it is too late for France." Schuschnigg's suppression of Austrian Nazis was provocative, Hitler declared. He could not be expected to stand by idle "when people are thrown into jail in Austria merely because they sing a song that you don't like or because they salute each other with 'Heil Hitler.' The persecution of National Socialists in Austria must have an end or else I shall put an end to it."[64]

To resolve the increasingly dire situation, Schuschnigg decided to call a plebiscite, not to legitimize the constitution, but to assert the people's will to maintain Austria's independence. The referendum was, however, forestalled by the German invasion of 11 March. Schuschnigg decided not to offer armed resistance. "Did I do everything that could have been done?" he asked rhetorically, "and above all, was what I did right?" He had no definite answer, but insisted that "no matter what course one would have taken in those days, the result would materially have been the same … armed resistance would have in all likelihood increased the number of victims."[65]

The day after the invasion Schuschnigg was forced to resign and was replaced by the Nazi sympathizer Arthur Seyss-Inquart. Austria ceased to exist as a country and became the "Ostmark" – the eastern province of Germany. Schuschnigg himself was arrested by the Gestapo and remained in captivity until 1945.

After the war, Schuschnigg bristled at the suggestion that his autocratic government had brought about Austria's downfall in 1938. He categorically denied that domestic struggles had provided Hitler with an opportunity to intervene: "That this view is erroneous has been shown by what happened to other countries which did not have to contend with similar difficulties and yet fell a prey to Nazi expansion." He insisted that he himself, as well as "Austria was a victim of foreign aggression."[66]

3. The Sources

For my study of Schuschnigg's strategies of coping with his seven-year imprisonment, I am drawing primarily on two sources: his diaries and a collection of letters addressed to his brother Artur and his uncle Hermann Wopfner, respectively.

Schuschnigg's recollections are atypical in several respects. Unlike most writers recording their experiences in Gestapo prisons and concentration camps, Schuschnigg was no amateur. He was a published author.[67] Also, most first-person accounts are memoirs. Few were written during captivity, either because inmates lacked the necessary writing materials[68] or were too worn out by forced labour, malnutrition, and mental anguish to muster the energy to write. It was "an unthinkable luxury for the Jews," Primo Levi writes, "and a possibility of no interest to criminals."[69] Schuschnigg had the impulse, the leisure, and the privacy to write. Few inmates – even among special prisoners – had control over their daily routine. Most of them were locked up in cell blocks and depended on the whim of their guards, like Pastor Martin Niemöller or the English agent Sigismund Payne-Best, who was routinely handcuffed at night, or Mafalda of Hesse, who shared a primitive barrack with the Breitscheids and other prisoners in Buchenwald.[70] By contrast, the house assigned to Schuschnigg resembled a normal single-family home. Schuschnigg's case was singular, moreover, in that he remained in the house assigned to him for more than three years. This provided him with a certain stability, whereas the stay of other special prisoners was transitory. Each time they were moved to a different location, they had to go through "the strenuous process of change and adaption (*Umgewöhnung*) all over again," as Isa Vermehren noted in her memoir. Similarly, Payne-Best comments: "When one is a prisoner one becomes most conservative in one's outlook, and nothing is more upsetting than any change from the accustomed routine ... there is that curious feeling that so long as there is no change, one is safe." This sentiment is echoed by Primo Levi: "We all had a certain dread of changes. 'When things change, they change for the worse' was one of the proverbs of the camp."[71] The stability of place enjoyed by Schuschnigg no doubt facilitated his keeping a record of his life in captivity. Yet he was in constant fear that his writings might be confiscated by the authorities and that he would be punished for any criticism of the Nazi regime.

All prison diarists took risks when they recorded their observations. Even a child understood that. Twelve-year-old Zuzana Justman, who was imprisoned with her parents at Terezín

(Teresienstadt), remembers, "Because I was fearful that the diary could fall into German hands and bring harm to my family, I rarely expressed myself freely in it."[72] Odd Nansen, a political prisoner from Norway, reports that someone at the Sachsenhausen camp was found keeping a diary and suffered reprisals. He reflected, "I'm wondering whether I shouldn't leave off."[73] Schuschnigg himself said that he "was tempted more than once to destroy the entire work."[74] Fear of discovery put constraints on what he could openly express. The American war correspondent William Shirer was a free man when he wrote his diary, yet shared Schuschnigg's fear of the Gestapo. "I jotted things down from day to day," he writes. Some of the notes were lost, "others I burned rather than risk them and myself to the tender mercies of the Gestapo; a few things I dared not write down ... in a few cases I was forced to reconstitute from memory the happenings of the day, conscious of the pitfalls of such a method." Arnold Weiss-Rüthel, who had failed to take such precautions, suffered the consequences. The Gestapo searched his home and found his diaries. The contents supplied them with enough evidence to incarcerate him.[75]

Schuschnigg was able to smuggle his writings out of Sachsenhausen. He brought them along on the journey that took him to freedom and published them shortly after his rescue by the Allies. In a letter of 6 September 1945 to his brother he reported that he received an advance from the Italian publisher Mondadori "even before he had seen the manuscript. I assume the book will appear at the end of the winter in Italian, English, and French, but I don't expect a shower of gold – more like a sigh here and there."[76]

As Jeffrey Olick states in his study of memory: "The past is always remade in the present for present purposes."[77] This also goes for memoirs, which are written with hindsight and from the standpoint of a later self. The great advantage of diaries written in real time is their unfiltered contents. This advantage is, however, reduced in Schuschnigg's case by the complex, not to say bewildering, publication history, which suggests significant editorial interference. As Schuschnigg reports, the manuscript was acquired by Mondadori and brought out in 1947 under the title *Un requiem in rosso-bianco-rosso: Note del detenuto Dottor Auster* (Requiem in

Red-White-Red: Notes of the Prisoner, Doctor Auster).[78] By that time the original German text had already appeared under the title *Ein Requiem in Rot-Weiss-Rot: Aufzeichnungen des Häftlings Dr. Auster*, published by Amstrutz, Herdegg & Co. (Zurich, 1946).[79] Another German text was published by Amalthea after Schuschnigg's death under the title *Requiem in Rot-Weiss-Rot* (Vienna, 1978). In the colophon, the Viennese edition is termed the "first Austrian edition" (*Österreichische Erstausgabe*) and acknowledges the copyright of Mondadori. No reference is made, however, to the prior German-language edition published in Zurich, except in the most cryptic manner. Stephan Verosta,[80] who provided a preface to the text, called the book a *Neuauflage*, an ambiguous word denoting either a reprint or a new edition, and mentions an earlier German-language edition without giving title or place of publication, merely referring to it as "a book that went out of print shortly after its appearance in 1946."[81]

A comparison of the 1946 and 1978 editions shows that the texts are identical, with corresponding page numbers. This is, however, a sleight of hand, since a closer inspection reveals that Schuschnigg's introduction has been eliminated and replaced with Verosta's preface. To achieve a correspondence of pages in spite of the changes to the preliminary matter, the table of contents was moved to the back of the book.[82]

The more important question of course is, How closely does the published version of Schuschnigg's diary correspond to the original notes he made in prison, which are no longer extant? How trustworthy, for example, are the lengthy passages in the book recalling verbatim conversations Schuschnigg had with Hitler (seven pages) and Mussolini (ten pages)? Schuschnigg says he wrote them down "from memory" and "as literally as my memory permits."[83] Did he write them down while in prison or add them later when he readied the manuscript for publication? Few authors of prison diaries recognize or articulate the problem of the relationship between memory and truth, and between spontaneous and edited expressions of thought.[84] Schuschnigg at any rate recognized the value of immediacy (*Unmittelbarkeit*).[85] He also acknowledged the difficulty of maintaining authenticity: "To keep a diary makes sense only if it is in the long run reserved exclusively for one's own eyes. Otherwise, the subconscious regard for an unwanted and inevitable critique acts like a censor looking over one's shoulder. To be allowed at last to have no consideration [for outside opinions] serves inner truthfulness, but that is a gift of the gods which is granted only to the truly free spirit." He admitted that he did not have that privilege. He was required to submit everything he wrote to the Gestapo for inspection, although he managed to keep parts of his manuscript concealed from the authorities.[86] These circumstances affected both the phrasing and the content of his writings and made it necessary for him to edit the text in preparation for publication. He admitted that he inserted or rearranged (*nachträglich gereiht*) unspecified passages. He also added "slight (*geringfügige*) supplementary remarks and corrections."[87] Such editorial interference compromises the integrity of the material or at any rate robs it of its immediacy. This in turn complicates our interpretation of the diaries. Stephan Verosta, the author of the preface to the 1978 edition, acknowledged the fact that Schuschnigg had reworked (*umgearbeitet*) the text but did not address the implications of that reworking.[88] Anton Hopfgartner, a historian who made use of the diaries for his biography of Schuschnigg,[89] went a step further. He compared an extant typescript of some 200 pages with the corresponding pages of the published version of *Requiem*.[90] The typescript covers a section discussing the history of Austria between the wars, but unfortunately not the diary entries or the conversations with Hitler and Mussolini. Hopfgartner characterizes the differences between the extant typescript and the printed version of those pages as, for the most part, a softening of Schuschnigg's criticism of Austrian Socialists and the elimination of remarks that might suggest that he was tolerant of Hitler's regime. Such "updating" was to be expected and understandable in view of the climactic turn of events, Hopfgartner writes.[91]

So much for the German language editions of *Requiem*. More problems surface when we look at the English translation of the book. An English version was published in 1946 by Putnam's Sons in New York under the title *Austrian Requiem* and was reprinted a year later by Victor Gollancz in London.[92] The translation was the work of Franz von Hildebrand, who had been active in the resistance in occupied France,[93] but neither Gollancz' nor Putnam's edition mentions the rights of Amstrutz or Mondadori or comment on the text from which Hildebrand translated.

A comparison of the German and English editions shows significant differences – omissions as well as additions. The page count is 516 in German versus 321 in the English edition published in New York. The cuts and changes were at least partly suggested by Schuschnigg himself, as manuscript evidence shows: a note signed and dated "Rome, 26 Febr[uary] 1946" and three typewritten pages of changes requested by Schuschnigg.[94] But the changes listed there do not always correspond to the published edition. We may therefore assume that further negotiations took place between author and publisher. Yet, Schuschnigg claimed in his introduction that "most of [the text] remained exactly as I had written it down during my detention."[95]

A section in the book defending Schuschnigg's actions in the lead-up to the Anschluss may serve as an example of the editing process and its results. In the English text, Schuschnigg admitted to having pursued a "policy of appeasement" with the Nazis. Indeed he used this aim as an excuse, explaining why he appointed Seyss-Inquart, an avowed Nazi, to the post of state councillor. It was a "friendly gesture" to Germany, made only "to avoid friction." He offers no such explanation for the appointment in the German text.[96] Hitler had many followers in Austria in 1938. In the German text, Schuschnigg acknowledged Hitler's attraction: "Hitler is a phenomenon. It would be useless to deny that ... He exerts a magic power on people. Like a magnet, he strongly attracts them and does not let them go or just as vehemently repulses them ... [The latter group] saw the abyss and realized that there is no crossing it. I was one of them."[97] Schuschnigg added apologetically: if his own actions and policies were perceived by some people as ambiguous (*zweischlächtig*), it was because "only Austrians could truly understand Austrian affairs."[98] These comments are missing from the English text.

Generally speaking, political musings – extensive in the German version – are either curtailed or removed altogether from the English text. We can only speculate why Schuschnigg (or his publisher) chose to reword, shorten, or cut out those comments. The publisher may have wanted a book that appealed to a more general readership and decided that American readers were not sufficiently informed about or interested in the details of political and diplomatic manoeuvres in Europe. Alternatively, the editors may have speculated that American readers would not be receptive to Schuschnigg's right-leaning views. As the omissions and rewordings in the sample passage show, there was a decided effort to present the ex-chancellor as Hitler's antagonist and purge even the slightest suggestion to the contrary from the English edition. In any case, the majority of readers were likely more interested in the personal history of Schuschnigg as a Gestapo prisoner and inmate of a concentration camp than in his political analyses. Indeed, the more detailed political references were meaningful only to Austrians who had experienced the effects of Schuschnigg's actions as chancellor. The time of reckoning had come, and many passages missing from the English-language edition specifically addressed Schuschnigg's Austrian critics and had a purely apologetic function.

Stylistic considerations may have played a role as well in the editorial decisions. As we have seen, unadorned statements were generally equated with the truth. The fulsome, and in some places maudlin, expressions Schuschnigg used may not have struck the right note in the judgment of the American publisher. A number of passages that are banal or melodramatic, to say the least, are cut from the English language version, including the following lines: "Night turns into another night. The world goes on. The sun rises and sets again. The lilac blossoms and the autumn leaves swirl in the late warm breeze. Then suddenly there is another 'Happy New Year' and your fate rolls on mechanically in the grooves destined for you."[99]

The overall effect of the cuts and changes is significant enough to say that English speakers were looking at a book substantially different from the one their German counterparts read in 1946. Schuschnigg's admission that he reworked his notes for publication must serve as a caveat to the researcher using his book as a source. Because of editorial interference, the book lost some of its authenticity and turned into a curated product. In the end, however, we have to accept the subjectivity of all testimonial writing and apply to Schuschnigg's diaries the judgment Charlotte Delbo, a political prisoner at Auschwitz, passed on her own: "Today I am not sure that what I wrote is true [*vrai*] but I am certain that it is truthful [*véridique*]."[100]

The second important source for my book is Schuschnigg's correspondence, that is, the letters he (or Vera on his behalf) wrote during his captivity and immediately after his release. Some of them remain unpublished; most of them appeared posthumously, edited by Schuschnigg's nephew Heinrich in collaboration with the historian Dieter Binder. The editors emphasized that they rendered the texts in their original, unabridged form, "ohne Kürzung, Auslassung oder Streichung [without cuts, omissions, or deletions]."[101] In that sense, Schuschnigg's letters retain their authenticity and, as source texts, are preferable to his book, which was edited for publication. Like his prison notes, however, the letters were written with an eye to potential censorship and the risk of interception by the Gestapo. Sensitive material is therefore often couched in ironic terms to camouflage the meaning, or even stated in terms contrary to the meaning, but with a wink to the knowing addressee.

Of the 135 letters in the collection, the bulk are addressed to Schuschnigg's brother, Artur, and to his uncle, Hermann Wopfner. Artur (d. 1990) considered the correspondence too personal to be published during his lifetime. An unknown number of letters exchanged between the brothers are lost, moreover. Schuschnigg destroyed the letters he received to avoid any negative consequences for the writers, should the authorities get hold of the missives. He assured his brother, "To make this clear in advance – you may put your mind completely at rest. I immediately destroy your letters after reading, so there is no danger."[102] Artur did preserve the letters he received from his brother, but some of them were lost when the family's apartment in Berlin was destroyed in an air raid. Hermann Wopfner (d. 1963) likewise preserved the letters he received and kept them in chronological order. That part of the correspondence is therefore likely complete. The letters are very full and provide ample information on Schuschnigg's life in prison and on his state of mind. In fact, Schuschnigg was apologetic about the length and frequency of his letters. He had time on his hands, he told his brother, and "a need to write to you."[103]

In addition to the diaries and letters, which are the main sources for my study, the memoirs of Schuschnigg's son provide helpful information, complementing his father's prison diaries and letters. They were first published in German under the title *Der lange Weg nach Hause: Der Sohn des Bundeskanzlers erinnert sich* (The Long Way Home: The Son of the Chancellor Reminisces [Vienna, 2008]), then in an English translation in which he collaborated with his wife, Janet. It was published under the title *When Hitler Took Austria: A Memoir of Heroic Faith by the Chancellor's Son* (San Francisco, 2012). The recollections of Kurt Schuschnigg Jr confirm and, in some cases, flesh out his father's observations and provide context.

Finally, it is useful to compare Schuschnigg's diaries with the first-person accounts of other inmates in Nazi prisons and concentration camps. They too serve to corroborate Schuschnigg's experiences. Although these accounts are not strictly comparable since survival conditions varied, there are notable parallels in the emotional responses and coping mechanisms, perhaps because they are grounded in human nature and therefore unaffected by specific conditions. Indeed, I have found a surprising overlap between Schuschnigg's tactics and sentiments and those of other prisoners, regardless of nationality, race, or status in the prison hierarchy. There is a meaningful correlation between the accounts even if the protagonists were at opposite ends of the political spectrum, like the Communists Harry Naujoks, Wolfgang Szepansky, and Arnold Weiss-Rüthel, or came from a different national background like the Norwegian Odd Nansen and the British agent Sigismund Payne-Best. Equally remarkable are the parallels between the observations of Schuschnigg, an elite prisoner, and those of Jewish survivors who had overcome extreme conditions, like Victor Frankl, Bruno Bettelheim, and Primo Levi. In short, my study shows that survival strategies have a universal character.

In addition, I have consulted the memoirs of prisoners whose paths crossed with Schuschnigg's and who commented on him. He is mentioned, for example, by Fey von Hassell, Irmingard of

Bavaria, and other members of the Wittelsbach family, as well as Isa Vermehren, Antonie Breitscheid, and Leon Blum. These memoirs also serve as foils to Schuschnigg's writings.

I have arranged the results of my research in chapters elucidating the various reactions and coping mechanisms employed by Schuschnigg, taking my cue from Viktor Frankl who analysed his own experience as an inmate in Dachau. He examined the question, "How was everyday life in a concentration camp reflected in the mind of the average person?"[104] The first phase listed by Frankl is characterized by shock. Initially the prisoner is filled with the delusive hope of reprieve; then he develops a form of apathy, "a kind of emotional death" or a protective shell against suffering. Almost everyone entertained thoughts of suicide during this initial phase, Frankl writes.[105] In the second phase the prisoner develops strategies of survival: nostalgic memory, which lets him escape into a glorified past, a deepening of religious beliefs, and the acceptance that God or fate is his master. This "intensification of inner life helped the prisoner find a refuge from the emptiness, desolation and spiritual poverty of his existence." Prisoners also typically came to the realization that love is the "ultimate and the highest goal to which man can aspire" and would help them preserve their inner selves.[106] Although Frankl emphasized that his concern was not with privileged prisoners but with "the great army of the unknown," the reactions and strategies he describes apply to Schuschnigg's case and are reflected in his diaries and letters.

Chapter 1, "In Isolation: Living under the Enemy's Eye," describes Schuschnigg's imprisonment in Vienna and Munich, where he was kept in solitary confinement. It is well known that human contact and the opportunity to converse take on extreme importance for solitary prisoners. Because Schuschnigg was under 24-hour surveillance, he had continual, but unwanted, contact. This chapter deals with Schuschnigg's handling of his guards, with whom he was forced to interact. Some of them were sympathetic to his plight; others were cynical and sadistic. Detachment and irony were Schuschnigg's only weapons against their cruelty. The chapter will also consider the impact of his limited contacts with the outside world through his teenaged son, Kurt, who was permitted the occasional visit, and through his wife, Vera. The couple were allowed supervised meetings once a week, restricted to a few minutes at first, then extended to more frequent and private visits, which became Schuschnigg's principal source of emotional support.

Chapter 2, "The Sachsenhausen Household: Living *en famille*," describes the conditions in the concentration camp Sachsenhausen, where the Schuschniggs were permitted to live together in the house assigned to him. At this time, Schuschnigg's contacts with the outside world expanded. Vera was permitted to come and go freely and could therefore inform Schuschnigg of current events. During this time, he also kept up a regular correspondence with his brother, Artur, and his uncle, Hermann Wopfner. The letters provided him with an important emotional outlet. They allowed him to vent his feelings, voice complaints, and reminisce, although in a covert manner, since there was danger that his letters might fall into the wrong hands. Vera, however, remained Schuschnigg's emotional mainstay. The chapter examines the dynamics of Schuschnigg's household, which included a succession of maids, his infant daughter, Sissy, and his son, Kurt, who spent part of his vacations with the family. At Sachsenhausen, Schuschnigg also obtained access to his private library, which had been stored in a depot in Vienna (some 2000 books by his own count), and a radio, which had been doctored to receive foreign news. Since the house had a small yard, Schuschnigg furthermore had an opportunity to garden, another valuable aid in coping with his imprisonment.

Chapter 3, "The Comfort of Religion," examines the role religion played in Schuschnigg's attempt to cope with life in captivity. He was by education and personal inclination a devout man, but the experience of incarceration shook his faith. He was able to overcome his doubts, however, and return to his former, solid belief in God. Yet he deeply felt the lack of a spiritual adviser and, more generally, missed the comfort provided by traditional rites like confession, absolution, and communion. He also longed for the inspiration of church music and the aesthetic pleasure of contemplating church architecture.

The next two chapters concern Schuschnigg's engagement in cultural activities, which Maja Suderland identifies as a means for educated prisoners "to preserve human dignity by striving to realize certain aspects of their social identity" and to counter the uncertainty of their lives with something that had permanence, to "suppress the odor of death."[107]

Chapter 4, "The Consolation of Books," considers Schuschnigg's reliance on books for intellectual stimulation and for the spiritual support to be found in the timeless wisdom of the classics. During the first few years, Vera supplied him with books, often borrowed from friends at Schuschnigg's specific request. At Sachsenhausen, he was able to consult books from his own library. He read mostly non-fiction in the areas of history and biography, political science, and philosophy. His readings prompted essay-like reflections in his diary entries. As for fiction, Schuschnigg confined himself mostly to the classics: Homer, Virgil, Dante, and the "greats" of German and Austrian literature, Goethe, Schiller, and Grillparzer. He attempted, not always successfully, to induce his son to read literature during the vacations he spent at Sachsenhausen. Schuschnigg also refreshed and improved his knowledge of foreign languages and, in his diary entries, quoted from works he read in their original languages – English, French, and Italian. He was, moreover, regularly supplied with the official Nazi newspaper, *Der Völkische Beobachter*, which goaded him into entering caustic responses in his diary.

Chapter 5, "Music to His Ears," deals with the comfort and pleasure Schuschnigg derived from listening to music on his radio. The regular German programming – the only legitimate source – was heavily slanted toward popular music and was not always to Schuschnigg's liking. In letters to his brother, he belittles local programming but also expresses his pleasure in the occasional broadcast of music by his favourite composers, Wagner and Beethoven. In his letters, he also makes inquiries about singers and composers he had come to know personally during his term as minister of culture and who were endangered by their resistance to the Nazis or by their Jewish ancestry. The Nazi propaganda which was part of the official radio programming angered Schuschnigg and prompted sharp responses in his diary entries. From those entries it is also apparent that he occasionally listened to illicit foreign broadcasts and knew about the progress of the war. Thus the radio provided him not only with a soothing pastime but also with information, which in the final years of the war served to bolster his spirits. As the Allies advanced, he began to hope for a resolution and delivery from captivity.

Chapter 6, "The Use of Wit," examines Schuschnigg's sense of humour, "another of the soul's weapons in the fight for self-preservation," as Frankl puts it. Schuschnigg's humour is sometimes good-natured and self-deprecating, but more often ironic and directed at his captors. Sharing humour with his brother or uncle through correspondence helped to create a sense of community between them, since irony and sarcasm was meant to pass under the radar of the censors. Thus it excluded outsiders, yet drew those in the know into a closer circle through a complicit understanding. Using satire allowed Schuschnigg to vent his feelings in a covert manner and indulge in the relief provided by laughter.

Chapter 7, "Cherishing Memories," discusses Schuschnigg's use of memory as a way of coping with, and in a way, overlaying the dismal present. They allowed him for a short time to slip into the past and escape the confines of the concentration camp. Significant dates, such as anniversaries, birthdays, Christmas, and Easter, usually prompted him to indulge in memories. They often focused on his parents, especially his mother. Such nostalgic reflections and his glorification of the "good old days," both in his own life and in the history of Austria, were a source of bittersweet solace.

Chapter 8, "Schuschnigg's Political Reminiscences," looks at his reflections as an examination of conscience analogous to the first step in a sacramental confession. His political memories often have religious overtones. Imprisonment takes the place of "penance," and rehabilitation is the "absolution" he expected for his atonement. Schuschnigg admits to having made mistakes, but emphasizes that he always acted in good faith. He believed, moreover, that the events leading up to the Anschluss were fated and therefore inescapable. The conviction that he had acted with integrity allowed him to draw on his political memories as a source of comfort, in the hope that seven years of imprisonment by the Nazis would rehabilitate him in the eyes of posterity.

Although his expectations were disappointed – Schuschnigg faced criticism in his own time and remains a controversial historical figure – the personal conviction that he had acted honourably helped him cope with life in captivity, as did personal memories, a strong religious faith, active intellectual and cultural engagement, and a sense of humour. These strategies – whether employed consciously or unconsciously – clearly emerge from his writings. More significantly, these strategies parallel those found in the autobiographical records of other survivors and give them the universality that allowed Frankl to typify the psychology of prisoners in Nazi camps.

chapter one

In Isolation: Living under the Enemy's Eye

Schuschnigg was in solitary confinement for more than two years, held first at the Hotel Metropole in Vienna, where the Gestapo had set up temporary quarters, then in Munich, in a prison attached to the regular Gestapo quarters. The damaging psychological and physiological effects of solitary confinement are well documented in many first-hand accounts and in the scholarly literature. Humans are social beings. Living in forced isolation constitutes a harsher punishment than the mere loss of freedom. The prison diarist Odd Nansen speaks of feeling "bankrupt, confused ... out of contact with reality."[1] Yet, he had the company of fellow Norwegians in the barrack where he was housed. Prisoners in solitary confinement generally fare worse than those who share prison cells. Psychologists speak of them becoming "unhinged," not only mentally but in a broader sense of being disconnected from the outside world. Schuschnigg used the word *ausgeschaltet* ("unplugged" or "turned off") and *losgelöst* ("detached" or "uncoupled")[2] to describe his condition, although he was not totally cut off from the outside world. He received books – "Praise be to God!" he writes in his diary.[3] He was also supplied with a radio, and eventually was given access to a newspaper, albeit the mouthpiece of the regime, *Der Völkische Beobachter*.[4] He was allowed visits from his wife and, later, also from his son. His main human contacts, however, were unwanted. He was surrounded by guards.

Strictly speaking, Schuschnigg's detention in Vienna was not "solitary" at all. He was being watched day and night. The sentries were stationed in his room, with a change of guards taking place every hour around the clock. The room in which Schuschnigg was held at the Hotel Metropole had been used for drying and ironing laundry. It had barred windows, but no door: "In its stead a small corridor connected the room with [the hallway]." Schuschnigg shared a toilet located in the hallway with the guards, whose quarters were next door. In his memoirs, Kurt Schuschnigg Jr. describes the improvised cell in which his father was kept: "A straw mattress lay on the floor leaving space for the guard, a table and a chair."[5] Conditions improved after a personal inspection by Heinrich Himmler on 11 December 1938. "On the same day – without any request on my part – my cell was transformed into a kind of living room by the addition of appropriate furniture. It was rather modest but at any rate humane. I was also given a radio, all of which brought me great relief," Schuschnigg reports.[6] Eventually he was moved to a larger room. According to an inventory taken at the time, the new furnishings included tables with tablecloths, lamps, upholstered chairs, an armoire, a typewriter, and even touches of interior decorating such as oil paintings, mirrors, carpets, and vases.[7] However, this did not change the fact that Schuschnigg had no privacy. "A sentry stands in the room at all times. The light has to be on during the night. When a new sentry comes to take over – which is once every hour – firearms have to be ready for firing, safety catches unlocked."[8]

Officially Schuschnigg's only duties consisted of making his bed and keeping his washstand in order, but some guards enjoyed harassing him in numerous petty ways. They raised the temperature in the room to 104°F, loudly sang the Horst Wessel song (the Nazi anthem), and required him to make and unmake the bed half a dozen times until it was "according to Nazi regulations." They mocked him in conversation with each other: "Don't you think this room is too good for him? He is positively gaining weight." They made excessive noise, banging for hours on the walls, which Schuschnigg counteracted by "procuring Ohropax [earplugs] and so managed to fend off the worst." They wrote offensive verses on the wall:

> We will not rest
> Until the last Jew is hanging
> From the intestines of the last priest.

They put Schuschnigg's food down on the floor in front of the toilet, made him clean the walls and radiators, empty the slop buckets, and wipe them with his towel.[9]

Schuschnigg reacted to this harassment with sarcasm. When one of the guards made him stand at attention every time he entered the cell, Schuschnigg did so with exaggerated precision. "I acted the soldier, also with all the other guards, who were visibly surprised. ... Perhaps they even suspected that I was mocking them."[10]

Schuschnigg was a closely watched man, but he watched his captors in turn. He seems to have derived a certain satisfaction from observing his guards, perhaps because it gave him a purpose and provided him with a semblance of agency and control over his environment. Victor Klemperer, who was at first harassed by the Nazis, then briefly imprisoned, and finally restricted to living in a "Jews' house," points out the importance of staying alert and in control: "I was invariably helped by the demand that I had made on myself: observe, study, and memorize what is going on." Similarly Albert Christel, a prisoner at Sachsenhausen, noted that "to sharpen your senses ... to know what is going on around you, is of extreme importance." To know the enemy was to be prepared for his actions.[11]

It is well known that solitary prisoners tend to establish a relationship with their captors or guards in the absence of other permitted relationships.[12] This was never the case with Schuschnigg. He kept his distance and remained an observer. He put his mind to work and immediately began to categorize his guards according to age and life experience. "On the whole ... the older men were easier than the younger ones and ... those who treated me badly were also disliked by their colleagues." When the "stinkers" mistreated him, the younger men seemed to be embarrassed and were apologetic. "Don't think all of us are like that," one of the guards assured him. "Don't judge the SS battalion by the behavior of some of these young hoodlums."[13] Schuschnigg graded the behaviour of the guards toward him. One group acted correctly and did their duty impersonally, others were even humane, while a third group was disagreeable and harassed him.[14] He took note also of the regional and national origins of his guards on the basis of their accent, and made generalizations on account of these differences. Confidential information usually came from "Austrians, Bavarians, and Rhinelanders," he noted.[15] In his diary, he often referred to individual guards by their regional background ("the Swabian," "the Carinthian") rather than by name. In some cases, he may not have known their names, but even when he did, he generally used only initials. Not naming his guards may have been a way of distancing himself from them. His remarks at any rate are invariably made in a detached and sometimes in an ironic or amused tone. Thus he describes the harassment he experienced as "ceremonies" or "having a little fun." In describing mistreatment, he often uses metaphors drawn from the theatre – "production," "first night," "serial drama" – reinforcing the impression that he was a spectator rather than an actor in the events.[16] Without explicitly saying so, he makes the guards out as ignorant or boorish – that is, his inferiors. The "Swabian" was arrogant. "The Austrians have to learn a lot yet," he said, deprecating Schuschnigg's nationality. "They don't know what it means to work. But we shall teach them, whether they like it or not." Others had no understanding of contemporary events. The "Carinthian" thought Schuschnigg had been made a scapegoat. "The others who are really responsible for everything are still free," he said. "But we shall get them in due course." The "Swabian" believed that Schuschnigg was guilty of calling the French into the country and arming the Communists. The guards liked to talk politics. "How could you be so stupid?" one of them said to Schuschnigg. "You were lucky enough to be allowed to shake the Führer's hand. You met him in Berchtesgaden and you didn't use your chance. Today you could be governor (*Reichsstatthalter*) in Vienna."[17] A "Tyrolian" eyed a guide to the English language on Schuschnigg's table. He leafed through the booklet and commented: "It's a pity that you aren't more advanced. With your education, you shouldn't even have to consult something like this."[18] And a "West German" said naively, "I don't know how you can stand it here. This heat can drive a man crazy. I find it hard myself to take the heat, but at least I can go swimming." He then comforted Schuschnigg: He wouldn't be here long. He would soon be put on trial.[19] One of the guards, witnessing the harassment to which Schuschnigg was subjected, said, "Why don't you complain?" But Schuschnigg was determined not to give his captors the satisfaction of letting them know that he was bothered. "No, I won't complain," he writes in his diary.[20] This determination to suffer in silence may be regarded as another strategy to preserve his self-respect and pride.

Schuschnigg's health was poor at the time. He experienced "increasingly frequent vertigo and vehement headaches, neuralgic pain in his teeth and ears, vague pressure in his stomach, reminiscent of the feeling one has during a bumpy airplane ride."[21] He lost weight rapidly, in part because his daily food intake was sparse. "For breakfast I order a roll and a cup of black coffee, for lunch a soup or home fried potatoes. For dinner I have either a marinated herring or potatoes, sauerkraut, and a frankfurter. That is with a very few exceptions my regular fare." He did not eat more, he explains, because he had to order from the hotel's kitchen and pay for the food himself. "The hotel is rather expensive, and I have to order à la carte and pay the extra percentage for room service. I simply cannot afford to eat more." In the German version, he adds, "and in any case I soon lost my appetite completely."[22] Vera was not allowed to bring her husband any food, which would have helped. A further complication arose from the fact that the kitchen was closed on holidays, a hardship for the prisoner, especially at Easter, Christmas, and New Year's, when he could not order food for two days in a row. A diary entry for New Year's Eve 1938 notes, "I am getting extremely hungry. I saved a piece of bread, a small piece of cheese, and a chocolate bar. That was all I had during the Christmas holidays. Tonight the same problem faces me since the kitchen will be closed for two days. The policemen, however, are very friendly and each of them brings me something from his own provisions."[23] The official prison report suggested that Schuschnigg was deliberately damaging his health "to make a transfer to a hospital necessary ... Should he be released, he will most likely claim and spread the rumour that we arrested him and watched him slowly die of starvation." He was therefore ordered to eat three solid meals a day, for which the authorities would pay, starting 20 February 1939.[24]

From October 1938 on, Schuschnigg had mandatory visits from the prison doctor, but he decided not to confide in the physician after he was told that his problems "were incidental and not caused by an abnormal condition." Schuschnigg's reaction was a sarcastic "That's comforting to know!" and a defiant "I must cope with these symptoms on my own."[25] Interestingly, neither his sarcasm nor the passage expressing his determination to remain in control of the situation appears in the English version of his diaries.

His attitude toward the prison doctor is an indication that Schuschnigg was doggedly holding on to his independence of mind and did not allow himself to be drawn into familiarity with the enemy. He made a point of never initiating a conversation: "I never start the conversation; and, when I answer, I only say what is expected of me." Keeping his distance – facilitated by the fact that he clearly considered the guards his social and intellectual inferiors – was a coping mechanism that helped him maintain his individuality. The guards were "no match" for him, he said. "Four years of service during the [First] World War and four years as the head of the Austrian government have steeled my nerves. Although I am over forty now, my youthful torturer seemed to be far more affected by his antics than I." He even reversed the relationship and professed to feel sorry for the guards: "The world look[s] pleasanter when you find some human interest in your guards. They suffer too; and their routine is not an easy one," he wrote.[26] He does not ask them for anything that might go against regulation. "I have no intention of keeping a guard from his duty, for one thing because under no circumstances do I want to endanger him."[27] When "K" falls asleep while on duty and is punished for his negligence, Schuschnigg musters sympathy for him, feeling sorry "for the poor fellows" who are struggling to stay awake at night.[28] One of the guards helped Schuschnigg cut his hair, which had grown long. His colleagues promptly denounced him for the crime of favouring a prisoner ("Begünstigung eines Häftlings"). The guard was upset by the treachery of his colleagues, but Schuschnigg comforted him and "succeeded in calming him down."[29]

When Viennese policemen replaced the SS guards in September 1938, the nightly inspections and the harassment stopped, but the change of guard now took place every half hour. A year later, in November 1939, Schuschnigg was transferred to Munich and, although still kept in solitary, was no longer subject to 24-hour surveillance. His relief was palpable: "Anything is better than a guard in the room, even if he is very quiet, which is not the case for every guard. And even if he is quiet, he can't help moving around. He is not allowed to speak or read. So he is understandably bored. Every half hour there is a change of guard, which isn't exactly nice during the night. No, on the whole it is certainly better here! I had never even dreamed of this aspect when the popular topic of comparing Vienna and Munich came up. And how much Vienna meant to me then!"[30]

Generally speaking, the conditions in Munich were an improvement over those in Vienna. The Gestapo headquarters were in the Wittelsbach Palais, an imposing red-brick building dating from the nineteenth century, which before World War I had been the residence of the king of Bavaria. Schuschnigg was allowed to go outside for a few minutes every morning, and again in the evening to walk for half an hour in the garden. Vera followed her husband to Munich and stayed in a boarding house to be near him.[31]

It is instructive to compare Schuschnigg's approach to his guards and the use of detachment and irony as a way of coping with their supervision with that of Sigismund Payne-Best, who was held in a cell block at Sachsenhausen. Like Schuschnigg he was in solitary confinement and under 24-hour surveillance. The first cell assigned to him was a small room with elementary furnishings: a plank bed with a straw mattress, a table and chair for his use, and another chair and table for his guard. Officially he was allowed neither pencil nor paper, but as he reports, he "managed to annex one or two pencils when being interrogated and, as I was provided with a roll of toilet paper, I had the requisite materials to enable me to keep some sort of record of events." He was moreover given a deck of playing cards, supplied with the daily paper (the infamous *Völkische Beobachter*), and one book per week out of the prison library. He was allowed to go outside for an hour's exercise daily. Unlike Schuschnigg he immediately went about winning the favour of his guards. He constructed a skittle alley (nine-pin bowling) for their use and joined in their games. In the winter, he even engaged in snowball fights with them.[32] "I talked to my guards almost from the first," he writes in a witness statement for the trial of Camp Commander Kaindl. "A number of them became my really good and loyal friends whom I could trust in every way." Speaking of his favourite guard, he writes that "it was a great comfort to me to feel that I had this friendly gnome [Grothe] … a thoroughly decent fellow quite uncontaminated by any Nazi ideas." Like Schuschnigg, Payne-Best was given a radio but unlike him he openly listened to BBC broadcasts "without fear that my guards would betray me." He obtained all sorts of information from them. For example, he knew about the debacle of Stalingrad "weeks before anything was published in the press."[33] It would appear that Payne-Best's method worked well for him, although most political prisoners would have shied away from his approach and would have agreed with Harry Naujoks, who was also held at Sachsenhausen: "There was no room here for truckling to or, worse, submitting" to the guards, he wrote. Wolfgang Szepanzky, who spent some time in solitary confinement, simply said that one must learn to be self-sufficient: "You must seek consolation in yourself." That sort of equanimity was not good enough for Arnold Weiss-Rüthel. He thought it was important for prisoners never to forget that they were in the hands of the enemy. It was this attitude – resistance – that had given him strength and (he claimed) was respected even by the Nazis.[34]

While Schuschnigg's diary entries suggest that his approach of dealing with solitary confinement worked well for him and that he was coping with the situation, this may not reflect reality. Striking an upbeat tone in his anecdotal reports was in itself likely a mechanism of coping with a bad situation. Both Schuschnigg's wife and his son reported that the imprisonment left him depressed and physically debilitated as well. "The imprisonment had taken its toll: six feet tall, he weighed about ninety pounds," Kurt Schuschnigg Jr. writes in his memoir. He attributes his father's move from Vienna to Munich partly to considerations of health. "The Nazis did not want the past chancellor of Austria to die, a martyr, in prison."[35] In the letters Vera wrote in the first two years of her husband's incarceration, she describes him as "terribly apathetic," but this state may have been partially due to the fact that he was given three Lubrocal (sedative) tablets daily.[36] Yet Frankl also lists "relative apathy, in which [the prisoner] achieved a kind of emotional death" as a typical reaction to imprisonment, and a number of autobiographical accounts speak of the same numbness, "a dusky state and complete absence of thought," as Isa Vermehren put it. Joseph Joos speaks of the effects in similar terms: "The senses become dull, memory is lost ... you are no longer yourself." To look reality in the face was too hard. "One mustn't do it ... one couldn't go on [if one did]."[37] Schuschnigg recovered somewhat after his move to Munich; Vera told a relative that he was in better physical health, but the uncertainty of what the future might bring was "almost unbearable" to him. As his imprisonment dragged on, he began to lose courage. "The hopelessness weighs on him ... I can't bear to see him suffer."[38] In 1941 Vera reports that her husband "suffers from depression on account of his lack of activity and hope – I feel rather wretched about it."[39] But "depression" is not a word found in Schuschnigg's narrative. He continues to project the image of a man staunch in the face of misfortune. The façade cracks only once. On 30 October 1939, when he was told to pack up his belongings, he allowed himself to hope that "land was in sight," and was bitterly disappointed when he found that he was not released after all, but merely transported to another prison. "And yet I must go on. I must live," although he felt that life was no longer worth living and there was nothing left but to wait for death. "Perhaps it was wrong not to force this solution earlier," he writes. These words might suggest that he regretted not having committed suicide, but that is not his meaning.[40] Rather, he wished he had been tried in court and condemned to death, since under the Nazi regime it was futile to think that "a legal procedure ... would bring justice."[41] As a Catholic he would have considered it sinful to contemplate suicide, which is not to say, that he did not wish for death. "For me there is nothing to do but wait until nature makes a kindly end of it," he writes. "My existence as a human being has come to an end, and to continue as anything else is not particularly tempting. Even an animal needs certain basic living conditions," he writes. He adds a profession of faith: "I believe in God … and I hope that my fugitive thoughts will find grace before His eternal judgment."[42] At this time, the lowest point in Schuschnigg's personal history, the brief visits of his wife Vera played a crucial role in sustaining him. She is the one to whom he wants to open up, yet he is unable to put his thoughts into words: "My innermost thought, which I would want to reveal to my love, can find no expression."[43] Vermehren expressed this loss in remarkably similar terms when she writes in her memoirs, "The inability to speak prevails throughout the whole camp like a form of deprivation … it is impossible to conceptualize, to be cognizant of oneself."[44]

After his arrest, Schuschnigg applied to the Gestapo for permission to marry Vera. The wedding took place on 1 June 1938. This fact was not widely known, so that the couple remained "lovers" in the public perception. Irmingard, Princess of Bavaria, who was for a time detained at Sachsenhausen in the house next to the Schuschniggs, refers to their relationship in her memoirs: "[Vera] had left her husband to join her lover in the concentration camp."[45]

For some time, Schuschnigg himself was kept in ignorance of the fact that his application had been approved and the marriage had taken place by proxy. An agent of the Gestapo informed him of the fait accompli and, without providing further information, gave him a packet containing his wedding ring. Later that day he received a note from his wife telling him about the ceremony, which had taken place in the Dominikanerkirche in Vienna. Schuschnigg's brother, Artur, had acted as his proxy, his father and a sacristan as witnesses. As a memento, Vera sent her husband a small bouquet of lilies of the valley, which he kept on his table beside her photo.[46]

Subsequently Vera was given permission to visit her husband briefly every Friday. In his understated way, Schuschnigg declares, "I was very glad of it," and, in a more expansive mood, "I live from Friday to Friday" and treasure "these few minutes of intense joy."[47] His son, Kurt, writes that the visits were kept to "exactly three minutes." Schuschnigg variously refers to visits of four, six, or eight minutes.[48] The time was presumably governed by the whim of the presiding guard. In any case, it was too short. "What can anyone even say in three minutes?" Vera exclaimed. Schuschnigg describes the conditions under which the visits took place in his diary. During their brief time together, the guard stood next to them, afraid that he might miss a word of their conversation. "But we did not talk much anyway. We just looked at each other."[49] In addition, he was allowed to write to Vera once a week and to receive a letter from her. The time in between seemed very long. There were "six days, 144 hours of loneliness, worry, and hopelessness."[50] Mutual love, even in the absence of words, takes on enormous importance, Frankl notes. "It sustains the inner self." We find the same sentiments in the first-person accounts of other prisoners. Henri Michel, a political prisoner from Belgium, writes in a letter to his wife of the "blissful knowledge of our steady love. This strong feeling of belonging gives us strength." Conversely, the absence of love leads to nihilism, Vermehren writes.[51]

Vera was not only Schuschnigg's emotional mainstay but also instrumental in the eventual material improvements in his prison life. According to Schuschnigg's son, she initiated a letter-writing campaign, haranguing numerous officials, but with little success at first. "Not easily denied, she changed her tactics; she simply arrived unannounced at an official's office and waited. Vera was a lovely woman with a commanding presence, and she had two additional advantages: she was relentless and – like many beautiful ladies from well-known families – she was accustomed to getting what she wanted."[52] He credits her with obtaining permission for the weekly visits, although it is questionable whether any individual had an impact on the capricious moves of the Gestapo. Keeping prisoners guessing was part of their strategy and tactics of harassment. This was certainly the case in the handling of Vera's application requesting to be allowed to live with her husband. Promises were held out to the couple from time to time, then withdrawn and reinstated again. The supposed date of their reunion was a moving target and ultimately made them lose hope in 1940 – at which point the promise unexpectedly became reality. Similarly, Schuschnigg was at first given permission to correspond with his father and his son, a privilege which was suddenly withdrawn in the spring of 1939, as was the permission to listen to the radio, which had been given to him in December 1938 and was taken away again in March 1939. As Fey von Hassell, a fellow prisoner, noted, the Gestapo made many promises. "They were hard to gauge ... I must confess that I fell for their lies every time."[53] Mafalda, the Princess of Hesse, experienced similar shenanigans. She was duped into entering the German consulate in Rome on a promise that she would be reunited with her husband. Once in Germany it became clear that she was a prisoner of the Gestapo. Promises continued to be held out to her: she was told that she would be brought to a villa where she could live with her husband. The villa turned out to be a barrack in the Buchenwald concentration camp, where she died in a bomb attack.[54]

Schuschnigg was not taken in so easily. He recognized the tactic for what it was: clever manipulation. As he remarked in his diary entry of 31 December 1939, the new year would "probably bring a new promise, then a disappointment, then another promise, and so on, the usual method of one step ahead and three back. Why then do I wish for the new year?"[55] The answer is probably a nucleus of optimism which allowed him to believe in future possibilities in spite of past disappointments.

Vera's personal courage, initiative, and devotion to her husband's cause were impressive. Her energy and strength of purpose were immediately apparent even to people who did not know her well. Payne-Best, who met her in 1945 on the long evacuation trek, when a number of special prisoners were moved from camp to camp, referred to her as "our beloved 'Camp Angel' as she was soon called by all of us. I can never express the gratitude which I feel to this beautiful, charming, and brave woman." Fey von Hassell suggested that Schuschnigg retained his mental vigour because of Vera. Leon Blum likewise remarked on the fact that Schuschnigg was "perfectly master of himself, perfectly lucid and calm" and that he "showed a vigorous spirit and intellect in spite of his long captivity." In Fey von Hassell's opinion, Schuschnigg drew his strength of spirit from Vera, "a lively and cheerful woman, always ready to help others." Schuschnigg's son similarly acknowledged her role in maintaining his father's courage, commenting in his memoirs: "Vera kept his mind and hopes alive as she presented the possibility of a future, of a life beyond prison."[56]

Their future together preoccupied Schuschnigg's mind while he was in isolation in the Gestapo prison in Munich. Schuschnigg worried that the long time spent on his own would affect his relationship with Vera and his son and indeed "ruin our lives in the future."[57] Then, against all expectations, he was given permission to see his wife once a week for three hours without the presence of a guard.[58] In view of their earlier experience with Gestapo "favours," the couple hardly dared to believe that this was a permanent arrangement, but the permission remained in place until Schuschnigg was moved to Sachsenhausen and the couple took up residence together.

The only other person with whom Schuschnigg had personal contact during his imprisonment in Munich, was his son, Kurt. The boy was twelve years old when his father was arrested in Vienna in 1938. Schuschnigg reported that he was allowed only one brief phone call to his son and did not see him again until two years later in Munich.[59] This tallies with his son's recollection. He was attending a boarding school in Vienna and remembers being called to the office of the principal, who told him that his father had been arrested. "He then handed me the phone. Father sounded the same as he always did. He said we wouldn't be seeing each other for some time and told me to do my best in school and be a good boy. At the end of the school year, I would stay with Fräulein Alice [his nanny]. He loved me, he said, and then the line went dead."[60] We may discard the melodramatic story found in Sheridon's biography of Schuschnigg, which tells of the father fetching his son from school in person and taking him for a night-time visit to his mother's grave before saying farewell to him.[61]

Kurt writes of his father with great admiration, not to say a touch of hero worship. He paints a picture of his father as a brilliant man with a patriotic spirit. His keen mind, he writes, had been honed by Jesuit educators. In university he graduated at the top of his class. He entered politics with a sense of passion and duty. As the family lived in Tyrol at the time, the commute to the legislature in the capital meant that Schuschnigg was with his wife and son only on the weekends. "As with everything else he did, Father threw himself totally into this new phase of his life," Kurt writes, apparently without resentment about the long-distance relationship. He did have less happy memories though, for example, of a beating he received on damaging his toybox. He recalled the warnings of his mother "Wait until your father comes home." When he saw his father with a switch of twigs used to punish naughty children, he crawled under the sofa in the living room, but his father dragged him out. "What followed is too painful to relate."[62]

Schuschnigg, then, was largely an absentee father even before his imprisonment. Kurt entered the Jesuit boarding school at Kalksburg near Vienna at the age of 10 and spent his holidays mostly in the company of his nanny, Alice Ottenreiter. Relatives were allowed to visit boarders at the school once a month, but these visits "were divided between Grandfather and Fräulein Alice ... I had not seen Father since [the beginning of the school year 1936]." At that time, he had hopes of spending the Christmas holiday skiing with his father, but that expectation "turned out to be unrealistic." In June 1937 he was looking forward to his father's company during the summer holidays. He knew, however, that his father "had little spare time. His life was his work ... When vacation arrived, Fraulein Alice and I were on our way to [the summer resort] Sankt Gilgen, but without Father." The following Christmas, Alice picked him up, as usual, and explained that they would travel for a skiing holiday to the fashionable winter resort of Sankt Anton. They would go by train. His father would travel in the government coach, which was attached to the overnight train. "We are going to be on the same train," Alice explained, "but not together." His father would be with his ministers and aides and do government work. "I reminded myself that I had expected Father to be busy," Kurt writes.[63] In 1938, the year of Schuschnigg's arrest, the school Kurt attended was closed by the Nazis, and Kurt moved into Alice Ottenreiter's apartment in Vienna, which she shared with her parents, her sister, and her husband. It was hard on the boy. He discovered that the privileged life he had led was at an end and the world shunned him as the son of a "criminal." In his memoirs, he tells a poignant story about a former schoolmate's mother who refused to let the boys play together. "His type is not welcome," she told an indignant Alice. Kurt experienced a new kind of loneliness, "knowing that I had been erased from the minds of most of those who had known me. I had become anonymous."[64] In the winter of 1938 his grandfather died, and it was up to Vera now to make arrangements for him. It was difficult to find a new school for the boy.

"I can't send him to school here [in Vienna]," she writes. "That is, I can't get the approval to do so, and yet he must have a proper education."[65] For a while she hired private tutors and paid for them out of her own funds, but that proved too expensive in the long run. With the help of the Niedermayr family – relatives of the Schuschniggs – she found a school for Kurt in Munich in the fall of 1939. He felt it was "like reentering the land of the living." In the hands of his Viennese tutors (who had been state-approved and were therefore Nazi sympathizers), he "had forgotten how much [he] had loved school."[66] His joy (and his stay at the school) was short-lived, however. A newly appointed principal decided that the son of the "criminal" Schuschnigg was not welcome at his institution. Other arrangements had to be made. He ended up in a *Schülerheim*, a boarding house for students, where he was tutored by the principal for the rest of the school year. In his memoirs, Kurt describes his tutor as "a kind man and an excellent teacher, who together with the occasional substitute, produced remarkable results ... The instruction was untainted by propaganda, and this was, for the times, a rarity." Because he had no family home, he said, he developed a certain indifference to family-oriented days – Christmas, Easter, and birthdays – "perhaps as part of my [emotional] survival."[67] Schuschnigg himself keenly felt his son's disadvantage. Kurt needed to develop a sense of home. "I know how valuable a family relationship is," Schuschnigg writes in a letter to his brother.[68] Vera managed to have Kurt accepted at another high school, the Wittelsbach school, "one of the best in Munich and one of the very few with neither political nor military affiliations." With the help of his tutors at the boarding house, he had achieved the highest marks in the entrance examination. "I was deliriously happy – another chance to be just a boy at a normal school," he writes in his memoir. The Wittelsbach school was a day school, however. He therefore continued boarding at the Schülerheim Schmitt. Throughout the school year he performed well: "I was consistently at the head of my class – my marks reflecting the satisfaction that I felt with my life. I don't think Father expected anything less; both Father and Uncle Artur had excelled at their studies." When he achieved high marks in the entrance examination, "Vera and Father were very pleased."[69]

The Nazi authorities acquiesced in this placement. They did, however, limit the boy's visits with his parents. Vera was keeping the family spirit alive. While Kurt was in Vienna, she had taken him to the grave of his mother and grandfather on All Soul's Day, as was customary. It must have been a comfort to the boy to see the grave covered with flowers by anonymous sympathizers, who indirectly wished to pay tribute to Schuschnigg. In letters to Schuschnigg's uncle Hermann, who offered financial help, Vera expressed her desire to give the boy her motherly love. She was pleased to find him receptive and willing to love her in turn and "do everything to please her and make her life easier. The boy has a golden heart."[70]

After Schuschnigg was moved to Munich, Vera was allowed to take letters from Kurt to his father, and in the spring of 1940, he was finally allowed to visit him for half an hour. Kurt preferred personal to written contact with his father, not least because "he had taken to correcting my letters with red ink and returning them."[71]

His first visit, however, was traumatic. "When I saw Father, I tried not to show my astonishment at this shocking appearance. Vera had tried to prepare me, and I was almost fourteen – old enough to know that mental and physical suffering change people – nevertheless, I was simply not expecting him to look so altered." This was the first of several visits. What did they talk about? "Mainly about my studies and friends at the Schülerheim Schmitt. I could see how satisfying this was for him, so I told him everything that came to mind, even about the goldfish I swallowed on a dare. I was not used to having Father's full attention. I had never before been able to spend so much time with him."[72]

Kurt treasured his visits and was deeply affected when his father was moved to Sachsenhausen in November of 1941, a move that would put him out of the boy's reach. Vera and his little sister, Maria Dolores ("Sissi"), born in March, would be gone as well. Kurt felt abandoned. "My studies began to suffer. I could not concentrate."[73] Vera tried to reason with him – he should be glad that his father was moving to the new location. It meant an improvement in his living conditions. Rationally Kurt agreed with her. On his last visit, he pretended a happiness he didn't feel, and on the way back to his boarding house he was barely able to suppress tears.

We don't know what Schuschnigg's reaction was to the separation from his son. There is a hiatus in his diary entries between 31 December of 1939 and 23 March 1941, that is, from the time the visits of his wife were extended to three hours to the birth of his daughter, Sissy, fifteen months later. He does not explain why he stopped writing. In fact, the entry for 1 July 1942 suggests that he had continued to write every day. "There is nothing going on here. Thank God, because an event is the worst thing that could happen. And yet, the monotony of the forced daily routine is never completely paralysing. There is no *dies sine linea* [no day without writing a line]. Astonishing, is it? No, just a matter of mindfulness and modest self-reflection."[74] It would appear therefore that Schuschnigg kept writing, but not in his diary. Perhaps he now shared his thoughts with his wife and described his experiences in the weekly letters he was permitted to write to her. The English edition simply states, "I have not kept a diary for over a year." The German version sounds more ominous: "But here the personal fate of today begins to blend into a gray, endless ocean ..."[75] The phrasing suggests weariness or depression.

While the hiatus is total in the English edition,[76] the German offers three entries for the year 1940. At Easter 1940 Schuschnigg's written testimony was requested for the trials of his aide Franz Schier on charges of fraud. Bits of his testimony were quoted out of context in the *Völkische Beobachter*, he notes, with the purpose of making him look bad. The verdict "amounted to an acquittal. The judgment against Schier was for a trifling matter, to save face ... too bad for the newspaper hacks!"[77] In June Schuschnigg reports yet another promise to be assigned new quarters where he could live together with his wife. At Christmas he notes that his wife is still living by herself, in a rented room; he himself has been given more space. He now occupies the former dayroom of the guards. Throughout the year 1941, his diary entries remain sparse. Whereas he made almost daily notes in the preceding years, we have only seven entries for 1941, one dealing with a renewed promise that he would be assigned quarters where he could live with his wife. There is also a lengthy entry referring to a newly appointed manager involved in "a little prison intrigue."[78] Under the manager's tenure the food served to the prisoners was significantly reduced. Apparently, he pocketed the savings, but was removed after the cook lodged an official complaint against him. Finally, at the end of 1941, Schuschnigg was moved to Sachsenhausen, where he was joined by Vera.

On the evidence of Schuschnigg's diary for the prison years in Vienna and Munich it is obvious that he used certain tactics for his psychological survival. He seems to have held his own against his captors by regarding them either with detachment or irony and retaining a sense of superiority over them. It is clear, however, that his contact with Vera, even if severely restricted, was of crucial importance for his psychological survival. Comparing the account Schuschnigg gives in his diaries with the impressions registered by his wife and son and the official reports of the authorities, it is difficult to say whether the tactics he used were successful. In his own eyes he was defying his captors and, as his quiet and determined style suggests, even triumphing over them. By contrast, the shocked reaction of his son on their reunion and the worried letters Vera wrote about Schuschnigg's state of mind tell a different story. On balance, it appears that the years of solitary confinement were more damaging, emotionally as well as physically, than Schuschnigg was willing to admit, even to himself.

chapter two

The Sachsenhausen Household:
Living *en famille*

On 9 November 1941, Vera was told to go to Berlin and prepare to move into new lodgings in Sachsenhausen, where she would be able to live together with her husband. A day earlier, on 8 November, Schuschnigg had been transported to Berlin on the night train, guarded by two Gestapo men, and was driven from there to the Sachsenhausen concentration camp. The couple and their child moved into the quarters assigned to them and set up household. The new arrangement brought a measure of relief, *ein Aufatmen*, as Schuschnigg put it. "I feel blessed," he wrote, "mainly because ... I can go outside or stay indoors, as I please. That in itself is of immense value."[1]

The house was fully furnished and equipped. In addition, Schuschnigg eventually received some pieces of furniture and cartons of books that had been stored in a depot in Vienna. He took great pleasure in unpacking this treasure trove. The nature of the books he owned and the satisfaction he felt in rereading them will concern us in more detail in another chapter.

His diary entries, which had been sparse over the past two years, become more frequent from June 1942 on: 29 for the second half of 1942, 53 for 1943, and 39 for 1944. In 1945 he returns to almost daily reports, describing his evacuation and liberation in May, but the notes for the final year are short and impersonal, often amounting to no more than a sentence or two on the progress of the war and the expected collapse of the regime. They tell us relatively little about Schuschnigg's personal thoughts and experiences. Another source comes into play at this time, however: the letters to his brother, Artur, and his uncle, Hermann Wopfner, which do reflect his thoughts and feelings.

Although mail "was only a poor substitute for conversation,"[2] as Schuschnigg told his brother, writing and receiving letters was a crucial element in the psychological survival of prisoners in concentration camps. "A letter meant an immense deal," Weiss-Rüthel said. "Waiting for mail was exciting, an anticipatory joy. The letter itself was supreme comfort and happiness." In Nansen's diary, as well, we find repeated expressions of gratitude for this "blessed help." Writing to his wife, he said, was "such comfort – and then the time goes fast." The letters he received were "a living breath of home, as it were from another world" and a "gleaming light in the darkness." No one in the outside world could possibly "understand the meaning of a letter from home." In the same vein Schuschnigg writes in his diary that the best birthday present he received during his solitary confinement was a letter from his wife. Such a message of love and loyalty "helps overcome everything."[3]

The main recipient of Schuschnigg's letters during his stay in Sachsenhausen was his brother, who could fully enter into his cultural and intellectual interests. Artur Schuschnigg (1904–90) was well versed in literature, music, and visual arts. He had obtained a doctorate in art history in 1928 and found employment in the Austrian Broadcasting Agency. Eventually he was put in charge of music programming and came in contact with many prominent performing artists. In 1934 he married Marianne Ulrichs, with whom he had five children, the last born in 1946. After his brother's arrest, Artur was spared *Sippenhaft* – the routine incarceration of close relatives of Nazi captives – through the intervention of Hermann Göring, who had Artur assigned to a post in the Kaiser Friedrich Museum in Berlin. He moved with his family to Berlin and soon established contacts there with the local arts community. Indeed, his apartment became a meeting place for writers and performers and, more generally, for Austrian émigrés. Artur carefully guarded his privacy. He refused to have a radio in the house and kept the phone covered with a pillow at all times for fear of implanted listening devices. Even so, he did not escape surveillance. Records show that both he and Vera were constantly shadowed by agents. Every step they took was registered by the Gestapo.[4] In 1940 Artur was drafted into the German army.[5] As a FLAK (anti-aircraft defence) officer in Berlin, he witnessed the bombing and destruction of his own apartment in November 1943. Fortunately his family had been evacuated shortly before the air raids began. After the war, he became program manager and, later, director of radio broadcasting in Tyrol, where he lived until his death in 1990.

Schuschnigg's second correspondent was Hermann Wopfner (1876–1963), the brother of his mother. Wopfner studied history at the universities of Innsbruck, Vienna, and Leipzig and obtained a doctorate submitting a dissertation on the Tyrolian peasant revolt of 1525/6. His interest in the subject was fostered by the history of his own family, generations of alpine farmers that could be traced back to the fifteenth century. From 1914 on he taught at the University of Innsbruck and did research on the economy and culture of Tyrolian farmers. He also undertook a number of carefully planned treks through the Tyrolian Alps, which inspired him to publish numerous illustrated works on local history and culture. Although Wopfner openly resisted the Nazis, he was able to maintain his position because his subject area, *Volkskunde*, folk history, was a shibboleth of the German Reich. Nevertheless he requested and was granted early retirement in 1941. He had bought an estate of historical significance (the "Plumeshof," first documented in 1305), where he spent the rest of his life. His contributions were recognized by the province of Tyrol, which awarded him its highest honour, the *Ehrenring* (1949). He was, moreover, appointed an honorary member of the Austrian Academy of Sciences (1953). Although Wopfner did not see eye to eye with his nephew in matters of politics, kinship triumphed over differences in opinion. "In the past we often clashed and sparks were flying," Schuschnigg writes about his relationship with Wopfner. "It would still be like that if we ever strayed into contemporary questions." When Schuschnigg was chancellor, Wopfner frequently wrote to him to ask favours for others. "On those occasions he never omitted to say: 'You and I hold largely different opinions, but I want the best, and it would not be to my credit, etc.'"[6]

Letters between Schuschnigg and his relatives were either delivered in person by Vera or mailed by her from outside the camp
to avoid censorship. In spite of geographical proximity and considerable effort on both sides, the brothers were unable to obtain
permission from the authorities to meet in person. "Unfortunately
I am not allowed to meet with Artur," Schuschnigg wrote to his
uncle in 1942. "Don't ask me why, it doesn't make sense."[7] In 1943
a meeting of sorts was arranged, but it amounted to no more than
the brothers catching a glimpse of each other. Schuschnigg referred
to the meeting in cryptic fashion to elude potential censors: "You
were in disguise, I so to speak in other circumstances." The "disguise" is a reference to Artur wearing the German uniform. "Other
circumstances" is a pun, since this is the German idiom for "being
pregnant," but Schuschnigg meant it literally, "in rather different
circumstances" than when they had met the last time in Vienna.
Artur was allowed to come to the gate of the camp to take "Mrs.
Auster" and her child for a walk. There he was able to catch sight
of his brother through the open gate, without, however, daring to
wave to him or give a visible sign of recognition.[8] Another meeting
was approved by the authorities in 1944, but cancelled at the last
minute. "We were very sorry that nothing came of the meeting you
initiated," Schuschnigg wrote. "I hope you received Vera's message in time."[9]

Thus it was left to Vera to carry letters between the brothers.
Since she had followed Schuschnigg to Sachsenhausen voluntarily,
she was not considered a prisoner or subject to prison regulations
and was allowed to come and go freely. Officially, the letters she
carried were not subject to censorship. Yet a certain caution pre-
vailed in Schuschnigg's exchanges with his brother, as we have
seen. He used subtle satire or camouflaged his meaning, using
code words – just in case the authorities decided to stop Vera and
check his mail after all.

About once a month, Vera visited Artur and his family, taking the
train to Berlin. She used the opportunity to shop for commodities
lacking in the camp and to supplement the food rations allocated
to them. Schuschnigg comments on the lack or shortage of certain
goods: "I was prohibited from using ink, which is part of the prison

ritual. Right at the beginning I asked for pen and ink. My request was denied. With much difficulty and as a special privilege I was granted permission to have the permanent use of a pencil."[10] Eventually these privileges were extended, and by the time he moved to Sachsenhausen, he also had a typewriter at his disposal, but obtaining ribbons remained a problem.[11] They also lacked certain household implements. "Laundry pegs would be most welcome," he wrote to his uncle, who offered help. "We don't have any at all, and the maid goes on and on about it! A clothesline would be welcome as well, but I suppose that's not to be had. I could also use an implement to wash the dishes. Too bad, carpet beaters aren't available, but the vacuum cleaner has been repaired, and so we can manage." In another letter, he notes: "It is really awful how many superfluous things I own. Yet I lack things that are necessary in everyday life: broom, pail, carpet cleaner, dust rags – and all the rest we gave little thought to until the onset of the 'freedom fight.' We took them for granted."[12]

Of course Schuschnigg was aware that in these war years, the outside world was no better off than the elite prisoners in custody. His brother's family also suffered deprivation. "And how are things food-wise? Do you receive care packages?" he asks Artur. "The way Vera looks after me is rather moving. I lack nothing. I don't know how she does it, and I'd rather not ask too many questions. Especially not about the price of all these things." He marvels at Vera's ingenuity in putting food on the table. "Twice now we even had genuine, excellent Tyrolean gnocchi." Apparently Vera also supplied her husband with cigarettes. "If I could only shake the stupid habit of smoking, which is a luxury! That cuts into our savings. But I don't think I can do it ... Who would have thought that all of us would have to find our way back to a more primitive life!"[13]

Vera occasionally shared the fruits of her foraging with neighbours in the special section. In a radio interview, Franz of Bavaria, who had been interned at Sachsenhausen as a child and lived with his family next door to the Schuschniggs, recalls his mother constructing a crèche for Christmas 1944. A guard had supplied the necessary materials: a saw and pieces of plywood. She painted the figures with watercolours, a gift from Vera. The crèche was still in his possession, he said, and had become a treasured heirloom brought out each Christmas.[14]

Vera was now her family's main provider, financially and materially. In a letter of December 1941 to his uncle, Schuschnigg speaks of his financial concerns. The accommodation, including electricity and heat, were free, he said, but there were other expenses. It was of course ironic that the Gestapo would charge (or rather, deduct from his confiscated accounts) any incidental costs, including food and the transportation from Munich to Sachsenhausen. "We had to pay for everything connected with our captivity," he writes in the diary entry of 23 July 1942. "Sixty marks a month go to the storehouse in Vienna where my furniture was taken in 1938. The journey from Munich to Sachsenhausen was also expensive."[15] In an absurd turn of events, he was promised a government pension. "For months now I hear about a distribution of support payments," he writes. "So far however it is only an institutional rumour. Too bad, because the money I lose each month is irretrievable, since the usual principle of retroactive pay doesn't exist here. By contrast it appears that I may eventually get access to my slim savings, but not yet. I don't mean to complain. I know very well that, comparing my life with that of many others, I have no reason to complain." Three months later he received 450 marks and was informed by the Central Security Office that he would receive a monthly pension in that amount from thereon. Schuschnigg likens these payments to "the thirty silver pieces of old," that is, the money paid to Judas Iscariot for his betrayal of Jesus. Half of it went to Kurt's private school in Munich, Schuschnigg notes, and sixty marks went to the storage company in Vienna. "On the whole, I have found that it is just as costly to live in a concentration camp as outside."[16]

Life was difficult for everyone, and Vera had her own cross to bear. She missed the company of the children from her first marriage; they were in Vienna and she could visit them only occasionally. In 1939 one of her daughters fell ill with typhus and came close to death. In 1940 her beloved mother died, and she herself developed serious health problems that eventually required surgery.[17] Schuschnigg consistently expressed gratitude and admiration for his wife and took a decidedly romantic view of their relationship, to the point of becoming maudlin. He describes their first meeting: "A new and wonderful dawn appeared on the horizon of my life ... a mild and transfiguring starlight shone upon my ponderous and solitary gloom. A man hungry for any light – be it ever so remote and vague – throws open the window of yearning and is filled with the shy and timid hope of meeting with a miracle. And it was like a fairytale ..."[18] These tender beginnings led to a solid relationship. Throughout Schuschnigg's ordeal and throughout the difficulties of life at the concentration camp, the couple remained mutually supportive. A letter to Artur, written in August 1942, shows that Schuschnigg himself was resigned to life in Sachsenhausen, but sensitive to Vera's suffering. After all, she was staying there voluntarily. "She probably imagined life to be easier ... the various inconveniences, the noise, smoke, shots being fired, every kind of disturbance to our night rest, and with the SS people and the prisoners, those poor devils, the only humans in sight, etc. etc. – none of this makes much of an impression on me because I have seen much worse. But for Vera it is a great deal to bear, and when I see her so unhappy, my usual contentment breaks down ... but please don't tell her of my lament. It would only make it harder for Vera, and in the end, we are so attached to each other that everything is bearable and we will always keep each other afloat."[19]

During the school holidays, Schuschnigg's son, Kurt, joined the household in Sachsenhausen. It is enlightening to compare how father and son, respectively, experienced the family dynamics. Kurt remembers his first visit to Sachsenhausen during the Christmas vacation of 1941. His father hugged him. "I could feel all his bones in that embrace, but the arms around me were as strong as ever. It was wonderful to be home."[20] Clearly home was where his father was. Schuschnigg reciprocated his son's feelings. He wrote of his hopes to see his son in Sachsenhausen, "to have my boy with me again ... in part for selfish reasons, but also because it is high time for Kurt to have a home again."[21] His first application to obtain permission for Kurt to visit him was denied. A few days before Christmas 1941, after he had already arranged for the boy to spend his vacations with Artur in Berlin, he received permission to have him join their household in Sachsenhausen for the duration of the school holidays.

In his memoirs Kurt stresses his cordial relationship with his stepmother. He unfailingly speaks with deference of Vera as a woman "born into an aristocratic life of privilege and ... a family that had been rich for centuries" manifesting a spirit and personal courage which was "contagious and had an effect even in the camp."[22] Yet, his father's diary entries for the summer of 1942 indicate tensions. Kurt's earlier sporadic visits had been awkward: "We are on tenterhooks the whole time, don't know where to begin, and are merely anxious about the time passing."[23] In 1942, Kurt was given permission to spend his summer vacation with them and stay with the family for five weeks. "It might be nice and turn out to be quite tolerable," Schuschnigg comments, but he was anxious. The surroundings were not conducive to a "*Sinfonia domestica* [domestic harmony] ... because every Largo is invariably beaten out by shrill Furiosi." This assessment of the family dynamics, which appears only in the German version of *Requiem*, is shortened in the English translation to a vague "Try as we may, our 'happiness' is forced and unnatural."[24]

A candid letter to Schuschnigg's brother explains the problem more clearly, however. When Kurt arrived for the summer holidays, Vera, was close to a nervous breakdown. The atmosphere was tense. "My dear Vera is the main sufferer of course. And I am a co-sufferer, because if there is anything I hate, it is tension at home," Schuschnigg writes. He felt helpless and "sat around listlessly." Vera was too drained even to look after their little daughter. Kurt volunteered to babysit. "The boy was really good. He pushed around the stroller every day for hours." He also did all the local shopping. "His only entertainment was fishing or swimming for two hours after the midday meal. He really didn't have a very pleasant vacation. I certainly don't close my eyes where the boy is concerned. Although he is very dear to my heart, he is a great scamp, forgetful, careless, sloppy, often so indolent it makes me shudder – that's all true, but thank God he has a solid core. And fundamentally he is easier to get along with than I would have been under such circumstances and at his age. In addition, one must take into consideration that for years he was floundering on his own and even now does not benefit from pedagogical principles. Materially, he is certainly well off in the home for students, much better and more comfortable than in other boarding schools. But from a pedagogical point of view, neither the home for students nor the school is worth a penny. He draws almost exclusively on his natural talents." As for any advice from his father, "naturally he thinks he is much wiser and more practical than I. He considers my opinions slightly dated – all that is quite all right, indeed, is it any different elsewhere? As for the rest, we are very attached to each other." It was painful for Schuschnigg therefore to see his "former suspicions confirmed once again: Vera doesn't quite get along with the boy. It's not a lack of kindness. She does her best and makes a great effort to pull herself together, but she is a bundle of nerves, and so we have, almost daily, a tempest in a teapot. Thank God Kurt hasn't taken notice of it so far, but I feel it deeply, and am considerably bothered ... As a result I am fundamentally glad that I finally have my peace and those ongoing excitements are over for the time being."[25]

Contrary to Schuschnigg's assertions, Kurt did take notice. He once caught Vera in tears.[26] He may not have connected her stress with his presence, but even on his first Christmas visit to Sachsenhausen he commented on how tired she looked and offered to take Sissy off her hands. She gratefully accepted his offer, so she could take a nap before making dinner. Kurt was astounded. "It had never occurred to me that Vera might be able to cook. In fact, I could not imagine her in a kitchen. I had always thought her too beautiful, too glamorous for such chores. Her lovely hands with lacquered nails seemed to belong to a world quite remote from kitchens."[27]

While Kurt managed to feel at home in Sachsenhausen, and his father, too, valued the opportunity to be reunited with his son, the visits did not always go smoothly. Like any teenager, Kurt engaged in risky behaviour and was therefore a constant source of worry. The upstairs bedroom window overlooked the general camp. Kurt witnessed the brutality of the guards, "enough brutality for a lifetime of nightmares."[28] He owned a camera and, defying all prohibitions, took clandestine photos of the watchtower and the house. He tinkered with the family's radio, ignoring Vera's alarmed reaction: "Kurti, if you break that radio, I personally will kill you. That is your father's most important possession." The radio was designed to have a limited range of reception, restricted to the official German stations. Kurt managed to pick up BBC broadcasts. Listening to enemy transmission could have serious consequences.[29] In this case, however, the family ignored the risk and listened to the daily "enemy" newscast, huddling under a blanket to mute the sound.[30]

Maintaining personal relationships and, more generally, contact with the outside world, was of prime importance for prisoners, but in this particular case Kurt's visits served an additional purpose. Every good parent – free or imprisoned – is concerned about bonding with their child. Schuschnigg's effort at bonding took the shape of sharing his own interests with the boy by providing him with reading material. It was also a way to fulfil his obligations as a parent and provide for his son's intellectual and moral education. Schuschnigg took these obligations seriously. He had been unable to do anything about the difficulty of finding a school for his son when he became persona non grata with the regime, a felon imprisoned for "criminal" activities. Vera had to cope with that dilemma, and the Niedermayr family had provided Kurt with a home away from home in Munich. Schuschnigg thanked them for their care in a heartfelt letter and asked them to continue keeping an eye on his son, to "keep him on the strait and narrow, as is customary in our families and as we always thought essential, and for good reasons, so that a young man will turn out not only honest and industrious, but also happy." He asked them specifically not to pamper his son, for "hard discipline is perhaps the most difficult but also the most useful and promising school of life." After the move to Sachsenhausen, Schuschnigg's brother, Artur, took over the guardian role and welcomed Kurt's visits to his home in Berlin during school holidays. Schuschnigg made a point of thanking his brother for exposing Kurt to culture on those occasions: "Many thanks for taking my Kurt to the opera! Please keep an eye on him if you can and it's not too much bother for you. I would like him to develop some interests beyond airplanes and tanks! The boy gives me cause for concern sometimes. Of course things aren't entirely his fault. In the end he is a victim of the times. V[era] troubles herself a great deal about him, but she can't work miracles. He is basically a good soul, but easy-going and immature. I am very attached to him! Well, you know yourself how much wife and children mean to a man! And sometimes it would seem that nothing else matters."[31]

Now that Kurt was a teenager, Schuschnigg worried about sexual temptations. "I must count myself lucky if he doesn't slip occasionally now that he is at a dangerous age," he wrote to his brother. "If he does, I couldn't even be angry with him, although it would pain me." But his focus was on Kurt's intellectual development and his performance in school, which he feared might be sidetracked by an interest in girls. As he said, tongue-in-cheek, flirting was bad for the boy's marks: "Girls might make Latin even less attractive to him." At the end of the school year, in July 1941, Schuschnigg wrote to his brother, "Remaining stuck (*sitzen bleiben*) in class, as Kurt usually is, is less of an evil than being stuck in life." The German words mean literally "to remain seated" and denotes a failing mark in a subject which does not allow the student to move on to the next grade. Schuschnigg adds "usually," which would indicate that the problems were of longer standing than Kurt's memoirs indicate. The difficulties, however, seem to have been restricted to language studies. In a letter of Christmas 1941, Schuschnigg reports to his uncle, who was contributing to Kurt's school fees: "[Kurt] is a rascal – as boys sometimes tend to be. He is forever battling Latin, and generally speaking the opposite of a model student. Yet it is striking how well he does in mathematics, and on the whole he is clearly not stupid. Mainly, he is a good boy at heart, but unspeakably frivolous and thoughtless. Yet he also has some good traits. For me he is quite a bit of trouble, but also often pure joy!" A year later, Schuschnigg comments on Kurt's progress in school in a letter to his brother: "He seems to have gotten away with the usual black eye, except that he once again got a failing grade in German. Between you and me: that does not especially bother me. According to his teachers, he regularly fails the now popular essays on the unity of the people [*Volksgemeinschaft*], etc. Well, that can happen! And as far as his style is concerned, I am well informed. Judging by his letters, I find his progress quite 'sufficient.' Nevertheless, I'll make a point of striking him with some private thunderbolts, even though I have no illusions about their effectiveness."[32]

During Kurt's visits to Sachsenhausen, accordingly, Schuschnigg tried to interest him in the authors he himself enjoyed. For their first Christmas together in 1941, he asked Artur to get him books that might be suitable as presents for his son. "If there is an opportunity, could you obtain for me a good book as a Christmas present for Kurtl? I am thinking of a handsome classic or a book about Austria (cultural, geographic, historical – if possible in the old style!) – The other day he connected Adalbert Stifter with the building of St. Stephan's! When he saw my astonished face and heard my weary groan 'Rudolf, [not Adalbert]' he just said, 'Well it involved some Stifter or other!' – I wonder whether a book by Stifter would be a suitable present for him. I remember reading that author with enthusiasm at his age. But it may be too early for Kurt. If he finds Stifter too boring, he may simply be deterred from reading, and that would not serve the purpose. Otherwise he has fortunately changed for the better, as far as I can judge. I would be especially keen on providing him with a correct and broad picture of our Austria, for he is interested in that subject as well! So, if you have an opportunity, please do so!"[33]

During Kurt's visit, Schuschnigg tried to develop the boy's literary tastes. He suggested reading Franz Grillparzer's Ahnfrau (The Ancestress), a Gothic family drama – perhaps not a bad choice, but the young man preferred science fiction. "I tried very hard to get Kurtl to read the Ahnfrau first. Unfortunately he got hold of some book about research into crocodiles and a futuristic novel about technological developments; so Grillparzer was put on the reserve shelf for the time being."[34]

The following year, Schuschnigg was wondering whether Kurt would be able to spend the summer with them at all. The young man might have to report to work, he mused. "School apparently doesn't count for anything anymore. The boys have already been requisitioned [to work] from 1 June on – after they have been on vacation for half the winter because of a scarcity of coals. Even Kurt took notice of that. Well, I suppose it's best not to worry my head about his future; the young people will find it hard to catch up one day. If only he stays healthy, in body and soul! So far he seems to have no problems." Kurt describes the situation in his memoirs: "My services and those of all sixteen-year-old boys were required by the fatherland. There was a shortage of farm workers, and Wittelsbach students were assigned to two weeks of picking hops." Neither he nor his classmates had seen hops before. It seemed easy work until he tried it. In the end he bought his freedom – paying another boy to pick in his stead.[35]

When Kurt was able to visit after all, Schuschnigg realized the need for a little diplomacy in developing his taste for literature. He got together a selection of books out of his own library – the cartons of books that had been delivered to him from the depot in Vienna. He included books about military history; the moralizing plays of Karl Schönherr; the works of Nestroy, a popular comic dramatist; Stifter once again; and an unspecified "book about cultural history written in an easy style. I had to gently nudge him to read at least part of this last book. He showed a 50 per cent liking for reading Schönherr's prose. As for Stifter, he immediately stored him away *honoris causa*. He baulked at Nestroy at first and would have liked to skip to lighter fare, but, strange to say, he suddenly conceived an interest in him. Finally, he read almost all of the twelve volumes; and in between he read a volume of Raimund, and could hardly be persuaded to put him down. In passing he also absorbed the *Ahnfrau*. And finally, I thought of showing him Goldoni (perhaps not entirely a happy thought). That, too, was a hit. Looking over his shoulder, I saw that he was deep into *Skandal in Chioggia*. I hope by God he was deceived by that nice title, which he deliberately selected. I am ashamed to confess that I don't know enough about it."[36]

In 1943, Kurt was informed that his age cohort was eligible for military service. Accordingly, he was assigned to FLAK units in Munich.[37] His tasks included setting the searchlights of the anti-aircraft gunner with the coordinates of the incoming Allied aircraft, to feed ammunition into the anti-aircraft guns, and to clean them. Naturally, Schuschnigg worried about his son, and not only because of the physical danger. The military discipline might be good for him, he mused, but it came too early because he had not yet developed a solid inner core (*innerlich gefestigt*). Kurt's schooling and future education were affected. The hours of instruction had been curtailed, and sometimes teaching was suspended entirely. Of course, Kurt himself was glad to escape the classroom, even if he pretended regret, Schuschnigg wrote. "But what will become of young people in future?? After all, they have to have some knowledge and skill, even if everything remains as it is now and nothing changes."[38]

In May 1943 Schuschnigg reported that "after much back and forth ... Kurt was given a three-day leave and permission to visit here. He looks good and seems to lead an orderly life. Apparently they work them hard, which isn't necessarily a bad thing." School hours had been reduced to a minimum, however. Instead of instruction, the young men were given paramilitary work. "His age group is supposed to be drafted into regular service by August. He will be 17 at the end of May! Certain things displease me, for example, that the young people are occasionally given an excessive amount of alcohol (which has otherwise unfortunately become rare); they don't receive tobacco rations because of their age, but cigarettes can be bought in the cafeteria at special prices."[39]

In October 1943 Kurt was assigned to RAD (national labour duty).[40] His task there was digging ditches and dams in the Westerwald. The work was back-breaking and the winter was especially cold, but Kurt managed to escape this duty eventually by feigning illness. Back in school, he finished his senior matriculation on a special wartime schedule, without exams. He was now 17 years old and liable to be drafted immediately. The father of a fellow boarder, Vice Admiral Kurt Slevogt, advised the boys to volunteer to avoid being drafted into the *Himmelfahrt* ("heavenbound") units. When Kurt told his father of Slevogt's advice, Schuschnigg reacted with exasperation. "These are extraordinary times when I find myself indebted to a German admiral I don't know and will probably never meet."[41] He agreed however that Slevogt's advice was good and should be followed. In January 1944 Kurt therefore reported to the recruiting office of the German navy. He was admitted to the Naval Academy and started training in marine engineering.[42]

While Schuschnigg was clearly anxious about doing his duty as a father and frequently wrote to his brother about his educational efforts and his worries for his son's education, Kurt recalls little of those concerns in his memoirs. His accounts of his last school years focus on his "adventures," the little tricks that got him out of scrapes and hard work. As for his father, he felt that the conditions of internment at Sachsenhausen were indeed a great improvement over solitary prison. "The listlessness produced by the years of confinement in Vienna and Munich seemed to have dissipated."[43]

Kurt's visits to Sachsenhausen ended in 1944 when he was drafted, an event Schuschnigg had anticipated with some fear. Kurt was assigned to the heavy cruiser Prince Eugen, a ship patrolling the Baltic Sea. In the entry of 15 January 1945 (missing from the English-language edition) Schuschnigg reports, "My own boy has for months now been serving in the German army."[44] In mid-January 1945 a Russian plane dropped a bomb on the cruiser. Kurt was wounded in the attack and obtained shore leave. He was able to travel by train for a visit with his father in Sachsenhausen. The widespread destruction he saw in Berlin convinced him that the war would soon come to an end. On his arrival in Sachsenhausen, he heard that the family was going to be evacuated the following day. He did not see his father again until after the war.[45]

All the information about Schuschnigg's relationship with his son comes from his letters. Kurt is mentioned only a few times in the diaries, and only in passing. The scarcity of references to his son, who was after all a person central to Schuschnigg's life, may serve as a caveat to the reader. It points to the selective nature of the information we can draw from this source.

At the end of January 1942, one other person had joined the Schuschnigg household: a maid. The woman assigned to them was a fellow prisoner. Already in the first letter Schuschnigg wrote from Sachsenhausen, he hinted that Vera could not be expected to handle all the household chores by herself. "In the long run it is completely out of the question for Vera to remain on her own. She tries as hard as she can and does a first-rate job. But to take even a moment's rest during the day is impossible. Both of us are kept in continual motion, playing housekeepers." Similarly, Vera writes to

Schuschnigg's uncle that they "have a terrible amount of work to cope with because we have no help."[46] Schuschnigg himself was full of admiration for his wife's good will: "Vera carries on as if she had done nothing else all her life but doing laundry, dusting, cooking, and everything else that's required; I myself am developing more spirit for household work than one might have thought."[47] To our modern sensibilities it is hard to see what all the fuss was about. Surely it didn't require an undue effort for two adults, neither of whom were employed, to take care of their modest home and their little daughter. But at the time, and in the social circles of the Schuschniggs, hired help was considered de rigueur – and unbelievable as it may be, the camp authorities agreed and supplied the Schuschniggs with help. Although Schuschnigg felt entitled to household help, he may have felt awkward about accepting this privilege since we find nothing about it in his published diaries or, for that matter, in his son's memoirs. All the information we have comes from Schuschnigg's private letters.

When the maid appeared, Schuschnigg was relieved. "It was a load off my mind. In the long run it would have been too much for Vera." Her health had suffered, and she finally collapsed with gall bladder problems. This created an emergency, not only because Vera needed immediate medical attention, but also because there was no one now to do the daily shopping for food, including milk for the baby. That is why they were finally assigned a maid. Schuschnigg was asked whether he minded if their employee had a criminal record. He had visions of a "kleptomaniac ... or maybe a sick gypsy," but the maid turned out to have been imprisoned for political crimes. "I couldn't very well say that I would welcome such a person. It has never been healthy to speak the truth indiscriminately, that is, to blurt it out," Schuschnigg quips. The 22-year-old woman was easy-going and an able cook. She was "as industrious as a bee, cooked, cleaned, dusted, laughed, and was obviously happy to escape the [general] camp." In a word, she was "just what we need."[48] The only flaw of this "gem" (as Vera called her), at least in the eyes of an Austrian, was her accent. "Of course she speaks the local dialect. Nothing we can do about that. But at least the Prussians know how to keep order."[49]

Unfortunately for the Schuschniggs, the capable young woman was soon replaced by a "clumsy oaf ... hysterical, abysmally careless, and with few skills."[50] She in turn was succeeded by a third helper. "The first impression was not reassuring since the girl came directly from the intake camp and hails from a rural home near Smolensk. Apart from her primitive nature, which is quite incredible by our standards, and her complete lack of a wardrobe, there are of course difficulties communicating with her ... other than by sign language. In spite of all that, the girl doesn't manage badly and obviously makes an effort – in marked contrast to her predecessor from Berlin." Schuschnigg put up with the imperfections of the new maid: "I still praise heaven that we don't have the former girl, and that we have a girl at all. The great advantage of the Russian girl is the fact that I can't really be angry with her. Such great and primitive stupidity is disarming. Nevertheless, such people have a good and decent core; no sign of depravity, etc., but we can hardly hope to teach her manners."[51]

Unlike her predecessors, the Russian woman was an *Ostarbeiter*, a worker from regions in East Europe occupied by German troops at the time. The conditions of employment for these workers were harsh, Schuschnigg notes. Their hours were not regulated, and they were not entitled to holidays. The "poor devils" were not allowed to visit movie theatres, inns, or churches. And they were paid a minimal wage of 9 to 12 marks.[52]

The assignment of a maid to the Schuschniggs was not a unique case. Other elite prisoners had help. Fritz Thyssen, for example, was registered in one of the special houses as "Fritz Thyssen with wife and companion." This third person was presumably a personal attendant they had brought along with them.[53] In another case, by contrast, a domestic who volunteered to accompany her employer, Fey von Hassell, was refused permission.[54] Mafalda of Hesse was assigned a fellow prisoner, Maria Ruhnau, as an attendant in Buchenwald. She diligently looked after the ailing Mafalda and earned her gratitude. Leon Blum, who lived in a house on the border of the Buchenwald concentration camp, had a *serviteur* by the name of Joachim.[55] Schuschnigg seemed to be afraid that the maid, or at any rate the first maid assigned to them, might report on them to the Gestapo. Her presence "probably means that we have to watch our words more carefully," he writes. Although he had no such fears about the Russian, he did not entirely regret her leaving in May 1944. It was better so, he said. "The house is too small for such trials – especially with an absolutely incorrigible person. The unimaginable Eastern stupidity, combined with other bad characteristics, made continued cohabitation quite impossible."[56]

The couple settled into a routine, described in a letter of March 1942 to Artur. Adopting a subtly ironic tone, Schuschnigg depicts a life of leisure and contentment. The couple got up at 8:30, looked in on the child, washed up, and breakfasted – "Vera very grouchy, I moderately grouchy. Then an hour goes by, I don't know how, but with much ado, and finally everything is in order and the morning begins." He takes a short walk in the grounds, such as they are, then sits down at his desk to read. From time to time he gets up and visits the child, taking the opportunity to do twenty kneebends. His visits to the child's room are fraught. If he goes, he is scolded for keeping the child awake; if he doesn't visit, he is told that "no one looks after the child." Vera busies herself with the household and in between does some typing. They eat at noon, "with passion and remarkably good appetite ... I eat as I used to in my earliest vacations." They end the meal with a cup of coffee. After that, the child is wheeled around in her carriage for an hour and put down for her nap. The couple then reads until 5:15. At that point the child is fed, washed, and put to bed by 7 pm. "At that time the two of us are again extremely hungry. After [eating], we make ourselves comfortable, talk a bit, and read again, and in that context muse how nice it would be to have a radio[57] or, even better, some alcohol." At 9:30 at the latest they wash up and go to bed and "jointly remark that it was a fine day." The routine is broken only on Sunday, when Schuschnigg dresses up *Salzburgerisch* (in traditional Austrian fashion) and reads through the canon of the mass in his missal. This routine may not be exciting enough for some people, Schuschnigg concludes, but "it's enough for me."[58] Payne-Best adopts a similarly light tone in describing his enforced leisure: "I rose at 5 a.m. and went to the lavatory to wash ... After shaving, I dressed and lay down on my bed for a nap. Breakfast was brought in at about eight o'clock ... I then either dozed on my bed, read, or played [solitaire] ... From noon to one o'clock I went out for exercise and when I got back my dinner was waiting for me on the table ... After dinner another snooze, and then I read or played [solitaire] till my supper was brought at about five ... From then until ten o'clock I would generally chat with my guard or read. Then to the lavatory, undress, get into bed, and the warder came with my wristlet and I was chained up for the night. A lazy futile sort of life for most of which I was only half awake, but it must be remembered that I had to snatch my sleep when I could, and that at least once every two hours I was awakened by the change of guards."[59]

What remains unsaid here is that both Schuschnigg and Payne-Best suffered from boredom. The mild irony they use in describing their "lazy" life covers up a certain embarrassment born from the knowledge that their complaint was trivial. The majority of the inmates suffered grievously and often fatally from malnutrition, hard labour, and overcrowding that prevented rest and sleep, whereas these men merely suffered a vacuity as absurd as that depicted in *Waiting for Godot*. Such enforced leisure might well induce brooding and even hopelessness, but lacks the intensity that touches the heart and the drama which elicit immediate compassion from the reader. Thus the slightly farcical tone adopted by the two men in describing their routine. Neither Payne-Best nor Schuschnigg were starving. The rations allocated to the Schuschniggs were supplemented with food Vera bought in Berlin as well as with occasional food parcels from Wopfner, who sent them apples and apricots. Sometimes Artur obtained cigarettes for his brother.[60] In addition, Schuschnigg received parcels from the American Red Cross and *Liebesgaben* (charitable gifts) from Tyrolian resistance groups. Schuschnigg welcomed them, not only because of the contents – coffee, chocolate, corned beef, and Chesterfield cigarettes – but also because they were addressed to him by his name rather than the alias the Gestapo had assigned to him. It was good to hear himself called by name, "but, above all, it is an immense joy and consolation to know that someone outside in the world thinks of us." The American parcel came from one Francis Hofer, whom he did not know personally. "These remittances were usually accompanied by several hours of 'inquisition'" by the Gestapo.[61]

Inmates of concentration camps were forbidden to receive parcels at first, but at the end of 1942 the authorities permitted such shipments at Himmler's directive, as an emergency war measure.[62] This measure was taken, not "for humane reasons, but for the sake of efficiency," Weiss-Rüthel pointed out. As war casualties mounted and industries suffered from a dearth of labourers, the authorities were suddenly concerned about preserving the physical strength of workers in the concentration camps. Nansen, for example, reports that inmates in his cell block now regularly received parcels from their families and the International Red Cross. The contents were shared among fellow prisoners, and it wasn't until 1944, when air raids disrupted the delivery system, that they were reduced to living on camp rations.[63]

It was difficult for all prisoners to obtain fresh fruit and vegetables. Schuschnigg countered that difficulty by converting his small yard into a produce garden. Obtaining food wasn't his only motive for taking up gardening. Nature offered special attractions to prisoners in their desolate quarters. They "experienced beauty ... of nature as never before," Frankl notes. "The mere thought of violets and lilies of the valley ... calls up the most wonderful pictures ... and nostalgic memories," Nansen writes in his diary. Edgar Kupfer-Koberwitz, interned in Dachau, wrote in his diary that the beauty of nature comforted him because it represented *das Draussen* (the outside world). Watching the swallows wheel above the camp grounds reminded him of freedom: "Soon they would fly away into the faraway South." And even Payne-Best, who generally adopts a waggish tone in his memoirs, strikes a softer note when talking about nature. "I scattered food and did everything I could think of to attract birds but they seemed to sense that this was no place for creatures as free as they. When one is free one takes so many things for granted, and generally one is not even conscious of the pleasure one derives from the presence of the graceful gifts of nature around one."[64]

Gardening not only put Schuschnigg in touch with nature but also provided him with creative work in its most basic sense. In the general prison population as well, physical debility and exhaustion did not keep prisoners from engaging in crafts for their personal satisfaction – carving, sewing, drawing, and other creative activities. While most prisoners found it difficult to muster the energy and make time for such work, special prisoners like Schuschnigg, who were not required to do hard labour, often felt time weighing heavily on their hands and welcomed activities that occupied them physically and helped them forget their surroundings. Work, Joseph Joos commented, "preserved one's mental balance." Others in turn engaged in physical activities to keep in shape. Thomas Cushing, a British soldier and one of the inmates of the *Prominenten-Baracke* (the barrack where special prisoners were housed) recounts that they were all in the habit of marching briskly up and down the yard "to keep fit."[65] One of his fellow inmates, Dschugaschwilij, the son of Stalin, liked to spar and taught him a few boxing moves. Some special prisoners engaged in crafts. As mentioned earlier, Franz of Bavaria's mother fashioned a crèche from plywood. She also designed board games for her children. Mafalda of Hesse made miniature clay plates and toy dishes, with the idea of bringing them home to her children upon her release. Some inmates at Sachsenhausen went as far as building a stage for theatre performances in their free time. On a more modest scale, Isa Vermehren busied herself cleaning her cell and keeping her clothes in order "to create dignified surroundings" and in hopes of creating a corresponding order in her mind.[66]

Schuschnigg took similar pleasure in the tidy vegetable plots and flower beds in the sandy lot around his house. He reports on his first efforts: "We are freezing regularly so far. That is, not in the house. That is still well heated. We enjoy that advantage at any rate. But outside there is no warming trend. Winds are blowing endlessly from the northeast. The sky is grey all over and it's raining as well! I am no longer as indifferent to miserable weather as I was earlier because I am very preoccupied with our garden. For a long time it looked as if we couldn't do anything at all because we lacked seeds, plants, etc. But the situation changed unexpectedly. Vera got together quite a stash of seeds in Berlin, and a loyal friend (a parish priest from the suburbs of Vienna, not known to me personally) sent me a large packet with all sorts of useful things. From red currant bushes to sunflowers, beans, peas, and carrots. He also included forget-me-nots and strawberry plants. Most of it was still usable. The shoots are putting out leaves, and even the forget-me-nots recovered magnificently. Plants to camouflage the many unattractive walls were particularly welcome. Unfortunately we won't be making much progress this year, quite apart from the fact that planting beanstalks along the wall met with disapproval. Still, it gives us great pleasure to see the daily developments and we are pleased with every new sprig. Spinach and peas are growing well, it seems. That's nice of them, given the climate! Now we have so many packets of seeds (lettuce, cauliflower, etc.) that we can't even accommodate them all. We are mainly interested in winter-hardy vegetables. We have already planted 25 kilos of seed potatoes. I'm curious what kind of harvest they will yield. That is of great importance to us, because we are great eaters of potatoes."

At first Schuschnigg had little success with his garden: "The weather is completely hopeless, nothing but cold and rain. Nothing grows – if the conditions are the same everywhere, one must fear for the harvest. Recently, moreover, our vegetables have been infested by worms, the potatoes are beginning to show the same problem, and there are aphids and the like on the flowers. So much work has gone into the garden, and now everything goes to ruin ... I just wonder how I am going to feed Kurt [on his visit], I am already worried about that because supplies are pretty tight here."

At last he reports moderate success: "I am still very busy with the garden. It is a former woodlot, worked for the first time, so that I must be satisfied with whatever success I have. It already looks quite grown in and green, which is the main thing for me, I think. The former sandy desert has disappeared. As far as it goes, I had quite a good harvest, especially of peas, beans, cucumbers, tomatoes, carrots, and, I am pleased to say, flowers. I wasn't lucky with salad greens or any kind of cabbage except turnip. In the spring the problem was that something was eating the roots, and now we have caterpillars which practically demolish the plants in spite of all my searches. Ants are also likely culprits. But, as I said, on the whole I am quite satisfied."[67]

Eventually Schuschnigg became resigned to life in the camp and even expressed contentment: "I am quite happy. I have everything I could wish for at this time. I am completely satisfied, and if I succeed eventually in my efforts to have Kurt [Jr.] with me here occasionally, I won't be afraid of the coming years at all." Of course, he may have been bluffing. Odd Nansen jokes about such letters being sent home. They contain "the usual phrases – 'I am fine,' 'I am well,' 'I am in good spirits.'"[68] These phrases were put in because there was always a risk of the letters being intercepted, but it seems that Schuschnigg found genuine comfort in the company of his wife and was much cheered by their little daughter.

The theme of comfort derived from human contact, especially with people who connected the prisoner with the "outside" world, is frequent in the memoirs of concentration camp survivors. An example is the account of Fey von Hassell, who repeatedly refers to the beneficial effects of human contact. "Just being able to exchange a few words with someone from the outside world was a comfort," she writes. The friendly community (*freundschaftliche Gemeinschaft*) of fellow prisoners, "their conversations, their mutual understanding was invaluable." Fabian Schlabrendorff, too, attested to "the single spirit of comradeship amongst us" when the special prisoners were evacuated in the spring of 1945. It was rare for anyone to transgress the code of friendship. Cushing's account is one of very few that reports disagreements among special prisoners. "The two Russians [Stalin's son and Kokorin Molotov] didn't get along and screamed insults at each other … once they even came to blows." Stalin seemed to have been particularly aggressive. When Cushing reminded him to flush the toilet, "he became physically aggressive, but I seized him and shouted 'Flush the toilet!,' which he finally did."[69] But such rough behaviour was unusual. As a rule, special prisoners maintained a sense of community, as von Hassell says. Yet hers was a community of strangers thrown together by circumstance. Schuschnigg, in contrast, enjoyed the closer, more intimate and meaningful relationship with a wife and child.

The will to help each other and a sense of cohesion cushioned special prisoners against the moral debasement they saw in the camp at large, where the fight for survival made any humane gesture a luxury. Indeed, they were alarmed whenever they noticed signs of callousness in themselves. Nansen sadly notes that seeing a dead body no longer made any great impression on him; by contrast, when he felt scared, he was "happy that [he] still could," that is, that he could still summon feelings. Renata Laqueur also regrets her inability to feel and that "everything was numb and dull." Similarly, Joos commented that he was glad to read Charles Dickens and "laugh and cry" with his characters. "May God grant that we all preserve the ability to do so."[70] Vermehren is distressed when she sees the humanity of prisoners slipping away and is deeply disappointed when theft occurs in her group because it "it clearly reflected our moral decline (*Verwahrlosung*)."[71]

As Joos notes, necessity forced prisoners to make a decision: did they want to fight for their humanity and appeal to their better selves, or would they allow themselves to sink to the level of animals. They had to "draw upon the last remnants of their moral strength." At this juncture it helped if they could fall back on their religious beliefs.[72] Moral decline was also one of Schuschnigg's concerns. He countered them by turning to his fundamental beliefs and to God.

chapter three

The Comfort of Religion

Victor Frankl speaks of most prisoners in concentration camps going into "cultural hibernation." This withdrawal, however, did not necessarily apply to politics and religion. Jews clung to their religion, even in the face of death. As incredible as it sounds, a group in Auschwitz managed to fashion a shofar and blow it on Rosh Hashanah. In some of the camps there were *Katakombenge-meinschaften*, underground Christian communities who found ways to express their beliefs and remain in contact with clergy. Masses were said, sacred songs were sung. Pastor Niemöller managed to give out communion. Isa Vermehren tells of a priest in her block who at a prearranged sign gave a general blessing, and Pastor Bonhoeffer, who was held in the Gestapo prison in Berlin, passed out scraps of paper with biblical passages as "words of comfort." Fabian von Schlabrendorff, a lawyer by profession who was arrested for his resistance activities, simply acknowledged: "Prayer can bring comfort." Nanda Hebermann, interned at Ravensbrück, found consolation in the thought of "nestling trustingly into God's fatherly arms." There is a strong consensus among concentration camp survivors that religious beliefs gave prisoners the power to overcome any obstacle and to transcend suffering.[1]

Schuschnigg was a professed and devout Catholic. Although expressions like "thank God," "God willing," "God grant ...," ubiquitous both in his and in Vera's correspondence, are too trite to be taken as expressions of religiosity, their frequency is notable and may indicate something more than the habitual use of a

commonplace. "Anyone who thanks God is better off and will not
be vanquished," Schuschnigg writes. It also seems more than a trite
phrase when Vera, who shared her husband's beliefs, expresses the
wish, "May God soon give us inner and external peace!"[2]

There are of course more definite expressions of Schuschnigg's
beliefs in his prison writings. More specifically he addressed the
role of religion in helping him cope with life in captivity in an
article published shortly after his rescue. In it he describes the
benefits he derived from faith during his internment. "It was inde-
scribably comforting" and "uncommonly calming," he wrote. Solitary confinement resulted in "the forced, but precious, reflections
that bestow the gift of inner balance." Reading biblical passages
brought him "blessed peace."[3]

The German (but not the English) edition of *Requiem* contains
two long disquisitions on Schuschnigg's beliefs and the role they
played during the time of his captivity. He contrasts people who
seek God independently with others who take the "easy" way
and follow the guidance of the institutional church. "I belong to
those who take the easy way," he writes. "I have no doubt that the
Church is God's messenger." Yet Schuschnigg faltered in his faith
during his solitary confinement, when he could not call on the support of the institutional church and on its rituals.[4] He missed the
holy images, the sacred music, the peace and quiet of the church
which facilitated prayer, and the "architectural splendour (*Formen-
pracht*) which spoke to the senses" with their beauty and harmony.[5]
He missed the counsel of a priest who might support him in his
beliefs and comfort him in his distress. In these sentiments he was
not alone. Henri Michel, a fellow prisoner at Sachsenhausen, also
noted,[6] "One cannot imagine what it means to a churchgoer, even
a lax one, to be without divine services, never to glimpse a church
or a belltower, even from afar."

Lacking this support structure, Schuschnigg wrote, "I was suddenly struck by doubts and strayed from faith for the first time in
my life." Solitary thought was dangerous and could lead to spiritual
emptiness, he noted. He began asking himself "crazy" questions:
Did God exist? And if so, was he punishing him when he experienced, in addition to loneliness, the "cruel fate of being deserted by

God"?[7] Arnold Weiss-Rüthel, a fellow prisoner at Sachsenhausen, used strikingly similar words to describe the doubts that assailed him: "Strange thoughts entered my mind: Is it true that there had once been a man by the name of Goethe? ... and the question of all questions: God! What kind of a God is that?" In view of the evil he permitted, how was it possible to believe in the doctrine of salvation?[8] Death was preferable to the misery of doubt, Schuschnigg wrote, paraphrasing the words of Christ on the eve of his crucifixion (Matt. 26: 39): "Your servant has experienced Calvary, has sensed the nearness of the abyss. His prayer to let this chalice pass from him went unheard. Deliver me! Deliver your servant who was hoping over and over again that he may be allowed to die of sorrow and a broken heart, while he remained a believer, not only because it is a consolation to believe, but because he felt the breath of God." The Calvary metaphor reoccurs in Schuschnigg's prison writings. "If the path of your life leads to Calvary, if you have ever said in your deepest despair 'Let this chalice pass from me,' and were not spared ... if there is no end to bitter experiences, it is not easy to collect your thoughts." Overwhelmed by misfortune, many sufferers lose their way, but those who are fortunate enough to look at life with the eyes of a believer, "will be blinded by the fullness of knowledge and bow humbly before God, for he is the One, and nothing is lasting apart from him." The sceptic, by contrast, will be left out in the dark and cold.[9]

Schuschnigg describes the emotional state of the believer/ doubter also in the article he published about religious practices in Sachsenhausen. The "absence of the accustomed ties [to the church] was the greatest hardship." Doubt brought darkness into their life, but God's grace brought back light. Schuschnigg's own misfortune destabilized his basic principles and beliefs, which he had never questioned before. Like many other inmates, he acknowledged the demoralizing effect of suffering, the loss of values, the numbing of feelings. "The situation was desperate, but thank God, I overcame the crisis. Not through my own strength, no! It was a divine ray of grace that shone into the darkness of my mind."[10]

Vera was aware of the consolation which faith afforded her husband and expressed her own hopes in religious terms as well.

Schuschnigg was often in a despairing mood, she writes: "I know that no help can come from human beings, and we have placed our trust and fate into the hands of our dear Lord. It was a great help to me to know that we think alike. If one does not have absolute faith in God and in goodness, one would have to despair." Like her husband, she firmly believed in an afterlife and the intercession of the dead on behalf of the living. In a letter to Wopfner, for example, she expressed the conviction that Schuschnigg's late wife, "dear [Herma], will pray to God for whatever is right for her child."[11]

Viktor Frankl describes submission to fate as characteristic of a certain phase of internment, as does Henri Michel, who was, like Schuschnigg, a devout Catholic: "One must yield to fate, not with the fatalism of orientals, but in the sense of yielding to what is preordained."[12] This sentiment is also borne out in Schuschnigg's prison writings. He believed in divine predestination and consequently the insignificance of the individual's efforts and desires. "Who nowadays can consider his own personal fate important! It is nothing but a tiny wheel which had to turn on its course so that predestined events and developments could take shape. I am certain today that [my imprisonment] was predestined and all agents were only tools in the end!" It was therefore foolish to call on God or invoke him in support of a cause. In the context of discussing the theory of historical cycles and professing his inability to judge how the present times might fit into them, Schuschnigg writes, "I can only think that the Lord knows where we are heading and why. Although it is certainly bizarre for people to drag him into human quarrels and to cite him when they perhaps thought of him very little earlier on. That is probably an error as old as human history." The course of his life had been determined long ago, and there was no use resisting it. Human beings could not hope to understand the larger purpose of the events they witnessed. Schuschnigg himself had experienced moments of yearning for death, but he was willing to submit to God's higher purpose. "What peace, what ineffable relief [to die], but I did not deserve it ... The moment of delivery was denied to me, and this cannot have been without a reason. It was obvious: I had not completed the task for which I was to serve as a tool in destiny's plan." The frustration and loss of hope he experienced in the face of his captivity was tempered by this submission to God's will. "We must be infinitely thankful to God and cannot ask him for more than he regards right for us at the moment."[13]

Although the faith Schuschnigg expresses is firmly rooted in the Bible, he occasionally speaks of divine will also in the context of literature and philosophy, connecting his beliefs with the words of Plato and Dante. Thus he quotes Dante's *Divine Comedy* on the concept of God's eternal love, which unfolds and becomes "the motor of everything that is great and beautiful and worthy to live for." The central role of love – though not necessarily in a religious context – is cited by a number of concentration camp survivors. Frankl calls it the "ultimate and the highest goal to which man can aspire" and of deep meaning to his inner self. To experience love and generosity in the dismal surroundings of the camp "helps preserve something in oneself which must not be lost." Conversely, Vermehren notes that the absence of love leads to "nihilistic radicalism." There is no human dignity without love, Schuschnigg says emphatically, and rejects any philosophy or *Weltanschauung* based on hate, negativity, threat, and violence, or rather denies that this constitutes philosophy at all. It is merely a tactic and will stay in force only as long as the regime applying it remains in power. At the end of his life, a man will look back at the milestones of love in his life: the love of his mother, the love of God, and patriotic love. Schuschnigg also takes from Dante the idea of patient suffering and atonement as well as the distinction between religious ideals and human practice. "It was a fortunate coincidence that put Dante into my hand half a year into my solitary confinement," he writes. Dante's unconditional faith revived his own beliefs. This in turn allowed him to overcome the spiritual turmoil and the doubts he was experiencing and brought him peace of mind.[14]

Schuschnigg found inspiration also in Plato, "the pre-Christian herald of Christian ethos."[15] He recalls his youthful fascination with the Greek philosopher, and in particular with his concept of the immortal soul. "Apart from the many Christian thoughts [Plato expressed, he also] believed in the migration of the soul ... The subject still interests me today, and I would like to know if it is possible to incorporate it into our [Christian] doctrine in some form. The same immortal soul in different forms? Those are just speculations of mine, I know. As for the rest, I have only now come to see the beauty of the gospel – and the liturgy! I take great pleasure in reading my missal," he writes to his brother.[16]

When Schuschnigg was arrested and allowed to pack only absolutely necessary belongings, he had put the missal into his suitcase, and now it was his "priceless constant companion." Later on, when the cartons of books he had in storage in Vienna, had been delivered to him, he also found the missal that had belonged to his mother. Since he could not attend mass, he used these books to go through the appropriate readings on Sundays. "Reading my old missal is of course only a small compensation for what people like me are used to and miss, especially at Christmas."[17]

Easter was another time when he particularly longed for the aura of the church and the inspiration of Catholic traditions, such as the Holy Sepulchre displaying a sculpture of the body of Christ, in a recess or on a pediment during Holy Week to commemorate his death and resurrection. "Do they still have a Holy Sepulchre and good church music?" Schuschnigg asks his uncle wistfully. He treasured the memory of the candles on the altar, the sound of the bells, and the sight of the consecrated chalice being raised up during mass. He read the Bible not only for its comforting message but also for the "aesthetic pleasure it afforded him as a literary masterpiece." Reading biblical passages furthermore evoked memories of paintings depicting biblical scenes – Michelangelo and Pergolesi – and the church music of Verdi, Mozart, and Berlioz. Schuschnigg fondly recalled the last time he visited the Burgkapelle in Vienna and heard a Schubert mass. He was deeply moved when he heard the same mass sung on the radio in 1944, when he was at Sachsenhausen.[18]

Schuschnigg's yearning for the comfort of church ceremonies is not unique among prisoners of the Nazis. As mentioned earlier, underground masses were held in concentration camps. Schuschnigg was not permitted to mix with the general prison population and therefore had no opportunity to attend any of these clandestine ceremonies. Instead he asked his son, who was about to visit him in Sachsenhausen, to call on the bishop of Berlin and ask to be entrusted with a consecrated host, so he could take holy communion in his house. Kurt Jr. complied. "He brought me the sacred host in a small golden container. Every room of our exile became a chapel for a few short moments, and I received my Easter communion." It was a memorable experience also for the teenager, who recalls the occasion of smuggling the host into the camp "in an envelope." He undertook the risky mission because it was of crucial importance to his father, he said. "His faith had sustained him these many years; but for the devout Catholic, to be denied the sacraments was a great deprivation." In Munich, too, Vera smuggled a host into her husband's cell after she had first arranged for his absolution. A priest agreed to walk at a prearranged time along the wall of the prison, where Schuschnigg could see him. "It was a matter of concentrating my mind [on confession]," he wrote, so that he might receive from the priest the unspoken general absolution. When Vera came to visit Schuschnigg in the Munich prison with the gift of a consecrated host, they spread a handkerchief on the table and lit two Christmas candles so that he could consume the host before a makeshift altar. Unfortunately their devotions were interrupted by the entry of an SS man – they were able to extinguish the candles and remove the "altar" just in time.[19]

Schuschnigg's respect for the church and the comfort he found in its ceremonies does not mean that he was blind to the faults of church representatives. We must distinguish Schuschnigg's personal faith in God and his belief in Christian values from his views on the earthly representatives of God. In a letter to his brother in 1942, he comments negatively on the clergy. He clarifies, however, that he does not mean to make a blanket judgment. "Conditions were certainly good in Tyrol (the Brixen area), Upper Austria, and Vienna, to a certain extent, but all the worse in several other provinces, especially in Styria and Carinthia. The church was too well off in our country – I am certain that's the explanation. You see the same phenomenon in all purely Catholic countries.... That reminds me of the good joke (vintage Stockinger) about our 'Unnitzer' ... But we should have known that earlier. After all, we knew him in Vienna and not in Rome. And at that time we still had a considerable say in the matter. Let us hope that all that will improve! But when?"[20] The fallibility of the institutional church preoccupied him especially during his earlier solitary confinement, he writes, and such thoughts were not without danger. He did not like to dwell on the imperfections of the clergy. Such thoughts led to "inner distancing; and the end result is emptiness."[21]

One of Schuschnigg's first acts on gaining liberty in 1945 was to visit the chapel of the alpine village of Niederndorf. He went out "over the crisp, hard-frozen snow to a nearby chapel in the forest for a quiet prayer." There was no organ and no hymns, but there were candles and flowers and a picture of the Madonna, he reports. He felt "completely happy" and at peace. His first public appearance was equally focused on faith. In an address, broadcast from the Vatican on 6 September 1945, he appealed to his listeners to practise the tenets of Christianity. The speech is a remarkable expression of his faith. Indeed Schuschnigg almost adopts the tone of a preacher:[22]

> It is great for a simple man, a German-speaker, to know he is at this hour and in these times in the company of brothers and sisters who think like him, who are linked by the same faith and the same determination. A man who is granted that experience will be grateful for God's merciful disposition.
>
> ... We are right to feel completely optimistic if heart, conscience, reason, and memory work together in all matters, inextricably and in fourfold harmony. Then we may forget the past, and indeed, praise it. At this point everything is still in flux and very few things, or nothing at all, has been decided. It would be a mistake to expect miracles from the great powers [the Allies], as they lay the foundations of future peace one step at a time. Even the best agreements are in themselves only groundwork. The durability of peace depends on the nations and countries, indeed on each individual being prepared to build a new, better, more peaceful order worthy of humanity. The path to a better future is secure only when the principle of "power as will and idea" no longer dominates our thoughts.
>
> None of these ideas are new. They are merely the old Christian ideals. Let us look back and remember the frequently used antithesis: Christ

on one side, Antichrist on the other. This is often an oversimplification of the problem. Too often, the idea of practising Christianity is conveniently cited, replacing any further search for a solution. But practising Christianity is much more difficult and much more challenging than it might appear at first blush. We can only assess this difficulty correctly when the fiery breath of hatred and lies push us hard up against the edge of despair. That is when we discover how difficult it is to think like a Christian, something we thought was self-evident, and how difficult it is to obey the Christian commandments. True Christian thought is not bound by time and occasion. It cannot be nationalized. It is faith in the possibility and necessity of a true and effective right of nations, of humane thought and the consciousness of humanity. After all God did not conclude his work of creation on the sixth day by creating animals. Thus Christian thought leads us to the Great Four: heart, conscience, reason, and memory.

If all of the millions of people who profess to be Christians go beyond the purely formal profession and think of the Christian practice, they will come to understand the immense dynamic inherent in Christian thought, and more importantly, will come to understand how much they have in common, an understanding which goes beyond national borders and social rank and lies in common ideas and goals. If that comes to pass, these millions of Christians will be holding the keys to the future in their hands.

Thus Schuschnigg's religious convictions not only served him as means of coping with his years of imprisonment but also put a lasting stamp on his character. As Hans Ehrenberg, another internee at Sachsenhausen, averred, anyone lacking inner strength, was left without refuge, but "anyone who arrives here in camp with some kind of belief ... will grow in understanding and humanity." The survivors of Nazi prisons agreed that the specific creed they professed was of no significance compared with the importance of believing in something, of having convictions and the will to fight for a cause – religious, philosophical, or political. As Niemöller put it, "Human beings who have no solid point of view have given up on themselves."[23]

chapter four

The Consolation of Books

> He'll miss out on dessert
> As long as he may drink
> From the fresh and sparkling
> Fountain of a book.
> With tender love he holds it in his hand.
>
> Heinrich Christian Meier, concentration camp prisoner[1]

This chapter and the next are concerned with the consolation Schuschnigg derived from books and music. In his pursuit of culture, he displayed the pattern of a typical *Bildungsbürger*, a culturally engaged bourgeois. Men of his social class were the product of an education that promoted elitist values. Such schooling functioned largely as a means of preserving, rather than transcending, class differences. Schuschnigg's education and his approach to culture rested on the broad assumption that culture was capable of enhancing life and that its acquisition was an ongoing process of self-improvement.[2] Although culture was seen as purifying the mind and was thus endowed with a quasi-religious quality, the practical advantages of receiving a good education no doubt also played a role in the mind of the *Bildungsbürger*. Pierre Bourdieu first introduced the notion of a "cultural capital"[3] and the idea that education was a resource which, though immaterial, could produce material benefits. It could be converted into gentlemanly language and behaviour, making the individual comfortable in sophisticated social settings and enhancing one's career. Like

material goods, culture was restricted to the privileged. In 1911 –
four years before Schuschnigg graduated – only a little more than 1
per cent of 19-year-old men completed secondary school. Yet education was fundamental for a career in the civil service, the church,
and the more complex forms of commerce. *Bildungsbürgertum* is
often associated with specific professions, notably law, medicine,
and teaching – in that respect, Schuschnigg fits the pattern. As the
author of several books, however, he exceeds the aims of a typical
Bildungsbürger, who was generally a consumer rather than a pro-
ducer of culture. The education of a bourgeois in Schuschnigg's
time was typically humanistic, rooted in the study of classical civilization and proficiency in the classical languages Greek and Latin.
It was moreover oriented toward acquiring a knowledge of history, philosophy, and literature, with the sciences relegated to second place.[4] This slant is clearly reflected in Schuschnigg's cultural
preferences, as we shall see. The foreign language of choice taught
in Austrian secondary schools was French, although Schuschnigg
also acquired facility in English and Italian. His tastes in books and
music bear out the rather restrictive bourgeois preference for high
over popular culture, education over entertainment. In this context
it is interesting to note, for example, that he often reminisces about
visits to theatres, concert halls, and opera houses, but never mentions going to the cinema, which saw a steady rise in popularity in
his time. Like others of his generation and class he was presumably
ambivalent about the cultural value of the cinema and may even
have regarded it as below his dignity to be entertained by such
fare.[5]

"The books and the radio are my staff of life," Schuschnigg
writes from his solitary prison in Munich. Joseph Joos echoed these
sentiments: "Books are the joy of my free time."[6] Reading was an
important aid in keeping Schuschnigg's mind focused on spiritual
and intellectual matters and distracting him from the disturbing
events of the present. Reading the great books – the ancient and
modern classics – enabled him to "ascend step by step the ladder
to heaven. It took his thoughts far away from what is called life, but
which was for him only torture, pervasive pain and sorrow." He
was comforted by the contemplation of ideals that had remained

constant in the midst of turmoil. Communing with the great minds provided "ineffable consolation and immense help to a man whose soul was dying of hunger and in danger of losing her sight, and who desperately reached for a saving hand … thank God for Plato, Dante, Shakespeare, and Goethe, and for the existence of books, and for the fact that I am allowed to read them."[7]

We find similar thoughts expressed in the diaries and memoirs of other intellectuals imprisoned by the Nazis. John Lenz, a Catholic priest interned at Dachau, read Dante and found it consoling in the cultural desert surrounding him. Delving into the *Divine Comedy* served as a reminder of the existence of another, cultured, world. It allowed him to reach back into his past and for a short time escape prison. Another priest at Dachau spoke of reading the Bible as an act akin to "touching the chalice … to taking communion." Similarly, Paul Neurath, a prisoner at Buchenwald, recited the poems of Hans Christian Morgenstern while working in a clay pit, "passing them along to our friends as an important contribution of something that did not smell of clay."[8] Thus books provided a distraction from the back-breaking work routine and acted as an *Aufputschmittel* (stimulant).[9] The journalist and theologian Walter Gross, who was interned in Dachau, rhapsodized about books: "Yes, you have become our true loves, comforters in our solitude, the only visitors who are allowed to join us poor and abject people, and to whisper to us words full of encouragement, strength, and determination."[10] Some prisoners read to find inner strength, others to escape the present. Wolfgang Szepansky said that reading meant being transported "into another world if only for a short while." The pacifist Carl Ossietzky read Knut Hamsun to escape from the real world into "the intellectual world … which exists purely for itself … knows no borders and can't be kept out by barbed wire or walls." Some political prisoners, however, disapproved of flights into an imaginary world of beauty. Walter Hornung reports reading the art historian Jakob Burckhardt's book on the culture of the Renaissance and being told off by a fellow prisoner, "Leave that garbage alone, you get the best education looking around you. No need to read that antiquated tome!"[11] Primo Levi's account of reciting Dante – "You were not born to live as a brute, but to follow virtue and knowledge" – contains a similar warning. Looking back to the classics, he suggests, provided a "deceptive continuity" with the past. It was better to remain aware of the dissonance between the lofty sentiments expressed in classical literature and the ugly present lived in the concentration camp.[12] Not everyone read to escape reality. Political prisoners read books as a means of political education, regarding it as a kind of revolutionary act and a continuation of the resistance they had exercised in the outside world.[13] Others read to further their professional knowledge, that is, to further their careers on regaining freedom.

Most of the camps had libraries, originally meant for the re-education of prisoners. Thus the regulations specified that the holdings must consist of books "in which readers will encounter what is right and decent in the German character, the German people, and the German state."[14] But these regulations were not always observed. Joseph Joos tells us that Dachau, for example, had a surprisingly large and well-stocked library. Some of the books, however, clearly went against Nazi philosophy. Presumably the authorities had not bothered to check them, or "more likely didn't understand their contents."[15] The attitude of camp authorities to the prisoners' access to books varied. Some raised no objection to prisoners receiving books in the mail. The Dachau Kommandant Eicke, by contrast, was principally opposed to reading and expressed his disgust for those *intellektuelle Wühler* (intellectual moles) who requested books.[16] In any case, the process of obtaining books from camp libraries was cumbersome. Prisoners were not allowed to enter the library.[17] They were required to fill out a request and were permitted to borrow one book per week. They did not always get what they wanted. The books were dealt out to them, "taking into consideration, if possible, their wishes and the background of the prisoner."[18] Wolfgang Szepansky describes how the system worked. He placed a generic order: a book on the history of art and a work of literature to complement it. He received a biography of Michelangelo by Hermann Grimm and a novel on the sixteenth-century sculptor Tilmann Riemenschneider. Szepansky, who was a committed Communist, read the latter with great interest because it contained scenes from the Peasant Wars, that is, a "class war."[19] Paul Neurath, however, describing the book-borrowing process at Buchenwald, wrote that it took days for an order to arrive and the wrong book was often delivered. Reading after an exhausting day was difficult in the crowded day room. Prisoners were only allowed to move to their beds in the last half hour before the lights were turned off. Reading 15–20 pages was "a great achievement." Political prisoners were the most avid readers, he says, because they saw it as a duty and as a "weapon … for intellectual survival."[20]

The Sachsenhausen library, housed in barrack 10 together with the *Schreibstube* (the administrative office) and the architect's office, was considered a showpiece to impress official visitors and was well stocked. Weiss-Rüthel described the holdings: "It offered a wealth of valuable books. Apart from the works of the classics, I found a respectable number of sources for the history of German literature and culture. There were periodicals about art, handbooks, older, and contemporary novels – oddly many that were on the 'Index of Forbidden Books' of the Nazis, for example, the books of Sinclair Lewis and Upton Sinclair. There were also all kinds of technical books and an especially rich selection of travel literature – a treasure for which the few hours of my leisure time were not enough." Permission to borrow books was a privilege which entailed a waiting period. Weiss-Rüthel was exuberant when he finally received his reader's card after a year: "No one could have made me a better present. I still remember how greedily I attacked the first book … from that moment on every free hour had a rich and full context. I no longer felt entirely imprisoned. My spirit had found a path to freedom."[21] Some of the books in the library were bought after a collection had been taken up by the prisoners. Harry Naujoks reports that they submitted the money together with a wish list for a thousand books, "progressive authors – not completely fascistic – and scientific literature," but the library received only 450 books. The rest of the money was diverted into the pockets of the SS. Eugen Kogon also relates that "ten thousands of marks" were collected for the Buchenwald library, but only "a total of 1009 books were actually purchased." Reading books was obviously popular with prisoners, providing them with a measure of psychological relief, and cancelling library privileges was therefore used as a means of collective punishment.[22]

There is no evidence that Schuschnigg used the library in Sachsenhausen, presumably because he had access to his own books, which were ready at hand and better suited to his tastes than those on offer in the library. In solitary confinement in Vienna and Munich, by contrast, he had felt not only socially but also culturally isolated. The conditions in Sachsenhausen were more tolerable, but initially he felt "still badly off when it comes to culture," as he told his brother. Yet even before his own books arrived, he was not without reading material and acknowledged, "It makes things much easier for me that Vera is untiring in bringing me good books."[23]

The prison authorities in Munich had in fact supplied Schuschnigg with reading material as well, after he repeatedly asked to be given work. "This is what happened," he told his brother. "After begging for a long time and over years to be provided with work (I would have agreed even to breaking up stones!), I suddenly received an assignment from Berlin. I was to write a paper about 'a constitutionally appropriate new order on the question of German national groups in Hungary, Yugoslavia, and Romania.' That was in 1940. For this purpose, I was supplied with relevant literature in the holdings of the Munich State Library. I had my fill of those sources therefore. In addition, I also saw the occasional review in the V[ölkischer] B[eobachter]." He wrote the requested paper and handed in his research, but "never heard anything further about this homework of mine. It will hardly have rated a D!"[24]

Throughout the time of Schuschnigg's imprisonment, Vera made great efforts to obtain books for her husband, appealing to their local acquaintances and finally to Hermann Wopfner, Schuschnigg's uncle in Tyrol: "Would it be possible for you to lend him some books? That's his urgent request. I am to ask whether you have anything on the subject of law and political philosophy. Good books are such a help to him, it makes the many, many lonely hours pass more easily. Two years have gone by now [since his imprisonment], and you can imagine that it is becoming increasingly more difficult for me to obtain anything for him. He has already gone through all the libraries of his acquaintances!"[25]

Among the friends that lent Schuschnigg books was the Jesuit Theodor Hoffmann. As editor of the magazine *Stimmen der Zeit* (Voices of the Time) he fought a running battle with Nazi authorities. The venerable and influential monthly publication, founded in 1865, was shut down by the regime in 1941. A man of exceptional erudition, Hoffmann subsequently headed a project to translate the *Encyclopédie populaire* into German. Schuschnigg notes in 1941 that Hoffmann had sent him a number of recently published books which brought his readings up to date. "The books of Father Hoffmann are a great comfort to me," he wrote to Artur. He warmly recommended to his brother one of the books the Jesuit had sent him: Gustav Schnürer's *Kirche und Kultur* (Church and Culture, 1936). "If you get around to it – it's a most excellent book!"[26] Artur himself lent books to Schuschnigg or borrowed them on his behalf. He kept an eye out for works in which his brother had expressed an interest, among them the writings of Hermann Bahr, a playwright and literary critic of the Austrian avant-garde. His quest was apparently successful. Schuschnigg's diary entry of 22 August 1943 contains half a dozen quotes from Bahr's *Tagebücher* (Diaries). "I am working through them," he reported. "It is a real and genuine pleasure to read them. They provide relaxation. Reading them is like finally breathing pure and uncorrupted clean air." He appreciated Bahr's sense of what it meant to be Austrian. Austria, Bahr said, "could not be understood rationally – there will always be an ineffable element, to which only soul, sensibility, and mindfulness can provide the key." But Austrians could also be cynical, which was, according to Bahr, "almost always an inversion of anxious sensitivity." Bahr's characterization of Austrians struck a chord with Schuschnigg. It was incisive in his opinion. Bahr "put the finishing touches to my reflections on Austria, for which I can only show respect, humility, and admiration – I can add nothing to them."[27]

Schuschnigg also asked for works by Reinhold Schneider, a personal acquaintance of Artur's. The poet and novelist was inspired by Christian, more specifically, Catholic, thought. Schuschnigg asked for his non-fiction works, including *Philipp der Zweite*, a biography of the Spanish king published in 1931. He also borrowed Schneider's *Macht und Gnade: Gestalten, Bilder und Werte in der Geschichte* (Power and Grace: Figures, Portraits, and Values in History, 1940) and apologized for not returning it promptly. He wanted to "read the book at leisure and savour it," he wrote. "It is incredibly good." He expressed surprise that the publisher got permission to print it since Schneider was an outspoken critic of the Nazi regime. Indeed the author was prohibited from publishing books after 1940 and put on trial in 1945. His life was saved only by the downfall of the regime.[28]

Schuschnigg's interests were wide-ranging. He browsed through *Annuaria Pontificia: Schematismus der Weltkirche*, a handbook on the hierarchy of the Catholic Church. He mentions *Das Bildnis Beethovens* (The Portrait of Beethoven, 1931) a biography by the prominent musicologist and journalist Richard Specht. "A good book and a rare find," Schuschnigg commented. He also went through the five-volume work *Lehrbuch der Nationalökonomie* (Manual of National Economy) of Heinrich Pesch ("outdated," he regretfully noted), and announced that he would soon go on to Theodor Mommsen's multivolume history of the ancient Romans, a standard work at the time. Schuschnigg was interested also in the historical research of his uncle, Hermann Wopfner. "If they give you free author's copies of your *Bergbauernbuch* (Book of Alpine Farmers) in future, keep me in mind!" he wrote. "I would be very much interested and pleased to have a copy." However, the first volume of Wopfner's ethnographic work appeared only after the war, in 1951. Wopfner in turn recommended to his nephew Franz Schnabel's *Deutsche Geschichte im 19. Jahrhundert* (German History in the Nineteenth Century), a three-volume work published 1929–34. "I will ask Vera to look for it," Schuschnigg wrote. The work included sections on the history of art, which appealed to Schuschnigg. "If one can't see the paintings in their original colours, one can at least enjoy reading about them," he comments. "I find it good that recent historians often place cultural elements prominently into the foreground and attempt to convey the normal rather than the exceptional features of an era and the people living in it." His interests in the visual arts were eclectic, however: "I sometimes have a very strong desire for art and culture in any form (and broadly defined: from Titian to apple strudel!)."[29]

Schuschnigg read widely, that is, he read whatever books Vera could organize for him, yet the list of titles he mentions gravitates toward certain subjects. His requests reflect his personal and professional interests. Not surprisingly, given Schuschnigg's career, many of the books he sought out dealt with the recent political and economic history of Austria and Germany. He borrowed the works of the historian Franz Schnabel, whom his uncle had recommended, and read the essays of Anton Kuh, *Der unsterbliche Österreicher* (The Immortal Austrian, 1931). The book was in need of an update, Schuschnigg commented. He was hoping for a new edition – unaware perhaps that Kuh, who was Jewish, had been condemned by the Nazis and had emigrated to America in 1938.[30] He went on to list a slew of other authors he read and used as sources for a book on which he was working. He does not specify the subject of his research, but the list of sources suggests that he was writing about the history of Austria between the world wars. In that context, he refers not only to Heinrich Pesch, but also to the works of the economist Friedrich Hertz and the social critic Hermann Bahr, whose diaries have already been mentioned. In addition, he read the works of the Austrian historians Joseph Redlich and Rudolf Sieghart ("not agreeable, but worth reading"). He added a wish list: the memoirs of the diplomat and statesman Ernst Plener and the works of the Austrian historian Paul Molisch, both of whom wrote about the multi-nation state and the rise of German nationalism. For Schuschnigg, these books were "unobtainable treasures, for which I am salivating." He expressed regret that he had discovered some of the books too late, that is, only after his incarceration, as they offered him new points of view.[31] In April 1944 he reported on his continued research: "I am fiddling around a great deal with a manuscript which I started writing years ago and which has become quite voluminous." He expressed doubts, however, that his efforts would ever come to fruition. They were "probably *ad usum Delphini*." The Latin expression he uses refers to a selection of Latin texts from the eighteenth century, simplified for the use of the dauphin (*Delphinus*), the young heir of King Louis XIV. In later usage the phrase often meant "expurgated."[32] Presumably, this was a hint that Schuschnigg expected the authorities to confiscate his manuscript or at any rate censor it. In the event, he was able to save his writings and may have incorporated his work in subsequent publications, notably in *Requiem in Red-White-Red*, which contains an analysis of the political and economic situation in Austria after World War I and on the eve of World War II. Since this analysis serves an apologetic and exculpatory function in Schuschnigg's book, it is possible that he read historical accounts during his captivity with this purpose in mind – to convince himself and ultimately his readership that he had done the right thing in 1938. This intent (and its strategic use to comfort himself) will occupy us more specifically in chapter 8.

Shortly after Schuschnigg was moved to Sachsenhausen, his own books were shipped to him from Vienna. He had earlier on borrowed the works of Reinhold Schneider from his brother, but now that his own library was at hand, he was searching for his personal copy. Artur had asked him to return Schneider's book because he wanted to reread it himself, and Schuschnigg encouraged him to do so. "I have been rereading books (forced by necessity), which I am sure I would not have taken up otherwise. So there is a positive side to everything." By now, he said, his library was "a little outdated, but thank God I have a few timeless and valuable treasures. They are mostly on art, political science, classical literature, and books on Austria – altogether some 2000 volumes. It is a modest number, but sufficient for me, and I will not suffer boredom for years ... You are right: Reading can be a great satisfaction and a support as well!"[33]

As for returning Schneider's book to his brother, there was a problem: "Although I was rummaging through the books during the winter and came across the said R. Schneider together with other books published by Hegner (all of them with the same binding), I have since lost track," he wrote. "The problem is that we can get only at a fraction of the books because of considerations of place and the need of putting up shelves, or rather the impossibility of doing so because we would need a cabinetmaker. The rest of the books are still in cartons in the cellar." This turned out to be an unfortunate arrangement as the basement was flooded the following winter, and the floor was several centimetres under water, as

Schuschnigg reported. "This is the consequence of a recent storm. To limit the damage at least, we placed all the cartons of books on top of empty boxes, so that I can barely get at them now. As soon as the repairs to the cellar are successfully completed, I can go on looking through them. But that will take time, as does everything here."[34]

Among the books he unearthed from the cartons and browsed with new interest was a standard work on the history of art, the *Propyläen-Kunstgechichte*, which appeared in 24 volumes between 1923 and 1941. There was a problem with Schuschnigg's set, however. "I discovered that I have two copies of Haupt's [volume], *Kunst der Hochrenaissance in Deutschland und Frankreich* (Art of the High Renaissance in Germany and France), among the 20 volumes. Either the edition has only 19 volumes or (I rather fear) one is missing. I guess it must be the one on the High Renaissance in Italy. That's too bad! It's typical that I didn't notice that earlier, although I paid monthly instalments on the work for 10 years. Unfortunately there is no index." Browsing through the volumes "in layman's fashion," Schuschnigg nevertheless began to develop an understanding of the history of art. "At least I know now the theory behind cubism, futurism, Dadaism, etc. That was new to me. Unfortunately the handbook[35] ends in 1925, so that anything about a more recent period is missing. – How does one label contemporary architecture and painting? Neorealism? Post-classicism? German Empire? – I talk like a blind man about colours, because I know contemporary art only from descriptions. I suppose some things are very good. But are they truly novel and authentic??"[36] There is, however, no follow-up to these questions in the extant letters.

We have seen that Schuschnigg was interested in religious thought, but there is little evidence that these interests extended to the more general topics of moral philosophy or teleology. In his letters, he does report that he "took much pleasure in reading Plato (in German, that is) … Recently I also read an excellent study of Nietzsche and Burckhardt." Schuschnigg shows a familiarity with the canon of philosophers, from the classics of antiquity to twentieth-century authors, but his interests seem to have been rather narrowly focused on political philosophy. As is to be expected, he commented negatively on Nietzsche, the Nazis' philosopher of choice. Schuschnigg emphasized that he rejected any political theory that was "built on Friedrich Nietzsche as a prophet and embraced his principle that Might Trumps Right." This principle, which had been adopted by Hitler, had left Schuschnigg no choice but to resign from his post as chancellor, he says in *Requiem*. The whole section, containing Schuschnigg's thoughts on Nietzsche's philosophy, is, however, left out of the New York edition. Significantly, the philosopher's name does not appear anywhere in the English text. The assumption was presumably that readers might be offended by, or at any rate had no taste for, the questions raised by Nietzsche: whether genius justified amorality and whether might trumps right. "Machiavelli and Nietzsche accept the principle," Schuschnigg noted. "Kant and Goethe, Leibniz and Schiller, Plato and Aristotle deny it. And Christ ...?" The brutality the Nazis engaged in was the result of "deifying Hegel and taking Nietzsche literally." But it was not right to identify Nazi politics as "German." Rather, "it was a horrid distortion ... aided by a too literal and therefore wrong interpretation of Nietzsche's philosophy."[37]

Mussolini was another admirer of Nietzsche, Schuschnigg noted, or else he took his lead from Machiavelli rather than the German philosopher. He reflected on the influence this kind of realpolitik may have had on Italian politics. "Mussolini may have recalled the dictum 'Any pact can be broken if that is useful' (Machiavelli Disc. I. 59)" when he deserted Austria because the Rome-Berlin Axis was more advantageous for Italy at the time. The Austrians should have remembered that Machiavelli and Mussolini were countrymen! However, Schuschnigg himself quotes Machiavelli repeatedly, and not always with disapproval. "What Machiavelli says of the individual in his *Discorsi* may also be applied to international relations: 'People tend not to be either purely good or evil. They prefer to take the middle path, which is the most detrimental of all.'"[38] Another quote from Machiavelli in Schuschnigg's diary entry of 28 October 1943 is meant to serve as a commentary on the retreat of German troops after suffering heavy losses on the eastern front: "'The most unfortunate situation that may befall a country is a state in which it can neither accept peace nor continue war ... But such a situation can befall a country only if it has followed a clumsy and mistaken policy, and if it overrated its own forces' (Machiavelli, Disc. II, 24)." This quote is included in the English edition. Indeed, here Schuschnigg is reading Machiavelli, as he ought to be read – not as a philosopher like Kant or Nietzsche propounding their own convictions, but as someone describing how the business of the state works in practice, in a less-than-ideal world.[39]

The philosophy of Immanuel Kant was another subject that did not make it into the English edition. Schuschnigg quotes Kant in his diary entry of 28 May 1944: "*Salus reipublicae suprema lex est* – the well-being of the state is the supreme law." Kant advocated the principle that "the well-being of the state must not be sought in the well-being of the citizens and their happiness ... but in the greatest agreement between the constitution and the principles of law." Schuschnigg comments on this quote from the philosopher: "Kant neglects to add that any constitution that does not conform with the principles of law produces perhaps temporary well-being and short-lived euphoria, but never true progress and lasting happiness." Like Nietzsche, Schuschnigg says, Kant was misused by the Nazis to prop up the sophistic principle of might is right.[40]

Plato the idealist was more to Schuschnigg's taste. He has high praise for the Greek philosopher. "From the Olympic heights of classical antiquity – far above the mountains and valleys of the history of humanity – he, the great pre-Christian harbinger of Christian ethos, taught what resounded through the ages." In spite of professing admiration for Plato, however, Schuschnigg was not uncritical in his reading of the philosopher. He observed, for example, that Plato might well have shared Hitler's and Mussolini's assessment of the masses as lacking knowledge, or even the capacity to acquire it, and therefore as being open to the influence of propaganda. "Plato would hardly have expressed it differently, except that in classical antiquity they did not express every thought and formulate it in a crass manner. But that's the only difference."[41]

We have seen that Schuschnigg pondered whether Plato's theory of the transmigration of souls could be incorporated into Christian beliefs. During the years of his internment, he seems to have made up his mind about that question and flatly rejected the idea.

"Plato is wrong, but however that may be, the creator has cast a veil over the mystery of life; the ideas of the philosophers only reach as far as that point; it may be the task of priests and poets to lift the veil. But no one can fathom it." This point of view would explain Schuschnigg's fascination with Dante, whom he often cites in a philosophical rather than a literary context, and as a seer rather than merely as a poet. He tends to quote him in a religious context, as in this example: "S'aperse in nuovi amor l'eterno amore [For the mark of God – of Eternity itself – is love!]" (Dante, *Divine Comedy*, Par. 29: 18). Dante's words appealed to Schuschnigg and stimulated him to develop his thoughts on the nature of God. "His faith ... the whole habit of mind of this great man encouraged me to reflect." Dante was one of those writers "whose immortality grew out of their faith." Dante taught or rather "heralded" (*kündet*) that even the great were not immune from "God's lightning bolt. He reminded them of the essential validity of the law in the decalogue, of the fact that time has no significance, ... that the soul is immortal."[42]

Some of the books delivered to the Schuschniggs in Sachsenhausen must have been from the personal library of Vera, who shared her husband's love of reading. She mentions recovering "a number of wonderful English books from long ago, which I dug out of my cartons and which I had already forgotten and am glad to read again now." During the last turbulent years, she said, she did not have the peace of mind to read and was happy to be able once again "to indulge my great passion for reading. When one is torn and full of cares, one doesn't have the proper peace and disposition to tackle a book. Now I can catch up." Schuschnigg shared her sentiments. He, too, commented on the circumstances of his life. Unlike Vera, he had not yet found the necessary peace of mind to read in a concentrated fashion or engage in any other serious intellectual activity. At Christmas 1941 he wrote to his uncle: "I am not in the right frame of mind to do serious work, but at least I earnestly study languages and know a little more in that area than before."[43]

Both in his diaries and his letters Schuschnigg mentions that he was trying to refresh his knowledge of languages. He therefore asked for dictionaries, a request that was apparently suspect to the Gestapo. During the first months of his incarceration in Vienna, any book he received was quarantined for a week or two while the authorities ascertained that it qualified under the rules. "I had special difficulties with a dictionary, and it took a long time to convince them of its harmless nature." In 1942 he read and was "completely engrossed" by Madame de Stael's *Dix années d'exile* (*Ten Years of Exile*, published posthumously in 1820). He quoted a number of French passages from the book in his diary entry of 23 August 1942, among them "One feels very firm in one's own conduct when it is founded on sincere convictions, but when it comes to others suffering because of us, it is almost impossible not to reproach oneself." He was surprised to discover how relevant Madame de Stael's observations were to his own time. In a way, however, "the parallels were banal," he wrote. After all, "History is usually much less original than we short-lived humans believe; more often history just goes through her old repertoire."[44] He mentions a number of English-language books Vera had supplied him with. At one time she brought him Duff Cooper's *Talleyrand* (London, 1935). A biography of Napoleon's chief diplomat at a time that was characterized by French victories was unlikely to meet the approval of Nazi censors. "When I think about the risk, I still get goosebumps, although it was an excellent and purely historical account. The authorities raised no objections at the time, however. The first page of a book is usually not very interesting, at least as viewed by the police. They were more suspicious of Dante's *Divine Comedy*, and rightly so, because the author would be my soulmate today."[45]

Schuschnigg also read Winston Churchill's *Thoughts and Adventures* ("much better than we are supposed to believe"). It is unclear, however, whether he read it in the original language or the German translation, which appeared in 1938. The names of other foreign writers appear in Schuschnigg's diaries and letters, although it is not always apparent how familiar he was with them, which of their works he was reading, and if he was reading them in the original language. He mentions Shakespeare's *Hamlet* and quotes from *Richard II* in English in the context of musing on death. Death releases a person from all sorrows and concerns, he writes. Once buried, a man no longer cares what happens to his grave. "Shakespeare may have had something like this in mind when he puts these words in King Richard's mouth: 'For on my heart they tread now whilst I live / And buried once why not upon my head?'" Shakespeare was timeless, Schuschnigg commented. He understood the human soul. "His King Richard plays could have been written in any age." Among English authors, Schuschnigg also quotes Milton (in German) and mentions Shaw, praising his wit and social relevance. More often than not, however, the names of foreign writers – Shakespeare, Molière, Dante, and Calderón – simply appear in lists of "great" authors without further characterization. A typical example is a passage on the subject of the immortality of the soul. This concept, Schuschnigg writes, was taught not only by the Catholic Church. "It was already taught by Plato. The great minds of all ages believed in it if they believed in anything at all other than themselves. The timelessness of characters in the works of Dante, Calderón, Shakespeare, and Goethe is rooted in that belief."[46]

In a letter of 27 April 1944 Schuschnigg asked his uncle for the works of Homer and Vergil, the iconic writers of antiquity: "Do you think you could somewhere acquire a Homer or Vergil (in German, I mean)? I especially want Homer 'badly,' to use the lingo of the poor people in Munich. I suppose one should be able to get those books since I can't imagine that the production of *Schmierer* [study aids and translations for students] has stopped. I am getting my comeuppance for sneaking old Voss out of my parents' library – if I remember those long-ago times correctly."[47] Wopfner must have been able to oblige his nephew since, soon afterwards, Schuschnigg quotes from Vergil and mentions reading Theodor Haecker's *Vergil, Vater des Abendlandes* (Vergil, Father of the West, 1931). He called Haecker's work "a magnificent book," and mused that "Vergil would be the right [guide] for a reborn ... well-tempered Austria." In his diary entry of 14 December 1944, Schuschnigg also lists Homer's *Odyssey* among his readings. The entry of 13 August 1944, moreover, consists of a quote from Homer: "How ready mortals are to blame the gods. It is from them, they say, that evils come, but they themselves in their blind folly create troubles beyond what is ordained."[48] In Schuschnigg's generation the Greek and Roman classics were on the high school curriculum and drilled into every student. The common experience created a bond among educated people. When Schuschnigg and other elite prisoners were evacuated in 1945, and transported from one concentration camp to the next, they preserved the esprit de corps by chanting the classics. "We sat on the benches in the yard in the last rays of the setting sun: General von Falkenhausen, Dr. Schacht, Mr. Best, and I. There was a momentary lull in the air raids, and suddenly without any introduction, Dr. Schacht began to recite from Homer's *Iliad*. Twenty, thirty verses in fluent Greek. Falkenhausen took up where he left off and continued for a while. When they came to an end, I began, timidly, *Arma virumque cano* [Of arms and men I sing] ... and both of them chimed in and showed that they were just as much at home in Vergil as in Homer. Finally, we quoted Goethe ... until we stopped and found ourselves once more facing reality – Dachau and Adolf Hitler."[49]

Apart from the classics, Schuschnigg read primarily non-fiction. He did occasionally mention modern poets and novelists, but often showed a preference for their occasional non-fiction writings. Theodore Fontane, for example, is best known for his poetry and fiction, which might be labelled poetic realism. Schuschnigg, however, read one of his prose works, a travelogue in which Fontane describes the area around Sachsenhausen. Likewise, he singled out for comment a non-fiction work by Anton Wildgans, an author better known for his poetry and his plays. Schuschnigg praised Wildgans' *Musik der Kindheit, ein Heimatbuch aus Wien* (Childhood Music: A Book from My Native Vienna). Schuschnigg felt a sense of homecoming on reading the book. It "spoke to his own memories." Elsewhere he mentioned reading a speech by Wildgans, "destined for Stockholm," a hint that the poet was nominated repeatedly for the Nobel Prize in literature.[50] He showed a similar preference for non-fiction works in the case of Eduard von Bauernfeld,[51] a writer of comedies and clever farces. Schuschnigg did not think highly of his comedies. He considered them "good workmanship, but dusty and ad hoc ... Hermann Bahr (not to speak of Shaw) proves that similar thoughts can be expressed more eloquently and in a more timeless, and therefore more cogent fashion." He preferred Bauernfeld's diaries, *Aus Alt- und Neu-Wien* (Of Old and New Vienna) for nostalgic reasons, but he disapproved of Bauernfeld's rejection of tradition. "No old nail is in the right place for this man who is full of 'progress' and 'new times' ... yet less open and modern, at least in matters of music, than the Viennese he likes to characterize ironically as enemies of progress." Most of all, Schuschnigg was annoyed by what he saw as Bauernfeld's "ultra-liberal" views and his anticlericalism. He complained that the author gave no specific reasons for his objections. "He does not go beyond labels. If you look for specifics, your thirst for being enlightened remains unslaked." Schuschnigg asked himself, What do people like Bauernfeld rail against? "Against absolutism, censorship, *System*, brute force? Of course, but only as long as they are not in the saddle themselves." Schuschnigg wonders how that "apostle of freedom and campaigner against anything that was censorship or appeared absolutist" would have fared under the Nazis. In another reference to Bauernfeld's resistance to *System*, that is, rigid, autocratic order, he comments, "Not that Austrians are principally against clearly drawn limits, against logic, order, and organization, although in its local meaning, *System* and 'systematic' mean a priori something undesirable. They would like order, but an order made easier by means of back doors and duplicate keys. Yet they don't want to be reminded of that and prefer to wink at it."[52]

Schuschnigg borrowed a number of contemporary novels from his brother, for example, *Die Göttinnen oder Die drei Romane der Herzogin von Assy* (The Goddesses, or The Three Novels of the Countess of Assy, Berlin 1903) by Heinrich Mann, the older brother of Thomas Mann. The three volumes describe the adventures of a woman seeking liberty, art, and love respectively. Heinrich Mann's novels generally take up themes of social significance. His most successful and widely known book is *Professor Unrath*, on which the film *The Blue Angel* is based. Mann, who was active in the resistance against the Nazis, was forced into exile. His books were publicly burned in 1933.[53] Mann's publisher was Paul Zsolnay, whose books Schuschnigg apparently favoured and bought in quantity.

In Sachsenhausen, he was reading through the "Zsolnay novels one by one." The Austrian publishing house was established in 1923. Among its roster of authors were Austrian writers such as Alexander Roda Roda, a popular satirist, and Franz Werfel, as well as international authors, including John Galsworthy, H.G. Wells, and Pearl S. Buck. The Szolnay Verlag was shut down in 1939, although the company had played it safe and began publishing pro-Nazi authors after 1933. In that context, Schuschnigg asked his brother what had become of the novelist Grete von Urbanitzky, "one of Szolnay's fail-safe authors."[54] Apparently she was not fail-safe after all. She collaborated with the regime for a time, but her lesbian-themed novels were banned in 1941 after she had fled to Switzerland.

Schuschnigg is clearly aware of the repressive measures taken by the Nazi regime against writers who did not toe the official line, and was curious to what extent authors collaborated with the regime. He raised the subject in a letter to his brother. "I'd be interested to know: Do you think Hamsun[55] and Jakob Schaffler[56] are putting on an act – for the sake of their readership and in the interest of the publishing house – or are they really serious?? Sometimes I am totally confused. After all I still remember the way Sven Hedin[57] talked to me, for example. It is surprising how much the milieu influences people."[58] In the context of discussing the difficulties of people in the arts obliged to truckle to the Nazi regime, Schuschnigg also mentions the popular actor Raoul Aslan, who managed to stay on the right side of the authorities and hung on to his engagements.[59] "By the way, I saved him from getting into trouble," Schuschnigg quips. "Shortly before the doors slammed shut [in 1938], he sent me a long telegram – at least six lines – expressing his agreement with me. If they had found that telegram, it would not have been very good for him. In a way I am sorry that I destroyed several notes of this kind." He further inquired about the novelist Hans von Hammerstein-Equord, who had been an administrator in the Austrian ministry of culture: "By the way, do you know anything about Hammerstein? A particularly high-minded and worthy man, and also a poet. I hear he got away with a black eye, and I'm heartily glad he got away. I believe you hardly knew him personally. I am sure you would have liked him." In fact, Hammerstein did not get away. He ended up in the Mauthausen concentration camp, was liberated by the Allies, and died two years later, weakened by the abuse he had suffered during his internment.[60]

We know about Schuschnigg's interest in novels and their publishers only from his private letters. None of these contemporary or near-contemporary authors are mentioned in his published diaries, and most of them are not well known outside the German-speaking world. The writers who do appear in the diary entries are those that have stood the test of time: the classics of antiquity – Homer, Plato, Vergil – and the great German writers, among whom Goethe was Schuschnigg's favourite, "truly the greatest and most significant of all Germans."[61]

From Schuschnigg's discussion of the authors he read, it becomes clear that his appreciation was for content rather than form, for an author's timeless wisdom rather than his style of writing. In his numerous references to books, there is only one (rather casual) remark about language: Bauernfeld's German "was undeniably good." Schuschnigg passes no judgment on the style of the great German authors Goethe and Schiller. He admires only their sentiments. In Goethe, he appreciated the grandness of his ideas, the fact that he did not address matters of concern only to the individual. "He consciously addressed and wanted to address all of humanity. Not only in his tragedy *Faust*, but also and in particular when he took his dramatic subject from ancient myths ... for then it no longer concerns the fate of a man from antiquity but the human being itself." Schuschnigg hoped that German readers would rediscover Goethe's wisdom and be guided back to the right path by his words: "Always aim for the whole. And since you cannot become the whole, join it and serve it as an organ." More generally, he praised writings which "in Goethe's spirit ... served the idea of a community of nations, the grand ideals of humanity and of peace." His references to Goethe usually appear in a serious context, but on one occasion he quotes lines from *Zahme Genien* tongue-in-cheek: "The axle suffers blows and, being inflexible, breaks at last." The passage in Goethe refers to the axle of a wagon, but the German word *Achse* can mean "axis" as well as "axle." Schuschnigg uses Goethe's line to pun on the Berlin-Rome Axis. Commenting on the progress of war in 1944, he remarks that "what we see on stage now is ... a travesty of *Faust* II." Still, Goethe's *Faust* promises redemption and, more importantly, so does Jesus in the Sermon on the Mount, he writes. The fact that Schuschnigg draws a parallel between Goethe and Jesus is indicative of the high value he placed on the German classic. Goethe's works were for him the secular equivalent of the Bible.[62]

Schuschnigg also pays tribute to Friedrich Schiller, the second grandee of German literature, and to the timeless appeal of his works. In December 1943 he tells his brother that he recently reread Schiller's drama *Die Räuber* (The Robbers). "Amazing how contemporary much of it sounds. Obergruppenführer (Sergeant) Karl Moor might and should write a lead article (but of course would hardly be permitted to do so). That's the classics for you!" In his diary entry of 1 January 1944 Schuschnigg quotes extensively from Schiller's play: "To start the new year, I listened first to Goebbels' New Year's speech, and then read Schiller's drama *Die Räuber*, which struck me as appropriate. There I read: '... Woe is me, fool, that I thought to embellish the world with atrocities, and to uphold the law by lawlessness. I called it revenge and right ... here I stand on the brink of a terrible life, and perceive with weeping and gnashing of teeth that two men like me would destroy the whole edifice of the moral world.'"[63] One wonders if Schuschnigg was aware that Schiller's *Räuber* was being performed at the time by fellow internees in camp. Wolfgang Szepansky, a political prisoner, recalled that the actor Edgar Bennert organized the camp performance. Although Szepansky had never acted before, he auditioned for a part. He was so nervous that his voice turned squeaky. Nevertheless he landed a part, playing a robber who had only one line to deliver: "Hark, a shot! And another one!" The performance was a memorable experience for Szepansky. Like Schuschnigg, he thought that Schiller's play had contemporary relevance: "Staging a literary classic, [we] represented the militant humanism of the present."[64]

Listing Schiller's play together with Homer's *Odyssey*, Shakespeare's *Hamlet*, and Grillparzer's *The Golden Fleece*, Schuschnigg declared that the unique merit of these classics lay in the absolute values they proclaimed. "Time is only a drop of eternity and every character, in spite of their individuality, brings a constantly recurring factor into the integral calculation of human life. But the world has always been forgetful. Therefore the drama remains eternal and the tragedy immortal in its constantly new variants." The classics were his daily companions, Schuschnigg wrote. "Every evening I read either Homer or Grillparzer ... or reread *Hamlet*." He had read these authors in school but it was only now that he truly understood their meaning and could appreciate their timelessness, "the uncanny fact that the world has remained the same and everything recurs in different forms."[65]

Schuschnigg enjoyed reading plays, especially now that he no longer had to envy people who were able to attend the actual performances. He joked about taking a malicious pleasure in their inability to see plays: "Other people can't go to the Burgtheater either – that's how mean I am!" Goebbels had decreed in the summer of 1944 that theatres must remain closed in the interest of the total war effort. That left people no alternative but to read plays, attending the "private theatre" of their studies. Schuschnigg took to rereading Franz Grillparzer's *The Golden Fleece* "and taking great pleasure in it ('rereading' is somewhat exaggerated because it is more than thirty years since I read it last – that hardly counts as rereading anymore)." Grillparzer, a nineteenth-century civil servant turned playwright, created historical dramas based on Austrian history and revived classical myths such as the tragedy of Medea and the story of the lovers Hero and Leander. His plays tended to be highly idealistic and moralizing. His political and philosophical writings, in which he rejected Hegel and closely analysed Kant, were published posthumously. Schuschnigg thought of him as a quintessential Austrian who understood the national psyche, for example, the reluctance of Austrians to embrace reforms – "their 'giving half-birth' as the ... immortal Austrian counsellor laments." Grillparzer furthermore recognized that the "Austrians had a quality you will search for in vain in Germany: true sentiment."[66] Schuschnigg quotes a number of passages from one of Grillparzer's prose works, *Kalender-Wahrheit* (Calendar Truth), because "they sound so typically Austrian," "so Viennese," and are "spoken from the heart." What Grillparzer said about the politics of his own time could easily be applied to the present time, Schuschnigg says, for example the bitter words "You are allowed to do what you are able to do. Laws do not apply to men like you." They were addressed to Napoleon, but could be used to describe Hitler as well. Like Goethe and Schiller, Grillparzer spoke "the timeless truth and truly suits our times."[67]

It would be useful to compare Schuschnigg's literary preferences with those of fellow inmates, but while their accounts make it clear that they regarded reading a valuable aid in their psychological survival, they rarely offer details about the books they had access to. Joseph Joos is one of the few writers who is specific about his readings. There is a definite overlap in Schuschnigg's and Joos' tastes and responses. He too is looking for eternal values. Thus he praises Grillparzer for his "unwavering belief in the existence of a power tying us to a moral order in the world and in creation." He applauds the French journalist and writer Albert Cahuet for the same reason and recommends his novels to his daughters so "that they may grow spiritually through his characters." Similarly, he sees in Plato's Socrates "the wisdom of the ancients representing the timeless ideas of the world," and he values the philosopher Wilhelm von Humboldt as a "reliable guide to self-knowledge." Not all the books he obtained were to his liking, however. We have seen that Schuschnigg believed that the Nazis misused Kant for their purposes. Joos, commenting on the classes his daughters took in university, expressed a dislike for Kant without specifying the reason, but it was presumably on account of the Nazis using the philosopher to justify their political actions. He also had reservations about Hermann Hesse, who was blamed by some people for not speaking out against the Nazis. In this case as well Joos refrains from any reference to contemporary politics. He left off reading Hesse's *Steppenwolf*, he says, because the novel struck him as "strange and sick" (*fremd und krank*). Like Schuschnigg, Joos regretted not having come across some of the authors earlier and thus missing out on an opportunity to discuss them with his friends and family.[68]

When Schuschnigg and his family were evacuated from Sachsenhausen in the spring of 1945, they were told to pack only the essentials. They had to leave the bulk of their possessions behind. Schuschnigg does not complain about losing "pictures, clothes, china, furniture, everything we own," but "hate[s] to leave behind the books." An episode he relates in this context once again confirms his close attachment to books. On the evacuation trek he made the acquaintance of Payne-Best and was overjoyed when the British agent made him a present of the Oxford Dictionary. "It is the first book I own since I lost my entire library, and although only one, it is a beginning," he writes in his diary entry of 17 April 1945. Because prisoners had few belongings, the act of gift-giving itself had special significance among them. It was an act of encouragement, reaffirming a sense of community and comradeship.[69]

Reading was no doubt a significant survival strategy for Schuschnigg, but it was a way out for a minority of prisoners. Torsten Seela, who investigated the subject in *Bücher und Bibliotheken in nationalsozialistischen Konzentrationslagern* (Books and Libraries in Nazi Concentration Camps) found that reading was for some prisoners "almost necessary for survival," but also noted that the vast majority of first-person accounts make no mention at all of books or of reading. Music, by contrast, held universal appeal, and will concern us in the next chapter.[70]

chapter five

Music to His Ears

Schuschnigg was a music lover. In his memoirs Kurt writes:
"Father could not do without music. In days gone by, he thought
nothing of rushing to the opera house just to hear a certain aria and
then returning to the chancellery to work far into the night." The
opportunity to listen to music on the radio – the only chance for
Schuschnigg to hear music during his years of imprisonment – was
no substitute for attending live performances. Nor did he have the
opportunity to make music himself. "I imagine it must be splendid to take your seat at the piano whenever you want or are in the
mood, and to be able in this manner to compensate for everyday
worries," Schuschnigg writes to his brother. "In any case, domestic
music is the best [way of listening to music]. In that respect former generations had the advantage over us. During my last years
in Vienna I sometimes hosted a philharmonic quartet, of which I
have lasting and beautiful memories." To accommodate Schuschnigg's work schedule, however, these house concerts took place at
unusual times, "starting at midnight and ending around 2 am."[1]

Listening to the radio was a clandestine operation for prisoners
in the general population of the concentration camp. It was possible
for Rudolf Wunderlich, for example, who worked in the office of
the Sachsenhausen administration to listen to foreign radio stations
early in the morning before his supervisors arrived. Naujoks also
mentioned that they smuggled in radio parts, put them together
and, "some cautionary measures being taken," were able to listen
to newscasts from London and Moscow. There were *Schwarzhörer*

(people with illegal radios) also at Dachau workshops, who were able to conceal radios among the tools and equipment.[2] They were not listening to music, however. Their purpose was to listen to the news and keep informed about the progress of the Allied troops.

Special prisoners were usually permitted radios. At Easter 1939, when Schuschnigg was in the Gestapo prison in Munich, he was supplied with a radio, which he enjoyed greatly because "it wiled away idle hours." Then, without warning or obvious reason, the apparatus was taken away again. The loss was bitter, but he vowed, "I won't beg for its return." After all, he said, it was only entertainment, the kind of pleasure he no longer wanted to indulge in. That was spoken from the depths of his depression, but once he recovered his balance, he seemed grateful for the diversion music afforded him. Throughout the years in Sachsenhausen he had the use of a radio – unless it malfunctioned. In February 1942, for example, it was out of order. He waited for months to have the radio repaired, joking that in the 1000-year empire everything was apparently calculated in 1000-year spans. In May, finally, he reported that the radio had been returned, but poorly fixed. The guard's considered opinion was, "That thing ain't gonna work for long." Even when the radio was in good order, the listening experience was not always satisfactory, either because of the tone quality and reception, the limited range of the device, or the content of Nazi programming. With all respect to Franz Lehár, Schuschnigg wrote, it was too much to listen twice daily to the aria "Life Is Worth Living"![3]

The musical offerings on the radio were a frequent topic of discussion in Schuschnigg's letters to his brother. It was a natural choice, given the fact that Artur had for some years been a broadcasting director with the Austrian Radio Corporation and, like Schuschnigg himself, was knowledgeable about music. "Do you actually listen to the radio?" he asked Artur in 1941,[4] and added sarcastically, "Your former colleagues must really reproach themselves when they consider today's fabulous opportunities for creating programs! Indeed I am under the impression that the great masses actually prefer what is called a 'concert' or 'music' nowadays. According to my observations, it is amazing how quickly they turn off their sets when Mozart is offered by mistake, or even Verdi. At the most they'll allow the often-repeated clog dance from [the operetta] *Zar und Zimmermann*." The average listener wanted something folksy. "Is it the same thing among you soldiers?" he asked Artur. "And, tell me, do you know all the so-ol-ol-dier songs, from 'two-three-Erika' to ... 'Mädchen Mädchen,' and 'Edelweiss'? Some of them (but too few) may be good, and those are a rare treat – Of course I am glad to own a radio at all."[5] Schuschnigg goes on, tongue-in-cheek: "I am merely concerned about the cultural experience provided for the people. Culture used to be the privilege of us 'System plutocrats.'" In the language of Nazi propaganda, *System* was the derogatory label used for the government preceding their takeover in Germany and Austria, and the term "plutocracy," literally "power through wealth," was used to denote a class that was removed from the common people, and indeed the practice of taking advantage of them by working the system. Radio programming reflected the general attitude of Nazis to high culture and avant-garde art, which was considered to be "degenerate." Because Schuschnigg had been minister of culture and education, his tastes were suspect. "During the first few months [of my incarceration]," he writes, "an SS guard told me that I would have 'to get used to family-style culture because the aesthetics and culture of the home were now highly valued!' And that man did not mean to harass me. He was one of the decent people who meant well! ... I would have enough material for an amusing little book! The moral of the story: everything can prompt laughter *once*."[6]

Complaints about the quality of radio programming are frequent in Schuschnigg's correspondence. He realized of course that official broadcasts were useless as a source of news. "As far as the radio news are concerned, I don't believe we are given a truthful impression. Apart from that, I don't have the courage to listen to news, perhaps I also lack the patience, or at least the understanding." He did, however, "listen to a little music from time to time," even if it was rarely to his taste. The radio "is not much help these days," he wrote in the summer of 1941, "but at least it's something! When I have to go without it for a time, I miss it a lot. Unfortunately my apparatus has a forbiddingly bad tone quality, and the program is usually beneath all standards. I keep asking myself over and over again, but in vain, Where is the 'culture of the people' if they ask only for the crap that's offered, and tolerate it! But my own observations confirm indeed that radios are turned off immediately everywhere if there is a modest attempt at a Schubert song or if an occasional piece by Liszt makes its way into the program by mistake. The program aired on the Leipzig station is by far the best, in my opinion. And on Sundays there is a really good program, *Schatzkästlein* (little jewellery box). But I rarely am able to enjoy it because at that very hour I am commanded to take a bath or go for a walk." The reference to this enforced schedule is meant to be a joke. It was Vera who determined when the bathroom was available and "commanded" him to take the baby for a walk around their small plot.[7]

While Schuschnigg complained about the sound quality of the radio he had at his disposal in Sachsenhausen, the device supplied to him earlier in the Munich prison seemed to have met his standards. Nor did he complain about the programming at that point. In his diary entry for 29 November 1939 he writes, "I am so glad I have a radio. The small *Volksempfänger* produces incredibly good sound. I have it on almost all day long. Music is unspeakably comforting because it allows for spiritual communication which no one can forbid and no one can control. As long as you encounter the memory of Beethoven, Mozart, and Schubert in the sad and lonely world of your mind, and as long as you have the strength to greet them with grateful respect, you retain the consciousness of your humanity."[8]

The importance of music as a memory device, a source of comfort, and a means of preserving one's humanity is a frequent theme in the memoirs of concentration camp survivors. It was a *Zauberheilquelle* (magic source of healing). "It was like a fairytale. We lifted up our heads ... we forgot for a moment where we were. We sang folksongs and student songs. Singing helped us a great deal. It strengthened our will to stay alive," a fellow prisoner at Sachsenhausen writes. Odd Nansen uses similar expressions to describe the consolation he derived from music. The inmates occasionally organized concerts. The performers were not professionals, their playing was anaemic, Nansen writes, but there were moments when he "forgot I was in Sachsenhausen and was going to turn [to my wife] and take her hand ... for a moment one could forget oneself." At those camp concerts, he reported, the prisoners listened to the music of Beethoven, Dvořák, and Borodin – music that showed that "beauty and harmony are strong and invincible in the human being." Rudolf Wunderlich, who worked for a time with a road-building crew, relates that they sang folksongs on their way home, in spite of being physically exhausted. "For us it was a means of feeling joy or shaking off unpleasant experiences and moods. It may be hard to believe, but we arrived at the barracks [tired and hungry] and nevertheless could sing those defiant songs with laughing faces." Similarly Henri Michel reports that a concert including music by Beethoven, Haydn, and Grieg was "received enthusiastically ... the music strengthened the will to hope, the joy of life ... in which the spirit triumphed over brutal force." Isa Vermehren likewise recounts that hearing music by the old masters evoked in them a soothing sense that they were listening to something "in the realm of pure and inviolable value." The music prompted thoughts "that mildness, goodness, and love still exist."[9] For Joseph Joos, classical concerts given by his fellow prisoners provided him with "a blessed hour, which allowed me to forget almost completely the squalor, the desolation of our immediate surrounding and the torture of everyday life."[10]

What were Schuschnigg's musical preferences? Richard Wagner ranked high on his list of preferred composers. Wagner's reputation has been tainted by his popularity with Hitler and the Nazi regime and the speculation that the composer's own antisemitic writings influenced their political thought. In 1850 Wagner published an essay entitled *Das Judenthum in der Musik* (Jewishness in Music), targeting his competitors Mendelssohn and Meyerbeer. It contained the infamous argument that Jews were incapable of artistic expression and were alien to the genuine spirit of the German people. The phrases Wagner used in arguing that the Jews should "annihilate" their nature and assimilate German ideals were interpreted by some readers as a call for the literal annihilation of the Jews, thus foreshadowing Hitler's genocidal policies.

Wagner in turn may have been influenced by the theories of Arthur de Gobineau, who claimed in his "Essay on the Inequality of the Human Races" that Western society had deteriorated because of miscegenation between "superior" and "inferior" races. While it is questionable that Wagner inspired Hitler's theory of the superiority of the Aryans and his enforcement of the "final solution," it is undeniable that he inspired his admiration. Hitler owned original scores of Wagner's operas and vigorously promoted the annual Bayreuth Festival honouring the composer's work. The association between Wagner's music and the Nazi regime was strong enough to evoke painful memories among Holocaust survivors and led to protests of performances of Wagner concerts in postwar Israel.

Schuschnigg himself addressed the question of the relationship between Wagner's music and Hitler's thought. He generally disapproved of linking music with politics, and specifically regretted the association of Wagner with the Nazi agenda. "Unfortunately people have made Wagner's music a matter of ideology – quite wrongly, it seems." He himself kept away from such associations and respected Wagner purely as a composer. In that capacity he was "unique," he said, and that *Tristan*, in particular, is an outstandingly beautiful piece of music. He regretted that he had not always been at leisure to give his full attention to Wagner. As chancellor, he had been too busy to attend an entire opera performance. As his son confirmed in his memoirs, Schuschnigg often snuck out of his office to hear at least a part of a performance. "I must honestly say that I never heard a really good performance [of *Tristan*]," Schuschnigg writes. "Perhaps because I lacked the right disposition which is absolutely necessary ... One can't really experience *Tristan* if one goes to the opera in passing and keeps an eye on the watch. I suppose that's the explanation."[11]

He recalls that he was a fan of Wagner even as a young man. On leave from military duty during World War I, he "went to the theatre twice a day if possible ... During my final leave I was keen on hearing the *Meistersinger* with Slezak, which impressed me more than anything else at the time. Everything had been taken care of [by his aunt] – tickets for the opera, tickets for the plays, even a borrowed military coat and the train ticket – when a telegram came cancelling all leaves ... I was very unhappy. Specifically on account of the *Meistersinger!*"[12]

Schuschnigg had moved in musical circles in Vienna and reminisced about discussing his tastes in music and the performances he attended with friends. "I often chatted about *Tristan* with Alma Mahler, who kept playing for us excerpts on the piano. The *Ring* attracts me every time. It makes an immense impression on me!" Schuschnigg was not uncritical of Wagner's operas. Occasionally he voiced reservations, although his quarrel was with the lyrics rather than the music: "I am bothered, though admittedly I'm not always unbiased. There are too many words, too many full beards, too many and too long monologues. And the many alliterations in the text!"[13]

In the context of discussing Wagner's merits, Schuschnigg also comments on the program of the Salzburger Festwochen. This Austrian music and drama festival was instituted in 1920 and, by the 1930s, had become a prominent annual event. The organizers, among them the author Hugo von Hofmannsthal and the composer Richard Strauss, had originally planned a program centred on Mozart, a native son of Salzburg. Wagner was introduced gradually, under pressure from Arturo Toscanini, who like Schuschnigg, was an admirer of the *Ring* cycle. Consequently, the Austrian festival came to be regarded as an event competing with the German Bayreuth Festival and was therefore disparaged by the Nazis as "loaded with Jewish and Anglo-Saxon snobbery."[14]

Schuschnigg himself "was very much attached to the [Salzburger Festwochen]. Some of the events were perhaps not as wretched as they [the Nazis] claim nowadays." He cited the praise of Wilhelm Furtwängler, the director of the Berlin Philharmonic and conductor at the Berlin State Opera, who had been keen on conducting at Salzburg as well.[15] In his letter to Artur, Schuschnigg also recalled Toscanini, who served as a conductor at the Salzburg Festival from 1934 to 1937. Toscanini was "an asset but also a great liability – the most difficult man I ever encountered." Unlike Furtwängler and other artists who put their careers first and collaborated with the regime, Toscanini was one of the most intrepid critics of the extreme right, both in his home country and in Germany. He resisted Mussolini, refusing to play the Fascist anthem at a concert in Bologna, and suffered a beating at the hands of right-wing thugs as a result. He refused to come to Bayreuth after Hitler came to power, ignoring a personal plea by the Führer, and he stopped coming to Salzburg after the Anschluss. While he was active at Salzburg, however, he was determined to add Wagner to the program – Schuschnigg called it his "idée fixe." While this initiative reflected Toscanini's personal preferences, he also meant to make the Austrian festival a rival to Bayreuth's, and undermine an event the Nazis were using as a cultural marker. "The Wagner content kept being increased," Schuschnigg writes. "First the *Meistersinger*, then *Tannhäuser* as well,[16] and it would presumably have continued in that vein" if Toscanini had not resigned in protest against Hitler's annexation of Austria.[17]

Schuschnigg, although himself an admirer of Wagner, objected to this shift in programming. He preferred focusing on Austrian composers, although not exclusively so. "I would have liked to see Rossini[18] in the repertoire as well as Mozart, Gluck,[19] and others, and a well-produced *Fledermaus*[20] ... But my efforts were completely in vain and hopeless, unless we were prepared to do without Toscanini. And so, in 1936 we had the premiere of the *Meistersinger* with Toscanini conducting!" As a matter of principle, however, Schuschnigg did not attend the performance. Nevertheless he "was burning with curiosity. And so my friend Rehrl[21] took me for a drive close to the festival hall in his little car, which had a first-rate radio. Just as the turbulent fight scene was on, we rounded a corner full speed and rammed a passing tram. Let's keep silent about the rest. It could have had a worse ending. Since then I haven't been to a performance of the *Meistersinger*!"[22]

Mixing politics with culture was problematic in Schuschnigg's opinion. "I keep worrying that someone will discover an irregularity in Johann Strauss' [family tree],[23] or in Lehár's,"[24] he jokes. "Wouldn't that be a shame? But it seems certain that exceptions are being made. Lehár's adaptability is remarkable, by the way. Let's forgive him since he is skilful and had quite a few good ideas ... That reminds me of the joke of Knappertsbusch[25] about the old Weingartner[26] conducting *Lohengrin*[27] standing up. 'You find that remarkable? That's nothing! For some years now Richard Strauss[28] has been conducting the whole of the *Meistersinger* crawling on his knees.'"[29]

Schuschnigg continued with these ironic and occasionally caustic reminiscences about the pressure the Nazi regime put on performers and the influence they exacted on the choice of cultural offerings. His remarks were rather daring, considering the risk of his letters being intercepted, but he may have felt safe by veiling them in irony. Quite frequently, he noted, there were last-minute changes in concert and opera programs. They were dictated by the authorities, who demanded that suspect singers be replaced with Nazi-sanctioned performers. In this context, Schuschnigg comments on the curious situation of Rosette Anday. The famous mezzo-soprano sang at the Vienna State Opera and at all the major opera houses in Europe. On account of her Jewish ancestry, she was banned in Austria after the Anschluss but seems to have enjoyed some leeway in Germany. Schuschnigg notes that she did well for herself. He had read about her repeatedly in the party newspaper. "I believe *Orpheus*[30] was scheduled; and on the opening day, there arrived, instead of the advertised [singer], a telegram cancelling her performance. Whereupon Anday was fetched by plane and actually performed. With her usual efficiency she immediately elevated this for us very enjoyable fact to a solid proof of her martyrdom. She came up with the most fantastic stories: She had an inflamed appendix, a raging fever, etc. etc., and yet she performed – In short, she deserved a medal from us … And the good woman dined out on that story in subsequent years." Schuschnigg also notes how skilfully she managed the question of her Jewish ancestry. "While all the others – there weren't that many in any case – carefully refrained from mentioning the race question, Anday practically paraded her persecution as a Jew. She was also supposed to have been a *Luder* (minx). But I don't want to impute miscegenation to her. I can only surmise that she managed to get Hungarian citizenship or something like that and was therefore served up to the guileless people of Munich as a reliable woman with impeccable grandparents." It is hard to say what to make of Schuschnigg's ill-natured observations. Was he not aware that

Anday was born in Hungary and therefore had Hungarian citizenship as a matter of fact? As for "miscegenation," a word he could only have used tongue-in-cheek, Anday was in fact married to an "Aryan," the lawyer Karl Bundsdorf, who acted as her agent after the Vienna Opera terminated her contract. Eventually Anday was forced to be more discreet about her Jewish heritage. Apparently it became too risky to mention it openly. When Artur Schuschnigg ran into her at the Berlin opera in 1939, she was cagey and declared that it was all a misunderstanding. She wasn't Jewish at all. In any case, she managed to hold her own while the Nazis were in power and resumed her career in Vienna after the war. The city honoured Anday by naming a street after her.[31]

Referring to the precarious situation of Jews in the arts, Schuschnigg noted that their treatment by the Nazis was uneven. "I always thought Mrs. Kern[32] was at least 50 per cent Jewish, and yet she plays a role here that goes far beyond what her voice deserves." Conversely, dissenters were treated harshly, regardless of race. Schuschnigg asked his brother about the fate of the star soprano Lotte Lehmann. Apparently Vera had suspected him of taking a romantic interest in her. "Do you have any idea what Lotte Lehmann is doing?" he asked.[33] "Incidentally, Vera still harbours dark suspicions of me – I think. Not justified at all, I should add. I merely thought Lehmann had the best voice, and she was also charming." Lotte Lehmann – the first woman to perform all three roles in the *Rosenkavalier* – was a frequent guest at the Salzburg Festwochen with Toscanini conducting. She emigrated to the United States in 1938, on the eve of Hitler's annexation of Austria, after running into difficulties with Göring. Presumably she feared for her stepchildren from her husband's first marriage, who were of Jewish descent through their mother. As for Vera's suspicions of Schuschnigg's romantic entanglement: Lotte Lehmann was indeed charming (Toscanini wrote her love letters), but she seems to have preferred women to men and, after the death of her husband in 1938, shared her home with the lesbian psychologist Frances Holden.

In spite of Wagner and the German national myth being promoted by the Nazis, tastes were changing in the 1930s in favour of Italian composers such as Verdi and Puccini. The list of the most popular and widely performed operas in the 1938–9 season is headed by Leoncavallo's *Pagliacci*. There is no indication that Schuschnigg followed these popular trends. Apart from Wagner, he esteemed Beethoven and Mozart. He believed that culture served as a bridge between nations and in this context specifically mentions the music of Beethoven. "It is interesting how leading French personalities have always shown the greatest interest and understanding for the master works of German art and culture. Barthou wrote important studies on Wagner, while Herriot, then president of the chamber of deputies and mayor of Lyon, wrote an outstanding work on Beethoven. There is really no reason why Frenchmen and Germans should not understand each other." When Schuschnigg was fortunate enough to hear a program on the radio that included Beethoven's music, he registered the occasion in his diary. On 1 December 1939 he writes, "Listening to the radio nonstop paid off. After a lot of oom-pah-pah they played Beethoven's Seventh in the evening." On 3 December 1939 he writes: "I enjoy very fine music on Sundays – a two-hour-long symphony concert in the morning. Today I heard Handel, Mozart, and Haydn." He adds that this program was followed by a Nazi propaganda piece, entitled "On German Religiosity." It was set to the music of Bach and Beethoven. Given the context, he says, Wagner or Richard Strauss would have been more appropriate, but Beethoven made any propaganda bearable for him, even the celebration of the Führer's birthday. At least they played the Ode to Joy on that occasion, although that celebration brought him no joy. "The combination [of the Ode to Joy with Hitler's birthday] in itself makes any commentary superfluous."[34]

Mozart shared Beethoven's high standing in Schuschnigg's estimation and indeed personified the spirit of Austria. The Hitler regime tried to impose Nazi programming, but "Austria stood by Mozart." Schuschnigg emphasized that his objections to German politics did not imply a rejection of German culture. On the contrary: "By letting Austria remain an open door to the world, with free access to the immortal treasures of that spirit which, couched in the German language, was at the same time servant and master of humanity, we only tried to promote the peaceful cooperation of all and at the same time serve German interests."[35] Schuschnigg's efforts to separate musical culture from Nazi politics were, however, naïve and futile. In practice, as his own letters acknowledge, the political orientation and ethnicity of composers and performers determined their success, and indeed their survival under the regime. Conversely, the continued practice of music in concentration camps, although testimony to the spiritual strength and heroic determination of the inmates, cannot be separated from the inhuman treatment to which they were subjected and cannot mitigate the crimes committed against them.

To return to Schuschnigg's preferences, they parallel his literary tastes for the great classics. He favoured time-honoured, grand and solemn music over the light popular music of Lehár and Johann Strauss, which he saw in a sense as belonging to a bygone era, the days of the Austro-Hungarian Empire. There was a time when "Master Lehár gave the world a new Viennese operetta almost every year ... but that was in the past." In a letter to his brother, Schuschnigg wryly remarks that Lehár had fallen in with the "wrong" people. The tenor role in his last operetta, *Giuditta*, was sung by Richard Tauber, who was of Jewish descent; after the Anschluss he was forced to flee to England. Schuschnigg himself owned a score with a personal dedication by Lehár – "which could be embarrassing for him nowadays." He merely lists, but has no further comment on, the light musical works included in the New Year's Eve radio program of 1942: Johann Strauss' operetta *Die Fledermaus* and Leoncavallo's *I Pagliacci*.[36]

Among contemporary operetta composers Schuschnigg also mentioned Paul Lincke, whom many considered Berlin's answer to Johann Strauss in the field of entertainment and dance music. The aria "Berliner Luft" (The Air of Berlin) was one of the most popular pieces and is sometimes labelled "Berlin's Anthem." Lincke's operettas, among them *Frau Luna* (Mrs. Moon), which featured the aria "Berliner Luft," were international successes and were performed to huge applause at the Paris Folies Bergère. Lincke remained in favour under the Nazis and retained his popularity into old age. On listening to a lengthy radio program of music and commentary devoted to Lincke, Schuschnigg sarcastically remarks, "I found his commentary in between the musical pieces precious. A typical Berliner! First-rate ideas (more than one – at least two or three), to which he has stuck for eighty years with unshakeable determination, iron consistency and an invincible impudence! And the dry humour he displays, patting his 'colleagues' Johann Strauss, Millöcker[37] and Lehár on the back. I particularly like the business of them being his 'colleagues.' He has the skill and the knowledge, and what's more: he has the nerve. Really, I can well imagine Paul Lincke in a touristy Vienna *Heurigen* [rustic wine bar]. What distinguishes him from his colleague Lehár and also from *Schrammelmusik* [the typical *Heurigen* zither music] is the full use of schmaltz which is reserved for after midnight, when there are fireflies not only on the Isola Bella."[38]

Schuschnigg acknowledges that his musical tastes are eclectic. "I can't help it: I am sometimes rather one-sided and narrow-minded," he writes to his brother. "I know it very well myself (and feel rather comfortable with it), but in no way did I want to impose on you my pet music pieces. I hope you know that. The more open and understanding we are to enjoying and valuing what is beautiful, the more hours of happiness life will bring us. I quite understand that; and I also know that with my attitude – stuck in a rut – I am missing out and have missed out on some things. For example, you mentioned Debussy.[39] I am ashamed, but nevertheless readily confess that he remains a closed book to me in spite of all my attempts. And not only Debussy but what is even more reprehensible, the symphonies of Brahms, for example."[40]

Sacred music occupied a special place in Schuschnigg's heart, no doubt because it was connected with the religious practices he so greatly missed. He fondly remembered the tradition he used to observe in Vienna on 15 November, the feast day of St. Leopold. He always began the day attending a mass at the Burgkapelle and listening to a performance of Beethoven's Mass in C Major. He also recalls hearing a mass at St. Peter's in Rome, which to him was like "perceiving with your senses a piece of heaven ... Beethoven, Haydn, Mozart, and Schubert all knew that this is the only way human beings can indulge in their longing for heaven and their rapture of faith. That is why they wrote their concert masses in the way they did; that is why Master Anton Bruckner wrote his *Te Deum* and Antonín Dvořák his *Stabat Mater*. Even Richard Wagner worked with Palestrina's musical version of this text. That is also why Verdi gave to the world his grandiose funeral mass and the *Pezzi sacri*."[41]

He returns to his memories of hearing mass sung at St. Peter's in a letter to his brother: "Have you ever heard the silver trumpets at St. Peter's, by the way? Although the sacred music in Rome is often not very impressive, the *Marcia papale* and the transubstantiation, accompanied by trumpets from the cupola, always moved me enormously. Yet it is perhaps only a kind of Herms Niels, culturally enhanced and transposed into the baroque. But you know, of course, it's the combination of all parts that creates the effect! And so I draw a great deal on memories nowadays. Sometimes the music becomes quite audible to me, and some pictures spring to life again. The beauty of remembered experiences often transcends bitterness. I imagine your case is similar."

Since sacred music was not to the taste of the Nazi regime, it was a rare pleasure for Schuschnigg to hear it played on the radio. One day the paper announced that Beethoven's Mass in C would be on the program, but Schuschnigg suspected it was a mistake. "Goebbels would never permit it," he wrote and added sarcastically: "And he has not suffered a stroke, as was to be hoped." The announcement in the paper was indeed a mistake. Instead of Beethoven, the radio played Flotow's "Martha." More often than not Schuschnigg had to listen to popular music geared to lowbrow tastes. "Anything but what reminds us of the Valhalla movement with oompah music!" he exclaimed in exasperation.[42]

In any case, listening to sacred music on the radio fell short of listening to it in the inspirational setting of a church. "I very much envy your enjoyment of church music," he wrote to his brother. "I would give a lot to hear it. More than hearing an opera. I quite believe that you liked Orlando di Lasso and the Palestrina intermezzo – I suppose it was the beautiful *Tu es Petrus*. It is quite rare to hear these pieces well performed. They require a special choir culture."[43]

On another occasion, when he heard that Artur had gone to hear Mozart's Coronation Mass, he commented: "I believe the cathedral choir here is very good. If you have an opportunity, I recommend you attend the masses in E and A by Schubert. That is possibly the most beautiful music of its kind. But that beauty is lost if the performance is middling and the setting unsuitable. I always thought an impressive performance helps to get over the many unpleasant events of everyday life."[44]

As in the case of Schuschnigg's literary interests, patriotism played a role in his musical preferences. He often praised Austrian music and declared that the concept of the "classic" was best understood by Austrians. "Man muss vielleicht Österreicher sein," he wrote. "Perhaps one has to be Austrian to grasp the meaning underlying this word [classic]. Traditional form, universal validity, perfection itself may all be part of it, but it isn't the whole." The determining mark was the human spirit. There were classics in literature, in the arts, and in music. Schuschnigg was willing to concede that northern and central Germany had first claim on literature and the arts, but "classical music has made its home in Vienna on the Danube."[45]

The evidence presented here for Schschnigg's strategic use of books and music to cope with his imprisonment bears out the importance of the education he received for his ability to draw on cultural resources. His preferences for the classics and, more generally, "high culture" are clearly connected to the specifics of his education, that is, a humanistic education in which the "great books" were central. They could serve as a template for the cultural pursuits of a *Bildungsbürger* even in the special and restrictive circumstances in which Schuschnigg practised them.

chapter six

The Use of Wit

Reflecting on life in Dachau, Viktor Frankl considered humour one "of the soul's weapons in the fight for self-preservation." In spite of the dire circumstances, some inmates of concentration camps managed to retain a sense of humour and found in it a measure of relief. Josef Berg, a Norwegian interned at Sachsenhausen, was one of them. He recognized the beneficial effects of humour, noting that occasional evenings of entertainment organized by the inmates, and especially the performance of skits, raised the spirits of the audience – "even of people whose soul was shattered. They laughed and forgot." He himself was told by a fellow prisoner, "A man with your sense of humour will definitely survive the concentration camp." Fey von Hassell, who describes her imprisonment by the Nazis in the autobiographical *Niemals Beugen*, mentions that she and her fellow prisoners decided to tell jokes and amusing stories as a way of keeping up their spirits. Similarly Josef Müller (called "Ochsensepp"), a political prisoner kept in solitary confinement, wrote that "gallows humour saved him in this precarious situation." He decided "to make fun of himself once every day." Odd Nansen likewise told of the prisoners' efforts in Sachsenhausen "to get their spunk up" by joking, but he noted that "it was no healthy laughter; we could just as easily have wept with rage and indignation." Still he acknowledged the healing power of laughter. When fellow prisoners gave him a spirited birthday party, he felt good. "It was marvelous to have a laugh again."[1]

The observations about the effects of laughter in first-person accounts have been confirmed by the research of psychologists studying the origins and functions of humour. They found it provided a range of benefits, from emotional release and easing of stress to building self-confidence. Humour is widely recognized as a coping strategy in stressful situations and as a means of reducing the impact of negative life experiences. Psychologists distinguish between various uses of humour. Three categories in particular seem to fit Schuschnigg's case. The superiority theory postulates that the person making a joke or witty remark is showing contempt for the person or institution being lampooned and, in a way, celebrates his or her own superiority. Zany humour can be a form of defiance, moreover. This type of humour works if the audience shares the joker's contempt, as was the case in camp when the authorities were made the butt of a joke. It established a bond between teller and audience as members of a "clique" who understood the point of the joke. The incongruity theory examines another type of joke in which amusement arises from incongruity, that is, the deviation from an accepted norm in logic or ethics. This kind of humour also fosters a sense of community in a responsive audience. It too serves to contrast "us" and "them" and confirms in the case of the internees that they subscribed to the same norm – honour, decency, respect – and recognized the deviation from this norm by the Nazis. The release theory focuses on humour resulting in an unburdening and easing of tension, as described in many of the first-person accounts of internees. In addition, psychologists have pointed out the effects of self-deprecating humour, which attracts sympathy and draws positive reactions and support from the hearer, creating a bond between narrator and audience.[2]

We find a considerable variety of humour in Schuschnigg's writings covering all of these categories and ranging from amusing anecdotes to sarcastic quips. In many cases, Schuschnigg's use of humour served a dual purpose: as a relief valve and as a method of disguising his true meaning. In letters to his brother, irony and satire functioned as a means of camouflaging the real message since such modes of expression were more difficult to understand and interpret than straightforward language. Criticism couched in ironic terms was therefore more likely to escape detection when read by outsiders – the prying eyes of Nazi censors. As Josef Berg put it bluntly, the would-be censors "were too stupid … to understand that they were being mocked."[3] Schuschnigg accordingly masked any criticism of the regime with irony, especially through the well-known ruse of saying the opposite of what he meant.[4]

It is notable that the instances of humour or irony occur mainly in Schuschnigg's private letters to his brother, whereas they are almost absent from the diary entries he published. This allows a number of interpretations. It may indicate that he considered humour inappropriate or even counter-productive to the purpose of the diary and may have edited his notes accordingly. While he was in prison, any amusement caused by the absurd behaviour or statements of his captors had to be hidden as a matter of course. "A florilegium [of their ridiculous statements] remained in my mind," Schuschnigg writes, "partly because they amused me greatly, even if secretly, since [laughing] was forbidden."[5]

To a certain extent, using straightforward humour in the letters to his brother may have been posturing to show a brave front. Schuschnigg wanted to avoid distressing his brother and at the same time keep up his own spirits. He may also have used humour consciously or unconsciously as a means of bonding with Artur. In the case of irony, he could trust his brother to understand what he said with a wink. Unlike the "enemy" – the Nazi censors – Artur would immediately and fully grasp the point of his joke and see the absurdity or the incongruousness of what he was saying. This understanding in turn would cement their relationship and strengthen their bond.

Schuschnigg's natural disposition seems to have been rather sober and reflective. In the numerous photos available online, he invariably looks solemn, not to say forbidding. The sole exception is an image which appeared on the cover of *Time* magazine, an artistic rendition of a photograph. It shows a smiling Schuschnigg, which must have struck readers as incongruous since the corresponding article in the issue was entitled "Austria Is Finished" – unless of course the editors wanted to imply that Schuschnigg was pleased with the Anschluss.[6]

Although Schuschnigg had little use for humour in his diaries, he was definitely aware of its healing and sustaining quality, as his advice to Artur shows. Reacting to the news that his brother had been drafted, he wrote, "Take everything as much as possible from the humorous side. I know: easier said than done! But certainly it's the only thing to do! The first principle in similar cases must be, Don't willingly give pleasure to anyone to whom you would begrudge it! For there are people who are only pleased to bully another man as long as they see that it bothers him. Believe me, I have some experience with that!" Similarly, he writes to his uncle: "One is best off by far if one looks at everything from a humorous angle."[7]

The target of Schuschnigg's humour varies. It is occasionally directed at himself and his daily routine, but more often at the regime and its representatives – guards and administrators. Nazi culture in particular is a favourite butt of Schuschnigg's jokes and the subject of his most sarcastic humour.

Among self-deprecating instances of humour are passages that make fun of the deprivations he was suffering. He puns on the conditions in Sachsenhausen. They were at any rate an improvement over the Gestapo prison in Munich, he writes. He and Vera were now leading the lives of "plutocrats," that is, of rich and carefree people. As mentioned earlier, the term was used pejoratively by the Nazis to refer to the upper echelon of the population, especially the aristocracy. Thus, Vera at any rate would have been an obvious target, but her voluntary stay at Sachsenhausen and her willingness to shoulder the hardships together with her husband made the label patently ludicrous and thus effectively a joke. Schuschnigg also puns on the beauty of their surroundings. He has gotten rid of all his prejudices, he writes. He used to favour mountains, forests, and lakes, but that was sentimental (unsachlicher Kitsch). He is perfectly satisfied now with the view from his window, a flat, sandy patch with two lonely pines, surrounded by barbed wire. He has come to fully accept his "undeniably charming and much envied surroundings." Schuschnigg's comments on his food rations are another instance of humour by inversion. "The ample official supply is well known," he jokes, and the "general food situation is splendid." In fact, the quality of the dinners "moves me to prayer." Schuschnigg also repeatedly made jokes about his enforced idleness. He was living the life of a "pensioner," he wrote. Only two things were missing to make his retirement perfect: a monthly pension and a coffee house to hang out in. In a letter to his brother half a year later, he again alludes to his "retirement." He is puttering around all day and taking a siesta at noon. "In a word, I lead a typical pensioner's life – a little prematurely, but well!" A joke about his teenaged son may be considered self-deprecating by extension. He notes that Kurt is not doing well in languages and will hardly go on to study humanities. The family tradition of acquiring a doctorate will have to be carried on by Artur's son – "if that title still exists in future and one isn't obliged to become a kind of intellectual Sergeant Major (*Hauptfeldwebel*)."[8]

Another self-referential joke concerns Schuschnigg's smoking habit. He repeatedly expressed regret about his lack of self-control and inability to stop smoking. However, the poor quality of cigarettes available to him was helping him shake off this "vice," he quipped. Although tobacco was native to the area of Sachsenhausen and grown there in abundance, "only straw is being dried for the purpose of smoking. Small comfort, I know!" Schuschnigg's assessment of the quality of tobacco is confirmed by other inmates at Sachsenhausen. Payne Best said they tasted like "a bonfire"; Odd Nansen, referring to the cigarettes for sale at the camp's commissary, called them "as nasty as camel dung and in normal circumstances unsmokable. But here they are as welcome as new bread."[9]

The succession of maids assigned to the Schuschnigg household was also a frequent source of jokes. One of the young women was from the Berlin area – that is, Prussian. Historically, there was tension between the Prussians, who were typecast as stiff and purpose-driven, and the more easy-going Bavarians and Austrians. It is therefore meant as a dig against northern Germans when Schuschnigg declares that the maid "did everything to reinforce my old and deep-rooted love for the true Prussian nature."[10]

The Nazis were intent on suppressing any news of prominent people being incarcerated to avoid agitation on their behalf. One of the measures they instituted was the use of aliases for the prisoners. The members of the family of Crown Prince Rupprecht of Bavaria who were for a time Schuschnigg's neighbours were given the name "Buchholz," Fritz Thyssen was registered as "Müller," Mafalda of Hessen was called "Frau von Weber," and all mail to the Schuschniggs had to be addressed to "Dr. Auster." The maid was told that she would be working for "good people," that Dr. Auster was working at the command post. Schuschnigg did not relish being associated with his captors ("painful for me!"). He did not want to be regarded as a collaborator, but he took the charade with a grain of salt. "I have no idea what the good girl thinks about all of this. She comes across our [real] name everywhere, from the label on the carpets to the ersatz toilet paper. I hope she doesn't think at all."[11]

The "pearl" who was assigned to them later – the Russian helper – was clumsy and broke things. Speaking of the life-threatening air raids in 1943 and the preparations made in camp, Schuschnigg adds this bit of black humour: "Here they are digging foxholes and bunkers, just in case our less-valuable citizens and contemporaries turn against [their captors] … as for the rest, we don't need to wait for bombs and bombing damage. When it comes to wrecking the remainder of our household goods, the mover and the people at the depot are on it with reliable precision, and Sissy and our Smolensk pearl are doing the rest." The sentence contains multiple digs in descending order – against the Nazis who treated their prisoners as an inferior species ("less-valuable citizens"), the carelessness of the moving company in Vienna that had stored Schuschnigg's furniture and returned it in damaged condition, the carelessness of the maid, and the rambunctious nature of little Sissy. The joke clearly worked on account of its absurdity, the incongruence between life-threatening air raids and the relatively insignificant breakage caused by an awkward maid and a spirited child.[12]

In another reference to the Russian maid (and her admirers), Schuschnigg declares, "We would have a ready-made operetta libretto, perfect for a Jewish author … All we are missing is a composer in the military, who can set the lyrics to suitable music, and the radio could once again provide a so-called amusing hour, and surely not the worst kind!" There are several allusions here that darken the humour of this jocular remark. The "Jewish author" is presumably the librettist Fritz Löhner-Beda. He collaborated on several successful operettas with the "composer in the military," that is, Franz Lehár, who began his career as conductor of a military band. In spite of Lehár's attempt to intervene on Löhner-Beda's behalf, his colleague was incarcerated at the concentration camp at Buchenwald and then at Auschwitz, where he was killed in 1942. Löhner-Beda's tragic fate was likely unknown to Schuschnigg, but spoils the joke for contemporary readers. He meant to ridicule the Nazis, who patronized Lehár and made his operetta *The Land of Smiles* a success, conveniently ignoring the fact that the libretto had been written by a Jew to whom they had shown no mercy in the end.[13]

The incidents that had given rise to Schuschnigg's cryptic remarks were indeed comical. The Russian maid was courted by the guards. "Recently we became aware that there has been an attempt at correspondence between the forbidding guard tower next to us and our Russian girl. Sweet little notes are being dropped directly on our lettuce beds. It's rather remarkable that such short-sighted men are accepted for service in the elite troop of the beloved Führer – you should see our little oaf! And it's funny that the young fellows from the Teutoburger Forest imagine that the 'cute girl' can read and write German, and have unfounded hopes that she will deposit a reply in the indicated hiding place (known to us from reading their notes). Now I am thinking that I should pen a strong reply by proxy. I only wonder how many additional years of incarceration I might get for such a frivolous undertaking."[14]

Much of Schuschnigg's hidden criticism is aimed at the cultural politics of the Nazis, that is, at their preference for popular over high culture and the consequent lowering of standards, at least in Schuschnigg's eyes. He had been complaining about the radio programing, but then suddenly noticed an improvement. His sarcastic explanation: Presumably the man in charge of the program "is on holidays, or has been drafted, or is otherwise occupied – may God keep him healthy, but far away! Things are more or less fine as long as Piefke's march ['Prussia's Glory'] isn't played too often." Joking about the prohibition against listening to foreign radio broadcasts,

Schuschnigg writes that he had to swear an oath that "they would listen only to the truth and nothing but the truth, so *nix* with foreign radio stations. But who in this place (or anywhere else) would think of something outrageous like that? Not even I!" The irony, impenetrable to an outsider, lies in the fact that someone "in this place" – namely Schuschnigg himself – was listening to foreign stations. Artur was presumably aware of that and laughing at his brother's fake indignation.[15]

"Ten years ago, all that would have sounded pretty crazy," Schuschnigg wrote. "Hopefully, it will again sound crazy in another ten years, assuming that we live to see such remote times." To calculate that time, he sets up an equation, using "4" to denote Hitler. "4er divided by Stalin = x. I don't think a professor has been born yet to solve this problematic equation." When that time arrives, however, he hopes that some benevolent soul will present Mussolini with a splendid edition of Nietzsche and a copy of the *Arabian Nights*, and the "4er" with an Old Testament with exegetical notes by the Nazi-friendly Austrian Cardinal Innitzer. "That would make us happy."[16]

In another poke at the regime, Schuschnigg reports that he was notified of his name being expunged from the ranks of retired World War I soldiers as a man undeserving of this honour. Luckily his rank wasn't very high, he quipped. "I had nothing more to lose than the title of lieutenant." He goes on to joke that there was in any case no logic to military arrangements, even in World War I. "To be assigned to the dental station, one had to be a dermatologist, and a trained surgeon was preferably put in charge of the administration of beds. But maybe that was only Austrian inefficiency."[17]

The Nazis tried to legitimize their government by connecting the Third Reich historically with the Holy Roman Empire. Projecting a long tenure, they referred to it as the *Tausendjährige Reich*, the "Thousand-Year Empire." Making fun of this notion and punning on his own circumstances, Schuschnigg writes, "Our trust in destiny and the Omnipotent as the protector of justice has now reached the prescribed unlimited measure. Whatever the future will bring over the next thousand years, we look at it with icy determination." The "Omnipotent" in this case is presumably

Hitler, to whom Schuschnigg refers elsewhere as "4er," punning on the resemblance of the German word for the number four to the word "Führer" as pronounced in the Austrian dialect.[18]

A letter Schuschnigg wrote to Artur on 1 April 1942 is dripping with sarcasm. "I feel excellent. I am no longer a pampered man and understand that things could be very different in this happy land. I'm therefore unreservedly content and have no objection to anything, not even the fact that the only people I have contact with are SS-people and the poor devils with the variously coloured triangles on their backs and the occasional B.V. [Berufsverbrecher, professional criminal]. My God, who is the real professional criminal, when you come to think of it? But of course everything is relative."[19]

He repeatedly comments on the attempts of the authorities to keep the presence of elite prisoners hidden by assigning them aliases. "By the way, our neighbour, whose name is strictly confidential, is the last president of the Social Democratic Party in Berlin and a famous former delegate in Geneva, as I found out with the help of my [encyclopedia] Der Grosse Herder." The neighbour in question was Rudolf Breitscheid, who was incarcerated with his wife. "The two old people will be quite distressed since they were unlucky enough to be caught twice, the second time in southern France when they already had passports in hand for an overseas trip. This last detail isn't in my encyclopedia. Rather, I got it from the guard. And now we are supposed to get a third 'settler.' It is a real blessing to be liberated at last! We have all been waiting for that."[20] Refraining from actually naming Breitscheid, yet clearly identifying him through referencing his position, Schuschnigg lampoons the Nazi efforts at secrecy. There is irony also in the fact that the guard freely talks about the so-called "settlers" as well as in the pretence that these settlers had been "liberated" or taken into protective custody.[21] In another reference to the regime's methods of rendering their victims invisible and turning them into non-persons, Schuschnigg muses about the restrictions placed on his contacts with the outside world. In the fall of 1943, his brother, who had been drafted into the German army, was stationed in Dannenwalde. Schuschnigg refers to the place as "Langenfelde (or whatever that little place is called)." The situation was absurd. Theoretically Artur had permission to visit his family. Practically, however, this was not possible because they had been evacuated to the south of Germany – "the rule being the further away the better." Vera would also have liked to stay in contact with Artur, but in her case that was not possible because she was a non-person "according to higher powers, although she does become visible with a certain effort." Any mail between Sachsenhausen and Dannenwalde (a two-hour ride on the local train) took two weeks to arrive. The long delay in mail delivery was made more poignant by another anecdote Schuschnigg relates. While letters from his family reached him late or not at all, hate mail was delivered promptly. "The letter I got was from a lady of whom I had never heard before. It was a registered letter and stated that her husband had been unjustly treated by the Imperial Ministry of War in 1917. None of the subsequent governments had done anything to right this wrong. Nor had I done anything about it, and therefore she expressed the wish, 'May thistles grow on your early grave and may not even a dog mourn your death. Heil Hitler.'" He kept the letter as a curiosity.[22]

Here as elsewhere in his letters to Artur, Schuschnigg protects himself well against any third-party reading. His puns are complex and riddling such that only an insider like his brother would readily understand them. The few instances of irony found in the published diary entries are in some ways easier to understand, yet the irony is more often contained in what Schuschnigg omits than in what he states. Thus he tells of his experiences in prison in a deadpan fashion, that is, without expressly noting the absurdity of the situation. The reader will, however, have no difficulty supplying the missing point. For example, he merely notes that a request of his was met with the suggestion, "Make an application." The reader, however, will understand from the narrative that this suggestion was ludicrous since Schuschnigg's applications were invariably denied. Similarly, when he was promised – once again – that his wife would soon be allowed to live together with him, he dryly notes the date: 1 April. The reader will understand that such a promise was worth no more than an April Fools' Day joke.[23]

Given the importance Schuschnigg ascribed to humour in coping with his situation, he was grateful for the gift of a book of humour from his brother. "A special thanks also for Bobby!" he wrote to Artur, presumably referring to an anthology of "Count Bobby" jokes. "Where have I met the dear man before – in person, I mean? But I believe he has died in the meantime. If not, our time would offer him a goldmine of material, mainly for his bon mots, and he would take great delight in them."[24]

Schuschnigg's question, "Where have I met this man before?" was meant as a joke, since the Graf Bobby figure, an obtuse aristocrat resembling P.G. Wodehouse's Wooster, was fictitious. The character was developed in Austro-Hungarian cabarets at the beginning of the twentieth century. No definite author is associated with the skits. Jokes involving Bobby and his aristocratic friends were revived after the war and reached a peak of popularity in the 1950s, when anthologies and films were made about the fictitious baron. Here is an example of a Graf Bobby joke from 1918: "I just don't understand it. We had such a beautiful army. The splendid horses! The plumed helmets! And especially the flags with their beautiful embroideries! Absolutely glorious. It was the most beautiful army in the world, and what did we do with it? We sent it into battle!"[25]

Schuschnigg declared tongue-in-cheek, "[Bobby's opinions] are certainly no more foolish than the average opinion of today's SS-*Obersturmführer* (First Lieutenants of the SS) – May God protect them and grant Bobby eternal peace." In recognition of the healing powers of humour, he adds: "It's always good to have something to laugh about nowadays!"[26]

chapter seven

Cherishing Memories

We all have a memory bank on which we draw from time to time in order to make sense of ourselves. We all have a need to see our lives framed in the past, to recreate the past in the act of memory, and perhaps even to transmute and refurbish our experiences, thus recreating ourselves.[1] Our memories may not always be accurate and reliable, but they are helpful when we are looking for purpose and direction in our life. At other times, memories operate outside the precincts of our awareness. We do not deliberately draw on them. Instead, they emerge from our subconscious, uncalled for and irrepressible, and bring on unwanted feelings. In either case, however, memory helps us define who we are.

Recalling the past takes on added importance in the wake of traumatic experiences and significant life changes which necessitate a redefinition, as was the case with the men and women who were interned in Nazi prisons and concentration camps. Schuschnigg's internment put an end to a successful career in politics and turned him from a man of action and authority into a nonperson, whose very name was taken from him. Although his misfortunes were not comparable in scale to the horrors endured by the general population of concentration camps, he shared with them the loss of all agency. Within days, Schuschnigg had moved from a life of privilege to one of deprivation. He was no longer in control of his actions. Prisoners in Sachsenhausen were told by the guards, "You are ciphers. We can do with you as we please." Their victims in turn spoke of being "erased" (ausgelöscht). Hans

Ehrenberg acknowledges that they were "depersonalized" (*wesen-los*) and deprived of dignity.[2] Schuschnigg expresses the feeling of facelessness in similar terms. He had been "cast aside, buried, yet condemned to go on living."[3] It is at times like these that memory enables the victims of violence to reconstitute their being and remain human despite their tribulations.

Schuschnigg's diary and letters are important sources for our understanding of how the memory process can be made to work for a victim. It is common for people to consider a day's events in their minds, to relate present to past experiences, or to judge ongoing actions by reference to the past. Keeping a diary – recalling the thoughts and events of each day in writing – is a deliberate act of creating memory and was for Schuschnigg a means of remaining conscious of who he was.[4] "Being alone and not socializing with others isn't the worst aspect [of solitary confinement]," he wrote. "The inability to express one's innermost thoughts is harder to bear." Keeping a diary allowed or even forced him to concretize his thoughts by naming them.[5] Schuschnigg's observations indicate, moreover, that he had a keen understanding of the uses and effects of his memories put into words and that he evoked them for the purpose of consoling himself.

On a more mundane level, Schuschnigg wrote to pass the time. The days in prison, with their enforced inactivity or limited sphere of action, dragged on. "Excuse the length [of my letter]," he writes to his brother. "– I have time." At other times, writing was just a means of spelling out his frustrations. Schuschnigg realized that retelling his experiences brought him relief. In his letters to his brother, he was able to give full vent to his feelings.[6]

Anecdotes from the past tended to enliven conversation, moreover. "Recalling one's own experiences always gives life and zest to a conversation," Schuschnigg writes. But even memories that remained unspoken and lived only in his mind were valuable and provided relief by removing him from his present, wretched surroundings. Like Schuschnigg, many prisoners used memories as a survival strategy; to mentally escape their confinement they focused their attention on the past. Remembered time became a substitute for real time. Viktor Frankl calls memories the prisoner's "refuge from the emptiness, desolation and spiritual poverty of his existence by letting him escape into the past."[7] For Schuschnigg, the flight into the past was also an intellectual exercise: "I concentrate on exercising my mind and have covered a remarkable distance." In that respect memories were akin to dreams and fantasies.[8] Schuschnigg allowed himself to spin out his thoughts and dreams, for example, when he was told that he might be moved from his prison in Munich. For a while, he thought his next destination was the Buchenwald concentration camp near Weimar. His reaction: "That wouldn't have been bad, at least for the trace of germs that may have survived there from the era of Goethe [who lived in Weimar]." In his mind, at any rate, he would then have been transported – not to another prison – but much further away, into the past and ushered into the mythical presence of one of his favourite authors.[9]

At the very least, memories helped him bury more distressing thoughts. "They displace many other things in my mind," he wrote. They reconciled him to a past that was irredeemable, that was "nothing more than silenced bells to me now." The memories which allowed Schuschnigg to escape prison for a while were sometimes as vivid and persistent as a lived experience. In the early days of his incarceration he called up visions of the past to relive the beauty and happiness associated with them. As his imprisonment continued, however, it became increasingly difficult to keep up these life-giving and sustaining memories. "It isn't so long ago that a kind of web of dreams animated the treasure of my memories. I chatted with them as with dear old acquaintances. What did I wish for with such intensity that my wish almost turned into a fixed, believable image? At first, a blue sky, a great expanse of water, and sunshine were the essence of my longing ... yes, those were my dreams at the beginning of my imprisonment ... then silence descended and became deeper. Gradually a veil dropped over the southern coastal view of my thoughts, and fog enveloped me."[10]

Of course, not all memories were pleasant or provided Schuschnigg with relief from his mental suffering. Sometimes they came to him unbidden and were hard to shake. The harassment he had experienced from the guards in Vienna continued to occupy his mind and vex him. He went over every word they said, their possible meaning and implication. These painful memories faded only gradually. "The darts aimed at me, transformed in a more forgiving moment of memory, lived on as mere discomforts in my thoughts. The memory was sometimes even accompanied by a slight laugh, though that gave me no relief. It was certainly not a memory I called up. Rather I could not rid myself of it." He tried his best to suppress painful thoughts, especially the memory of his arrest and imprisonment in the Gestapo quarters in Vienna. "It is no good dwelling on these things. I shall try to forget them."[11]

We all have memory props – for Marcel Proust it was the taste of a madeleine, which evoked childhood memories. It prompted the iconic passage in *Remembrance of Things Past* describing the exquisite pleasure he felt at the sight of the little cake, a pleasure that displaced the tribulations of life. Schuschnigg, too, confesses to an *Anhänglichkeitskomplex*, an almost pathological attachment to old things. He was pleased to find his mother's prayer book in one of the storage boxes sent to him in Sachsenhausen, and used it for his devotions on Christmas Day. In prison, he kept photos of his mother, son, and wife on the bedside table. Vera had brought the photos to him at Christmas 1938. "Now I sit here with the enlargement of my wife's picture in front of me. The lights are out except for the lamp on my table, which shines on the picture. It is my Christmas tree."[12]

Family photos recording events of the past were an almost ghostly reminder, he noted: "It gave me a turn when I saw [the photo of his parents and his late wife Herma], in each other's company, oblivious of what was to come – Mama wearing that fur collar ... and Papa with his stiff hat." Looking at a photo commemorating Christmas 1934 and seeing the family so *gemütlich*, "one could almost hear their voices." Looking at a photo of Artur's family, he detects his mother's features in his nephew's face: "Am I mistaken, or is there something of our Mama in his little face?" He fondly recalls his nephew's visit when he was only a toddler, and also remembers attending his baptism. He reflects how close the events of birth and death were at the time. A few weeks after his nephew was born, Schuschnigg's mother died.[13]

Schuschnigg's memory is often jogged by special days. Not surprisingly, Christmas was one of them. It is a time which tends to heighten memories and make people turn an occasion that was perhaps less than glorious into something picture-postcard perfect. Henri Michel, a political prisoner at Sachenhausen, writes that "on feast days we always felt more closely connected in our minds." The Christmas celebrations permitted in camp were emotionally gripping, especially the Christmas carols sung in several languages. Michel also marks other special occasions in letters to his wife: the anniversary of the day when he was taken away and separated from her, past Easter celebrations ("beautiful memories to draw on even today"), All Soul's Day, when "we remember our dear departed." The same emphasis is evident in Joseph Joos' letters. He marked the day of his arrest, the anniversary of his mother's death, All Soul's Day, Easter, and Christmas, which brought on a "blossom rain of memories." Similarly, Nansen noted special days in his diary: his wedding day ("it is of eternity and will never die"), his father's birthday ("he would have been 83 today"). His memories of home offered him something "dreamlike" that helped him overcome the reality of the camp, he wrote.[14]

Schuschnigg's memories were likewise triggered by special days, such as anniversaries and All Souls' Day, when it was the practice in Austria, as in many other countries, to visit cemeteries and commemorate the dead with prayers and masses. "All Souls' Day awakens in our minds familiar and loving images. One must be thankful to God for such beautiful and untarnished memories," he writes in 1942.[15] Another day that prompted memories was 12 September, commemorating the Holy Name of Mary, which had special meaning for Schuschnigg's mother. As a boy, Schuschnigg was allowed to carry a banner in the procession marking that day. The celebration took place in the village of Heiligwasser in Tyrol, near his uncle's house. "Should you turn in the direction of Heiligwasser on a nice evening, think of me," he writes to Wopfner. "Mama also liked that view."[16]

Indeed, Schuschnigg's mother seems to have functioned as a memory-bearer herself, reminding him to congratulate others on their birthdays, as he tells his uncle: "My mother would have said: Don't forget Uncle Hermann's birthday. And on all these significant dates I keep thinking: what would Mama have said now?"[17]

Both Schuschnigg and Vera regularly reference the anniversary of his parents' deaths. "Papa would almost be eighty now," he writes, and "I have thought a great deal about [what would have been] Mama's 72nd birthday." On the anniversary of his father's death in 1940 Schuschnigg had mass said in his name at St. Stephen's cathedral in Vienna. He thought of his surviving family members often, but death crystallized memories, he writes: "They come into focus only after the long goodbye."[18] At Christmas, Schuschnigg remembers prewar family reunions, when his mother welcomed the family to a special evening and was the perfect hostess. She knew how to make everyone comfortable, he writes, and how to create a feeling of coziness and joy, so that her guests went away thinking, "what an especially fine evening it was – and I still have that feeling today." He remembers Christmas 1934, the last he celebrated together with his parents. "Of course I thought a great deal of Mama and Papa [at Christmas]," he writes. His uncle, too, featured in this "most beautiful memory ... it was a very fine experience."[19]

Memories flood Schuschnigg's thoughts when he writes to his brother and uncle. An astonishing number of his letters – more than a third – contain references to his mother, who died in 1935. "It is terrible to lose one's mother," he writes, "... and when the dear eyes are closed, it is, as if a veil dropped down and a piece of one's own life sank away." A mother's death was the most painful experience, "perhaps the only wound that never heals over completely." Yet remembering his mother seemed to comfort Schuschnigg. In his correspondence he encourages his brother to reminisce with him and share his memories: "Please write again to me about our parents. Those thoughts are so good, and those memories such a treasure." At the same time, he acknowledged that they were bittersweet, but to his mind, the positive elements predominated. "We both enjoyed exchanging memories of former times, even if there is a measure of sadness in them," he writes. Similarly, he appreciated the reminiscences contained in the letters of his uncle, especially when Hermann Wopfner related anecdotes or quoted certain expressions used by Schuschnigg's mother.[20]

In his own reminiscences, Schuschnigg goes beyond recalling his late mother's actions and words, to the point of recreating her and attributing putative opinions to her. This too is a known phenomenon. People tend to integrate fantasies into their memories when they have experienced a loss, synthesizing wishful thinking with real experiences.[21] When his uncle fell ill in the late summer of 1940, Schuschnigg counselled him not to return to his teaching prematurely, citing the authority of his mother. "If Mama were still alive, she would beg you to delay returning to your activities at the university. You'd be taking a risk." When his daughter, Sissy, was born, he reflected on his mother's feelings. If she were still alive, she would have loved to see the child. On another occasion, too, he "inserts" his mother into a scene, making her a quasi-observer. On hearing that an acquaintance had died in an air raid, he expressed horror at the manner of her death – she was buried in the debris when a building collapsed. "If Mama had lived to know that," he adds, "she too would have been greatly affected." As the military action moved closer to Sachsenhausen and the area around the camp was threatened by air raids as well, Schuschnigg commented, "Sometimes I think, if Mama were still alive and forced to experience this, she would die for fear of what might happen to us all." His parents lived on in Schuschnigg's mind and were ever-present as ghostly bystanders. This is most apparent from a comment he made after political and military developments had uprooted both him and his brother, with him interned at Sachsenhausen and his brother obliged to move to Berlin. Their parents, he said, were now "the only ones left at home," that is, in a cemetery in Vienna. Although a figure of speech, the words clearly indicate that Schuschnigg's parents were to him symbols of "home" and remained a strong presence in his life, a concept that may be related to his belief in the immortality of the soul and the intercession of the dead before God on behalf of the living.[22] Vera, who was also a devout believer, shares the idea that the dead are, in a way, present and continue to take an interest in the well-being of those who are dear to them. They take on the role of advocates before God, interceding for their children. Schuschnigg's mother did not live to see the birth of her granddaughter, but she could nevertheless "guide the child from above" and ask God for whatever was best for them.[23]

Consciously or unconsciously, people show a "self-serving bias"[24] in selecting specific events from the wealth of their auto-biographical memories. They pick experiences that are salient to them and filter out the rest. Schuschnigg's reminiscences about his mother focus on three seemingly disparate themes: her educational methods, her housekeeping, and her last illness.

With a certain amusement he recalls her cautious approach to life, her difficulties in making decisions, her ifs and buts – an approach to life that was also reflected in her pedagogical methods. It was typical for her to say "no" to any request of her son – at least, that was her first, automatic reaction. Schuschnigg himself used the same method (or ruse) on his son in turn. "It served me wonderfully well as a protective wall, was educational, and gave me time to think." Like his mother, he pretended to a certain severity, but never held on to this fiction for very long and felt no lasting anger. Of course, children catch on to parental ruses, he notes. He himself saw through his mother's pretences, and so did his son, Kurt, when Schuschnigg feigned anger or denied his pleas. Kurt "therefore never worried too much about that first no. There was only one instance in which I used actual corporal punishment. That occasion he remembers to the present day. I remember Mama's last years – if I wanted anything from her, asking her to come to Vienna, for example, I would regularly set aside two weeks for a negative answer, but then it was high time [for a yes]. It worked every time!"[25]

Schuschnigg often mentions his mother's housekeeping and cooking skills with admiration. He compares the shortage of food supplies he and Vera experienced in the present situation with the difficulties his mother's generation experienced during and after World War I. With ongoing rationing, procuring sufficient or specific kinds of food was a daily problem not only for the

Schuschniggs, but for all families. "It was like that also in 1918–1920 ... I remember what a relief it was after those years to be able finally to have a normal dinner at home! And the wonderful, celebratory evenings Mama arranged so cleverly, with home-baked bread – but better not think about that now ... let's just be grateful to our parents!"[26]

It was hard to believe how good life had been only a few years ago and how naïve they were to think they would never experience the deprivations of wartime again. "Inconceivable, we said then!" Yet his mother had coped well with the shortages during World War I and its aftermath. She made do with whatever was at hand. "Do you remember her bean soup with cabbage?" Schuschnigg asks his brother. "Mama was so inventive and always managed to produce something tasty. We at any rate were enthusiastic. But I will never forget the shocked face of dear Cazin – our guest one Christmas – when she was served up the famous bean soup! I myself rather liked it – the bean soup, that is; what would I give to have it now! Yet I must honestly confess that in the present circumstances and for the most part I cannot complain about food supplies."[27] During World War I, both Schuschnigg and his father had served in the military. Sometimes they had access to extra food supplies, which they brought home on their respective home leaves. Once, Schuschnigg brought along a bag of unground corn, and his mother put it to creative use. "Mama pretended to be very pleased, but believe me, it was only to avoid spoiling my pleasure. I suppose it was enough for a proper polenta or corn gnocchi." Elsewhere, too, Schuschnigg pays tribute to his mother's cooking skills. Every time he was given home leave, he always felt that "everything was wonderful – including potatoes with baloney, my standing request every evening (and I have not enjoyed anything as much since!)."[28]

When he and Vera moved into the house on the grounds of the Sachsenhausen camp, Schuschnigg made an earnest effort to help with managing the household. It was a new experience for him, but he was making progress – or so he flattered himself. His mother, the perfect housekeeper, would not have been impressed, he surmises. "I can hear my mother's doubtful 'Oh my, oh my.'"

She had set high standards and would have been very unhappy with the state of affairs at the house in Sachsenhausen: "My good late Mama would not have been able to stop cleaning and wiping." He remembers how anxious she was to have her own home in pristine condition. Expecting a visit from her parents, she subjected everything to a thorough cleaning and tidying. "But I gladly labour over it," she told her son, "in the expectation of good things to come." Recalling her efforts and the pleasure she took in company, Schuschnigg adds, "I wish I could relive just one day with her – nothing has been as difficult for me to overcome [as her death], either in earlier times or now; I'm still not over it." He feels guilty about not having paid enough attention to his mother when she was alive. "It is terrible how tone-deaf one becomes to such things and how lacking in judgment as far as one's values and priorities are concerned," he writes to his uncle. "I wish I could talk to you about that."[29]

He took great pleasure in recalling his mother's meals, her perfect home, and remembered with some amusement her little schemes of keeping him in line. Yet his memories of her are also tinged with sadness because she died of kidney failure at the relatively young age of 63. The circumstances, moreover, disturbed him, even a decade later. "Really, one shouldn't ruminate about it," he writes, but goes on nevertheless to reminisce and indeed to agonize about his mother's last days. He recalls every detail: his question to the doctor whether he could in any way hasten her death to shorten her suffering, his father's emotional strength, the decision of the doctor to stop her heart medication. He recalls his mother's unwillingness to acknowledge that she was at death's door until she could no longer deny it. He quotes her words: "Now I know why I received the last rites." He raises the question whether they did enough for her ("we were all taking it rather easy"), whether the doctors made the right decision and acted quickly enough. Schuschnigg's brother was apparently not so keen on reviving these memories, and did not immediately react to Schuschnigg's prompts, but Schuschnigg was insistent. In his next letter he returned to the subject, reminding Artur, "You left a question of mine unanswered: Do you believe or have you ever heard that there may have been a medical error in Mama's treatment?? – I sometimes muse about that. The parents were staying with us at the time. Perhaps we didn't take the matter seriously enough in the beginning. I had no idea that it would become critical. Perhaps we called in the specialist too late? – He was certainly among the best Vienna had to offer at the time in that field. – Why wasn't she operated on in time? – Those are useless questions today of course. But they go round and round in my head. Today, I sometimes can no longer understand my actions! – It wasn't until the end of July that I realized how serious the matter was. Yet I realized it before the physician told me. May the good woman rest in peace! And our Papa as well. What he managed to do when he was 70 years old or older is incredible. I wish I could do as much! Today I sometimes feel that I was oblivious to our parents' getting old."[30]

If he was oblivious to the seriousness of the situation then, Schuschnigg compensated, or perhaps even overcompensated, for his earlier neglect by idealizing his parents after their death. In his prison letters, he expresses the hope that his own children will remember him in this fashion as well. "I think we can't ask for anything better from our children than that they will regard us in the way we regarded our parents. They were one heart and one soul throughout their lives and literally inseparable! There would be a great deal more to say of them in that respect!"[31]

Schuschnigg writes of his family with a deep sense of belonging. They are an extension of his self. The family's military tradition is one element linking the generations. Schuschnigg proudly speaks of their service to the fatherland: his grandfather's service, his father's, and his own. It is a tradition that lives on. Schuschnigg himself had fought in World War I. So had his father, who was eventually promoted to titular field marshal. His grandfather made a name for himself as commander of the regional gendarmerie. In 1919, when Schuschnigg was taken prisoner in Italy, "one of the carabinieri there noticed my name and began to speak of grandfather in terms of the highest praise." Schuschnigg's son, Kurt, refers to the family's military tradition in his own memoirs: "Father had volunteered to fight in the First World War and, like his father, had been taken prisoner. In deference to my Grandfather's high rank, the Italians interned them together. In the prisoner of war camp, they had orderlies who polished their boots and laundered their uniforms." Such anecdotes, handed down through the generations, contributed to a sense of belonging. After Schuschnigg's imprisonment, his father was a mainstay for Vera and Kurt. "I could always turn to him, and he helped us immensely," Vera writes. When he died in October 1938, the Gestapo rejected Schuschnigg's request for permission to attend his funeral. The veto deeply distressed him. The ritual meant perhaps more to him than just closure. His attendance would have been an act of reaffirming his belonging to the family and their collective memory.[32]

For Schuschnigg, the parental home was *the* home. "Oddly, considering how much I moved around, my memories increasingly focus on [their apartment]. Not so much on account of the years I lived there, but rather on account of what came later: the evenings with my parents." Not that he wanted to turn back the clock and live there again. Too much had happened since, he acknowledged. "Hallowed memory is the best part" of the past.[33]

Schuschnigg's memories often have a melancholic element and occasionally strike an eschatological tone. He looks at his own life and the history of humanity as preordained and part of a larger, divine plan. In Schuschnigg's eyes, the world was in decline. Although he was saddened by the death of his parents, he was also glad that they were spared experiencing the present, a time of horror and destruction. America had now entered the war, he knew, and Hitler's fortune had begun to turn, but in Schuschnigg's view, the malaise went beyond the war. America was not the answer to the world's problems and could not halt the decline of civilization.[34] "My mood is often affected by the tragedy of destruction. Especially because most of what has been destroyed is irredeemably lost, and what has been rebuilt is hardly of particular interest. It is quite possible that live-in kitchens and bathrooms will be more beautiful than ever, and may be quite practical and pleasant; and a new edition of a beautifully illustrated Grimschitz will perhaps have to suffice to evoke memories of the baroque style, and perhaps we might even have the ingredients for a *Kaiserschmarren*." But none of this could replace what was lost.[35]

Thus, while Schuschnigg's family reminiscences may have given him joy, more general memories of the "good old days" gave him a feeling of wistfulness and regret, which the anticipated victory of the Allies could not appease. "For decades now there has been much palaver about a break in culture, so that it really had to come to pass one day," he writes. "But it is rather tragic that America of all cultures remains standing. In the time of antiquity, there were heirs at any rate, and the causes were spread more broadly over time and diverse peoples; this time future researchers who keep an objective mind will not have an easy time to determine the why and wherefore."[36] He wrote these words to his brother in December 1944, but an apocalyptic mood and a lack of belief in the future had crept into his mind earlier. In a diary entry of 20 September 1943 he characterizes the time as a "an awful and precipitous step backward, worse than ... original sin." Yet, seeing this perceived fall of humanity in the biblical context of the original sin also allowed hope for divine redemption, "a shimmer of hope, no, a firm belief." Even at the nadir of civilization and of his own life, he was grateful for memories of an earlier, happier time, on which he could draw for the remainder of his life. "Even if it is only the memory of two candles burning on the altar, and the lost sound of the bells which calls the reflective mind to the raised chalice. The mere knowledge that these things exist and my reliving this mystery ... provide an ample and overflowing treasure."[37]

In a broadcast entitled "The Good Old Times" aired by Radio Vatican on 3 October 1945 – that is, almost half a year after Schuschnigg regained his freedom – he refers to this use of memories as an effective, but ultimately futile, survival strategy. When we experience hardship, he says, memories become "the most precious gift this life has to offer ... a transfigured past the poets called 'the golden age.'" The emphasis is on "transfigured" since the sufferer has a tendency to recall "only the light, not the shadows." Such memories therefore produce no more than a Cockaigne (*Schlaraffenland*). Yet, "the harder the present and the more menacing the future, the greater our tendency to forget and allow our mind to travel into the past." In retrospect, however, using memories as a palliative served as an "attempt at escaping reality, which was doomed to failure."[38]

chapter eight

Schuschnigg's Political Reminiscences

We have seen that memories played an important role in the struggle of prisoners to retain a sense of self. A special case may be made for political memories or the political conscience of internees, particularly when such memories yielded satisfaction, that is, the feeling of having done the right thing. Josef Berg, for example, who had been active in the resistance in Norway, wrote that it was "the fight for a cause ... that gave him strength." Similarly, Arnold Weiss-Rüthel says that his conscience was clear. He was innocent, perhaps "not before the Nazi laws, but in my own mind" and in the eyes of a "universal conscience" (*Weltgewissen*). Although this knowledge was of no material help to him, he writes, "it gave me the inner strength needed by a man in my situation," that is, an inmate of the Sachsenhausen concentration camp.[1] Prisoners who had been interned for their political views were sustained by the knowledge that they were suffering for the sake of a principle. Schuschnigg likewise took a certain satisfaction in having been detained by the Nazis on account of his political stance.

The terms of Schuschnigg's imprisonment in Vienna and Munich – living in isolation and enforced idleness – encouraged reminiscences. "In the silence of the cell my thoughts turn back constantly to the years which led up to the fall of Austria," he writes.[2] Unlike the fond memories of his parents and his home life, however, Schuschnigg's political memories were not comforting in themselves. He had taken the helm of the state during an emergency, after a failed coup and the assassination of his predecessor. He had inherited from Dollfuss a country in financial and political turmoil. He was diplomatically isolated and unable to ward off Hitler's invasion and annexation of Austria. Schuschnigg's memories of these years could only function as palliatives if he established in his own mind that his actions had been morally correct.

In this context we need to consider the question: To what extent are Schuschnigg's political memories reliable and to what extent are they wishful thinking or a prop to reassure himself? The reliability of memory is an issue relevant to Schuschnigg's narrative, but it also applies more generally to first-person accounts of Nazi prisoners. Some memoirists are sensitive to this problem and counter the reader's doubts with a plea for understanding. They emphasize that they lived in circumstances where common norms and expectations were suspended and ask readers to take into consideration the difference between "then," the Nazi era, and "now," the time of writing or publishing the reminiscences.[3] Schuschnigg uses a similar approach. He begins his autobiographical account in *Austrian Requiem* noting that the rise of Hitler created a "caesura of historical development." In 1946, "a new era was beginning."[4] He contrasts "then" – the "long and bitter night" of Hitler's regime – with "today," that is, the postwar period, when it was "easy enough to assert that all this was to be foreseen." He asks his readers to acknowledge that "a certain amount of time has elapsed" between writing and publishing his diaries. His observations may therefore seem "outdated" or "overstrained," whereas they do in fact accurately reflect the historical situation as he saw it at the time of writing. Schuschnigg's desire for credibility, his cry of "believe me" is typical, as Paul Ricoeur notes in his study *Memory, History, and Forgetting*. A gap remains, however, since "the witness has no distance, is a participant, and after all historical fact is not the same as empirical fact."[5]

Some memoirists also speak of a "doubling of person," a split between the person who existed "there" in the camp and the person who is "here" in the free world. For prisoners this doubling or compartmentalization served as a means of gaining distance from the gruelling experiences in the camps. They found relief retreating in their minds to a former self, one that had agency, was involved in cultural activities, and shared ethical standards with fellow citizens. In the aftermath of their ordeals these survivors required time to reconcile the two selves and consolidate them into one post-imprisonment self.[6] Schuschnigg may have gone through a similar experience at the beginning of his solitary confinement, when he sought release from the present through imagination. However, as the regulations governing his confinement were relaxed, and especially after he was allowed to live with his family, he made a concerted effort to stay grounded in the present and face his situation. He describes his progress through successive emotional stages. At first, he clung to fantasy and daydreams in an effort to escape the present. He aspired "not to freedom," which was unobtainable, but "to the illusion of freedom." Later he tried to numb himself and merely sought the "peace of oblivion." Finally, he decided to confront the present and engage with the situation at hand.[7] Thus he avoided the quasi-schizophrenic division experienced by prisoners in extreme situations.

Scholars studying the accounts of inmates also point out the problem of heroic memory, the temptation to recall triumphal moments and shape their memoir into a "narrative of redemption."[8] Yet unheroic memories persisted and surfaced later to distress the individual. In other words, the truth may have been too painful to be admitted or, being suppressed, may not have been readily available even to the memoirist. Thus the true feelings and thoughts of the writer remain hidden, forming a subtext that is difficult to fathom for the reader. Schuschnigg, too, presents a narrative of redemption, but one that is tinged with religious beliefs. Schuschnigg remembers not only his triumphs over adversity but also his failures, and makes his narrative one of divine redemption. His phrasing makes clear that the act of recalling his political actions had a religious dimension. He repeatedly invokes the grace of God. "The goal [of my reminiscences]," he wrote, "remains inner, balanced peace, reconciliation with God and the world – and with myself." He concludes another reflection on his political past with an expression of hope that God would accept his good intentions and "take the will for the act."[9] In approaching the subject of political memories, he uses the ecclesiastical vocabulary of "confession" and "penance." Looking back on the Hitler era after his release in 1945, he says that the lesson to be drawn from history "is incomplete if we are too easy on ourselves and do not raise the question whether and to what extent we must shoulder some of the blame and some of the responsibility (*Mitschuld und Mitverantwortung*) ... All of us, without exception, are called upon to examine our conscience." Those who recognized the danger and did not take timely action or closed their eyes to it must take some of the blame for the catastrophe. "How many people are free of this sin of omission? It is absolutely essential to confess the truth. There is only one way to do penance: confession."[10] In light of these explicit references to the rites of the Catholic Church, Schuschnigg's reminiscences in *Austrian Requiem* can be seen in terms of a sacramental confession and its four steps: examination of conscience, confession, receiving absolution, and doing penance.[11]

In terms of this analogy, Schuschnigg examined his past actions as chancellor, confessed his errors, invoked God's pardon, and considered his incarceration a form "penance meted out" in atonement for his mistakes. "The dark spots in my life required a purgatory," he writes. "Who knows, perhaps we suffer the hardest purgatory already on this earth."[12] He hoped that his arrest and internment would wipe the slate clean and restore him to "a state of grace," that is, restore his standing in the eyes of posterity. As he saw it, the years of imprisonment vindicated his claim that he was an enemy of the Nazis and had done his best to stave off the German invasion.

In a letter to his brother written in 1941, he said that he had no expectation of getting out of Sachsenhausen alive and returning to a life of human dignity, but he did hope that his name would be cleared. "From the point of view of maintaining our good name, [the internment] was the right thing – it will lead to my rehabilitation in history. I won't achieve it any other way ... if only the Lord helps me to do my part, namely, to remain true to my principles."[13] A diary entry of 11 December 1938 likewise makes clear that Schuschnigg was concerned about his historical legacy and the judgment of the world. On that day, Heinrich Himmler visited the Gestapo prison in Munich. Schuschnigg relates that he asked questions about his prospects of being released. The Reichsführer was evasive about the duration of his imprisonment and, indeed, the nature of the accusations against him. Schuschnigg then asked him to at least "stop the attacks in the press, as I was completely helpless here, and such attacks could not but harm my reputation."[14] Similarly, he explained why he had not fled and asked for asylum in a foreign embassy when Hitler's troops invaded Austria: "I was prepared to sacrifice everything, but not my good name as a man of honour." According to the Austrian constitution, the chancellor had the final say over political decisions. He therefore accepted responsibility for his actions as well as their consequences.[15]

In his introduction to *Austrian Requiem*, Schuschnigg expressly calls the book "a human confession" and makes a point of distinguishing it from historical analysis: "It is not the purpose of this book to ask the whys or the wherefores. Historical research we leave to others better qualified for such investigations. What has been done cannot be undone." The religious tone of Schuschnigg's introduction fits with with the "confession" trope. He calls the war years a time "in which Lucifer once more tried his strength against God" and an epoch which was "to play an important role in the divine world plan." The catastrophic events were "the answer of the Creator to the sin against the Spirit."[16]

A Catholic confession is a private act. In fact, according to the laws of the church, the priest is bound to secrecy. In handing his diaries over to a printer, Schuschnigg turned them into a public confession. It seems, however, that he was not entirely comfortable with this decision. The original foreword is missing from the 1978 German-language edition, as mentioned earlier. Comments within the text explaining the purpose of the book are obviously written with hindsight and do not always dovetail with the purpose stated in the introduction. One passage in the German text – omitted in the English translation – contains this disclaimer: "It is certainly not my purpose mainly to report my personal experiences or fate. That would be narrow-minded. In an era that was of signal importance and 'unique,' the fate of an individual should play no role ... This must not be an attempt at personal justification."[17] Another tortuous explanation for publishing his diaries is also omitted from

the English translation: "Unfortunately there is much purely personal material here and much more about me than I had wanted. I
truly realized this only when I read through the text. But in the circumstances, it could hardly be avoided, especially because I tried
in this indirect manner to defend myself, since the authorities had
not given me that opportunity. But perhaps I should call it more of
an explanation than a defence."[18] Such equivocations leave us with
questions about the intended purpose of the book. Was it a confession, as the English introduction said, or was it a justification for
his political decisions leading up to the Anschluss, as the passages
in the German text seem to indicate? I suggest that Schuschnigg's
original reminiscences had the character of a personal examination of conscience. In the editing process, however, they became,
or moved in the direction of, a political apologia. Schuschnigg was
motivated by frustration and what he saw as betrayals, notably by
Mussolini, who "preferred to write a blank check to the order of
Adolf Hitler"[19] and, in his own government, Seyss-Inquart, who
stabbed him in the back: "Until the present day no one has made
an effort to ask me personally what happened in March 1938 and in
the years leading up to it. Here is the truth: Seyss-Inquart assured
me even at the end of 1937 that an Anschluss of Austria did not
seem to him possible at the time and, mainly, was not desirable …
even on 11 March 1938, in the midst of all that was happening, he
literally wept and agreed … that no decent person could partici-
pate in this step. – Well, he did!"[20]

In his examinations of the past Schuschnigg frequently returned
to two points: His failure to preserve Austria's autonomy was predestined and the result of a fatal combination of circumstances; he
may have erred in his decisions, but he always acted in good faith
and had done his duty.

Reviewing his actions, he insisted, "I am clearer in my own
mind than ever that I have done my duty and was obliged not to
act in any different way." In another examination of his decisions
as Chancellor of Austria (a diary entry for 19 November, 1943) he
reflects at length on the obligation of doing one's duty and on the
benefits of a clear conscience as a result of doing so. "There is only
one true measure for everything: duty! Whatever duty requires

must be done, and we must live according to the dictates of duty, whether they require little from us or a great deal, whether they are easy or difficult, bitter or sweet." Acting conscientiously will result in inner peace. "Only conscientious fulfilment of one's duty, or at any rate the will to do so and quietly persisting in it, will lead to happiness."[21]

Reasoning in this manner, Schuschnigg was able to take comfort in his reminiscences. He was convinced that he had acted according to his duty. He "had never deliberately misled others. He had erred only in trusting them, for his calculations included only what was right and not who held power." It was important in Schuschnigg's eyes to establish and follow clear guidelines and recognize one's motives. "You must be clear about your intentions, the reason why you take a certain stance, and whether your conscience is clear."[22] He acknowledged the politician's need to be flexible, but strongly emphasized that flexibility must never come at the cost of abandoning one's principles. This had been the maxim he himself observed in his actions.

"Those in command, those shouldered with political responsibility, cannot afford to cling to prejudices, to unchangeable views, or to long-established immutable methods … Errors occur, but in politics as elsewhere it is better to err than to stand by with eyes closed and let events take their course. The statesman needs elasticity in his thinking, his planning, and his actions. Both sides of a question have to be carefully weighed and studied. But this elasticity must never degenerate to the point where the principles of a policy are sacrificed, where the goal is changed because the road is difficult. Elasticity in politics can be good or bad; it can be intelligent or stupid; but it must never be guided by opportunism alone; it must never sacrifice basic principles. And the worst policy is always a policy without principles."[23] Schuschnigg conceded that strong principles and personal convictions often resulted in intolerance of dissenting opinions and could even lead to the belief in one's infallibility. "I can say so because my own past has not always been free of this sin, even if I wasn't cynical enough to admit it openly to myself or elevate it to a principle to be posted." Personal convictions always entailed an uncompromising attitude – that couldn't be helped. "Only a man who lacks the passion to fight for his cause will avoid this sin altogether."[24]

Schuschnigg maintained that it had been his goal and duty as a responsible political leader to preserve an independent and free Austria. Unfortunately, he had not been successful: Hitler annexed Austria. In reviewing his actions on the eve of the Anschluss, Schuschnigg conceded that he and his ministers had made mistakes. He had no intention of covering them up, but the question was, "Were the actions taken in good faith, with best intentions, and without regard to personal interests; in a word, was it decency that motivated those at the helm?"

In the English edition the chapter containing these statements is entitled "Political Post-Mortem"; in the German version it is called, more descriptively, "Many If-and-But Scenarios." Comparing the English with the German text, we find a slight shift in tone, from justification to instruction. In English, Schuschnigg merely comments that hypotheses had no practical value, and it was easy to say in retrospect what should have been done. "Yet, some of the if-clauses are of historical interest and should be recorded here." In German, this turns into a lecture in historiography: "One must not project present conditions onto a time in the past when they did not exist. And one must not interpret conditions in the past as one would like to see them today to justify in retrospect the desired negative verdict."[25] Those who now blamed him for the Anschluss did not understand the circumstances. In his diary entry of 13 March 1944, he refers to an English radio program he overheard on the sixth anniversary of the Anschluss. The speaker asserted that "the Austrian people, the victim of a failed internal policy, faced the inroad of the German troops with equanimity." That description of the events was simplistic and assigned fault in a one-sided manner, Schuschnigg said. Austria was not annexed on account of the internal policy he pursued. Rather it "could not change the course of fate." In the diary entry for 14 December 1944, Schuschnigg again stressed the consistency of his policies as chancellor and his principled actions, which followed the "straight path of a solid and unchangeable conviction ... Only the man who grasps this concept, feels in all situations that final and never-failing help – the grace of God."[26]

That this catastrophe could not be avoided, and took place four years later, was beyond human control, Schuschnigg insists.[27] He strongly felt that the events over which he presided had been "predestined." This quasi-religious argument, combined with his insistence that he had acted with integrity, allowed him to take comfort in his political reminiscences. He frequently pointed out that he did not have a free hand in making decisions in 1938. He was constrained by circumstances beyond his control and should therefore not be judged without considering the historical context. His hands had been tied by a combination of factors, he insisted, and indeed by fate. "One should not speak of guilt and atonement, but rather of doom and fate. Was it possible to escape fate? Perhaps – but only if all participants had not only a correct understanding but also the real power and full liberty to make decisions within and without the country. But that was not the case, and so nothing can be done now except visit the graves." In the English version, this argument is presented much more succinctly, but offers the same conclusion: What happened was fated and could not be avoided. "I did not know in those January days of 1938 – and really could not know – that the die of history had already been cast as far as Austria was concerned. The timing and the direction of events was already in the hands of the Führer, who by sheer force held all the trumps of the time in his hand."[28]

Schuschnigg continued to emphasize that he made his decisions under pressure. "The compelling force of the hour" gave him few options. It was useless for him to explain his concept of "empire" and "state" at this point. "To do so is no longer relevant. History was the determining factor." What happened in 1938 was predetermined by what had gone before. It was "the intellectual legacy of the nineteenth century, which ended in the unfortunate bankruptcy of 1914."[29] In the years 1943–4 his entries manifest a new certainty and confidence, rooted in his religious beliefs. "Regrets? No!" he writes. "Some things were certainly wrong. I would give a great deal for the opportunity to write a 'make-up exam.' I believe that I would do many things differently and better – I mean in the purely personal and private aspects of my life. But what do we know? *Stat pro ratione voluntas.*[30] May my mistakes find a merciful judge." In his entry for Christmas 1944, he reflects on the causes of the war and goes as far as postulating that it was the consequence of moral decline and lack of faith in God. The war was result of an "overdose of secularization, which befogs the mind ... Justice and morality, written and unwritten law must never be subject to the will, but only to the consideration of a reasoned understanding of a time-honoured concept of the Good."[31]

Schuschnigg's concern for honour was not limited to his personal reputation. It included the honour of his country. Even as a soldier returning after the World War I, which spelled the end of the Austro-Hungarian monarchy, he "was searching for justice ... which made him go to battle once again to save the honour and sinfully maligned reputation of his fatherland." Connecting his experiences in World War I with those leading up to World War II, he writes in his diary entry for 1 September 1939, "War! Just twenty years ago today I returned from Italy as a prisoner of war." It was this experience, he says, that nourished in him a sense of loyalty to Austria.[32] Even after the Austro-Hungarian monarchy ceased to exist, Schuschnigg saw a special role for Austria, "her European calling," which had tragically remained a dream without fulfilment. Yet Austria's "special mission within a 'balkanized'[33] Europe remained, not as a power, but as a cultural focus of possible future development." Vienna was for Schuschnigg a *völkerverbindende Brücke*, a bridge connecting nations. The city was the cultural heir of the Habsburg Empire after all.[34] Leafing through a collection of his own speeches he savoured the patriotic phrases he used in 1935, although they were hardly salient a decade later: "Austria the guarantor of European peace," "Austria, a flagbearer wherever we hear the call to European community and collaboration."[35]

He cherished these patriotic thoughts, even though he was a prisoner deprived of agency and no longer in a position to make decisions or fight actively for the reputation of his country. Speaking of his impotence, he once again used religious language. He alluded to the Catholic belief of an afterlife shaped by the Last Judgment, which admitted the soul to heaven or cast it into purgatory or hell. He used the simile ("fable," as he called it) of a dead man who retains consciousness and finds himself in a kind of purgatory "to pay for his mistakes." He does not enjoy the peace and quiet normally following death and continues to be affected by "libel, ridicule, loss of honour, and slander." Yet he is powerless to defend himself. "He can do nothing ... he wants to speak, explain, ask, plead, but he must remain silent ..." He is experiencing a "living death." Suffering slander, then, was part of the penance the man in the fable (and by analogy, Schuschnigg) had to suffer to atone for his errors.[36]

Schuschnigg understood that his own fate was insignificant in comparison with that of his country. He did not want his personal story to dominate the narrative of his book, yet could not suppress "the understandable, though pitifully small wish for rehabilitation and justice." He was aware, however, that his rehabilitation would be a long process. It remains to be seen, he wrote, whether the "next generation will render a correct and just verdict based on their own experiences."[37]

From 1943 on, Schuschnigg's apologies and justifications taper off. As he saw it, the events proved his claims that he had done his best. Other countries too experienced Hitler's aggression and, like Austria, were unable to fend him off. Hitler's monstrous mind, his despotism and irrationality, had become obvious to the world. Schuschnigg, in turn, became more daring in his pronouncements. The diary entries for 19 November, 14 December, and Christmas 1944 are lengthy admonitions, no longer concerned with his own political decisions as were the earlier reflections, but rather with Europe, and beyond politics, with moral laws governing human actions. "Enough of this radicalism, this bestialization of humanity ... this conscious and deliberate corruption of the whole public atmosphere – those are the deep roots of degeneration, the true and basic reasons for the failure of democracy."[38] The long years of imprisonment had given him leisure to philosophize, he wrote. They had given him "a permanent seat in the gallery of the theatre of life." What was happening on stage, however, was "truly an 'Undivine Comedy'. ... One cannot do away with 70 million Germans if one wants Europe to survive. The establishment of a universally valid and truly international law, which applies to Germans as well as to everyone else ... will lead to a new order in Europe. Without it, chaos threatens."[39]

In these reflections on the past and present of Europe, Schuschnigg clings to utopian ideas about his fatherland. He saw the possibility of Austria "serving as a German link in the heart of Europe, a cultural bridge, whose existence could guarantee the existing peace and further its advancement."[40] Austria remained for Schuschnigg "the land of harmony." Indeed, he believed that his task was not yet completed, that he could play a role in the future development of Austria as a "European, a Catholic, a human being, that is, respectful, devout, conscious of past history and trusting in the future as a patriot. There will be a time when we need no longer be ashamed of our German mother tongue. ... The hour of Austria's *Verklärung* (transfiguration) will come. My God – I want nothing more than to live long enough to see that hour!"[41] Austria had always been the keystone of Europe, and "as long as I breathe, I shall see Austria that way. My heart and soul belonged to it once. Its end has been also my end. Perhaps Austria will rise again in spite of everything? Yes ... perhaps ... it would be wonderful. But only if Austria means a way and a will to Europe."[42]

In line with these sentiments, Schuschnigg concludes his book with the words, "I step back into the rank and file, silent and satisfied after I have done my duty and in the knowledge that my conscience is pure. I want to live long enough to see one wish come true: The *Anschluss* of Austrians to Austria."[43]

On the trek to freedom in 1945, when Schuschnigg and other high-ranking prisoners of the Nazis were being evacuated, they suddenly found themselves at liberty to engage in conversation. They took the opportunity to reflect on their political decisions. Schuschnigg recounts a conversation between himself, Hjalmar Schacht, Generals Franz Halder and Georg Thomas, and Colonel Bogislav von Bonin. The English version of Schuschnigg's diary entry for 8 April 1945 is laconic. It reads: "We were happy to find conversation partners."[44] The German version, however, relates the contents of the conversation. The men talked about the policies they had pursued prior to their arrest. Schuschnigg singled out Blum, whose opposition to the Vichy regime landed him in Buchenwald – "a sterling character, in appearance more like an English conservative peer than a radical labour leader." He praised Blum for his exemplary style of discussion, his calm and rational manner, and mused, "We certainly did not have the same goals in the past, but I know one thing: each of us wanted the best and did his best, each one in his fashion and in the domain in which fate had placed him. Each of us saw the disaster coming and aimed at averting it." In a later reminiscence, he likewise noted that "the human links forged by our common experience in concentration camps overshadowed all earlier enmities."[45] Blum likely refers to the same occasion when he recalls a conversation with Schuschnigg, in which he bluntly told him that they were on opposite sides of the political spectrum. He quotes Schuschnigg replying "What does it matter? ... History will judge which of us was right. We both wanted what was good for our country, we both wanted peace, and now we are no longer adversaries."[46] Schuschnigg furthermore declared that he was not only willing to confess his mistakes, but also to learn from them: "Much in the future is based on past and surpassed mistakes." He neither wished to lay blame nor to complain. He merely wanted to attest to his efforts and his good will. He had always been "true to himself, his statements, his beliefs, and his ideals ... he fulfilled his destiny out of inner conviction and true enthusiasm that made him speak the later often-cited words 'Red-white-red unto death!'" His aim had always been to act in the best interest of Austria and "to guard the Austrian heritage according to his best knowledge and beliefs."[47]

It is clear from Schuschnigg's statements that political memories played a role in sustaining him during his years of imprisonment. At the same time, he worried about his image and the judgment of historians. In this context, it was important to him to establish that his actions had been based on principles rather than opportunism. He was able to convince himself that his actions were not only morally correct but also fated and therefore inevitable. Thus he could use his political memories as a strategy to cope with imprisonment, casting his loss of freedom as a form of atonement for his mistakes and a guarantee for his rehabilitation. His remarks have decidedly religious overtones, as we have seen. They are couched in the language of a man examining his conscience in preparation for making a sacramental confession, and should be read in that sense rather than in the sense of a (disputable) historical analysis. As Delbo pointed out, memory is no stand-in for the past. It merely forms a trace of the past.[48] It remains for the contemporary reader to assemble these traces and convert them into a communal history lesson.[49]

Conclusion

Schuschnigg hoped that his internment by the Nazis would vindicate him in the eyes of posterity. It seems that he was successful in maintaining his reputation among fellow prisoners at Sachsenhausen. Henri Michel reports in his memoirs that Schuschnigg "was regarded by all prisoners of the SS as Number One in the resistance against Adolf Hitler."[1] In the outside world, however, the assessment of Schuschnigg's role varied considerably, as seen in reactions ranging from hero-worship, as in R.K. Sheridon's *Schuschnigg: A Tribute* (1942), to the bitter hostility of Socialist partisans, for example, in the anonymous screed *Ein Jahr Schuschnigg: Dokumente einer Diktatur* (One Year Schuschnigg: Documents of a Dictatorship, 1935) or the reproval expressed in the lead article in the Viennese daily, *Die Arbeiterzeitung*, of 13 October 1946, where Schuschnigg is described as *Haupt der Diktatur* (the principal agent of dictatorship), whose hostile actions toward the left must never be forgotten or forgiven by workers.

In a letter to his brother at Christmas 1944, Schuschnigg referred in general terms to the judgment of future generations: "Well then, on we go full speed ... into 1945! Too bad we can't tell what schoolbooks will say about all of this in 2000."[2]

To answer Schuschnigg's question, here is what the American historian Evan Burr Bukey had to say about him in 2000:

> [Schuschnigg] was a decent but myopic man who lacked the common touch and saw little need to broaden his own narrow political base. He

was also a zealous Catholic, but to a much greater degree than his fallen predecessor he regarded German identity as an essential component of the Christian Corporative order. Dreading an Austro-German conflict, he tended to be more receptive to Nazi deceit than might otherwise have been the case ... Whether Schuschnigg might have done more to strengthen Austrian independence through imaginative diplomacy or the extension of an olive branch to his domestic opponents must forever remain an open question.[3]

Schuschnigg may have taken comfort in the conviction that he had done his best and followed his conscience, but he did not succeed in clearing his name in the eyes of historians today. While they may concede that Schuschnigg's government offered resistance to the Nazis, "the character of the regime [itself] is still disputed by scholars," as Gerhard Botz noted in 2017.[4] Whatever term historians choose to describe Schuschnigg's government – Austrofascism, imitative fascism, parafascism, half-fascism, or the palliative "non-democratic regime" – no one, including Schuschnigg himself, denies that his government was autocratic.[5]

Negative assessments of Schuschnigg's term of government do not of course invalidate my findings that Schuschnigg used political memories, or rather the conviction that he had done the right thing, as a coping mechanism. On the whole, my study supports the conclusion that Schuschnigg used a number of strategies consciously and largely successfully in dealing with his imprisonment and in maintaining a measure of agency and self-possession. We have seen that two witnesses commented on his alertness and mental fitness after seven years in captivity. Although Schuschnigg went through the typical emotional responses outlined by Frankl, including shock and depression, he took a proactive stance in handling his problems from the beginning by analysing the conditions of his imprisonment and assessing the character of his keepers. He avoided truckling to them and managed to take an ironic view of their actions. In this manner he was able to preserve self-respect and a sense of superiority. Although he did not expressly refer to any "strategies," he showed an awareness and sometimes expressly acknowledged the benefits of certain beliefs and habits:

putting his faith in God, keeping a sense of humour, engaging his mind by reading books and keeping a diary, gratifying his senses by listening to music, and keeping active both mentally and physically. Even if he did not use the vocabulary of strategy, he recognized the needs he must satisfy to retain his sanity. He realized, for example, the danger of losing his faith in God and understood the role of rituals, such as confession and communion, in maintaining his beliefs. He recognized that a supply of books and the availability of a radio were saving graces and relished the classics of literature and music to which he had access. For his constructive use of these "devices" he could draw both on his native intelligence and on his sound education, which gave him an appreciation for culture and its aesthetic and intellectual benefits. Of course, as Wolfgang Sofsky observes, "personal resources are only useful if there are opportunities to use them."[6] Unlike most prisoners in concentration camps, Schuschnigg had those opportunities. He was fortunate, moreover, in being able to draw on personal memories, especially the memory of his mother, which provided solace, and to look back on his political actions with the conviction that he had acted honourably. He was fortunate also in having a loyal partner in his wife. He was able to rely on his relationship with Vera for emotional support and for the all-important connection with the outside world. Her initiative on his behalf made his life easier, both in practical matters and in supporting his intellectual interests. Finally, he had in his brother, Artur Schuschnigg, and his uncle, Hermann Wopfner, compatible and supportive correspondents with whom he could engage in a satisfying dialogue, sharing his memories and unburdening his sorrows.

While these means, used strategically, allowed him to cope with his internment, they did not facilitate his re-entry into postwar society. His political memories, which clearly helped him during his internment, did not carry weight in postwar Vienna, now dominated by the left, which he had shunned during his tenure. Other prominent internees returned to their former spheres of action on being freed. Leon Blum, for example, re-entered politics and became briefly prime minister of France; Martin Niemöller resumed his religious mission and remained a vocal pacifist, Odd

Nansen returned to his architectural career and became a co-founder of Unicef. The banker Hjalmar Schacht was acquitted at the Nürnberg trials and founded a private bank; Fabian Schlabrendorff, a professional lawyer, advanced to the position of judge in the Constitutional Court of Germany. Schuschnigg, by contrast, did not find it expedient to return to politics or to Austria, where he was regarded as a persona non grata.[7] Indeed he encountered considerable hostility from Socialists there and, when he embarked on an international speaking tour, repeatedly faced demonstrations organized by the left. Schuschnigg mentions these problems only in unpublished letters to his brother. On 8 April 1946, he reports on his speaking tour in Switzerland: "Sold-out venues everywhere in spite of furious resistance by the Reds in the parliaments of the cantons!" In a letter of 8 November 1946, he reports that there were "incidents" (*Zwischenfälle*) when he was speaking in Belgium. He alleges that they were orchestrated from Vienna with the help of the journalist Kaiser-Blüh. The man had tried to cause trouble for him also in Paris, but was prevented by the police there.[8] Schuschnigg insists that he "never had any thought of re-entering politics" and "did not know at the time that ... the US Military Government had placed a veto on political activity by any member of the last Austrian government." He had no plans to resume his old career, he wrote. "Apparently they cannot believe at home [i.e., in Austria] that I have no political ambitions ... Indeed, my homesickness is quite tolerable."[9] At one point a rumour circulated that he would be appointed Austrian ambassador to the Vatican. In a letter of 6 February 1946, he noted dryly, "That's what I read in the local newspaper. It was confirmed in letters from Cairo, Australia, California, and Holland – but not from Vienna!" In the end, Schuschnigg elected to emigrate to the United States – for personal reasons, he said, falling back on the explanation that "I had my family to consider." He was offered, and accepted, a post teaching political science at Saint Louis University.[10] It was only after his retirement in 1967 that he returned to Austria, where he lived until his death in 1977.

The obituary, which appeared in the *New York Times* on 19 November 1977, may be considered a marker of general opinion.

The notice affirmed that Schuschnigg "remained a controversial figure to the end, with historians divided over his role in the years leading up to the war. Though he was an opponent of Hitler, some say his authoritarian policies at home in the four years he spent as Austrian Chancellor created the conditions for a successful 'Anschluss,' or union, of Austria with Germany."

Chronology

Page numbers in **bold** indicate events reflected in Schuschnigg's diary. The references are to the NY edition.

	Schuschnigg's Life	Events in Austria or Affecting Austria
1897	Born on 14 December in Reiff am Gartsee, Tirol (now Riva del Garda, Trentino, Italy)	
1914		28 July: WWI begins
1915	Matura (senior matriculation) at Jesuit boarding school, Stella Matutina, Feldkirch	
1915–18	Served in Austrian army during WWI (rank: lieutenant)	
1918		Emperor Karl resigns; Austro-Hungarian Empire carved up into national states 12 November: Proclamation of 1st Republic in Austria
1918/19	Prisoner of war in Italy, released September 1919	
1919		28 June: Treaty of Versailles ends war between Allies and Germany 10 September: Treaty of Saint Germain-en-Laye reduces Austria to national borders, imposes crippling reparation payments

(Continued)

(Continued)

	Schuschnigg's Life	Events in Austria or Affecting Austria
1919–22	Studies law at the Universities of Freiburg and Innsbruck, graduates 1922; practises law in Innsbruck	
1922		Mussolini prime minister in Italy Ignaz Seipel, Catholic priest, chancellor in Austria; negotiates League of Nations loan of £30 million to avoid state bankruptcy; temporary stabilization of currency; presides over coalition of the Socialist Schutzbund and the right-wing, agrarian Landbund
1924	Marries Hermine Masera (1906–35)	
1926	22 May: birth of son Kurt	
1927	Elected parliamentary deputy of Christian Social Party in the Nationalrat (national assembly)	July: The two parties clash in a riot
1931		Collapse of the Credit Anstalt Bank; Seipel arranges a loan from England
1932	29 January: minister of justice	Death of Seipel. 20 May: Engelbert Dollfuss becomes chancellor, presiding over right-wing coalition of Christian Social Party, the Landbund, and the ultra-nationalist Heimatblock (political arm of paramilitary Heimwehr)
1933	24 May: minister of education	30 January: Hitler becomes chancellor of Germany; Austrian Nazi party gains strength August: Alliance Austria-Hungary-Italy. Mussolini issues a guarantee of Austrian independence October: Dollfuss escapes assassination attempt by Rudolf Dertill

	Schuschnigg's Life	Events in Austria or Affecting Austria
1934	February: Social Democrats suppressed; as minister of justice Schuschnigg is responsible for the harsh verdicts and imprisonment of rioters	February: uprising of Social Democrats. Dollfuss suspends parliament. 1 May: new autocratic Austrian constitution approved by cabinet; Dollfuss establishes Patriotic Front (Vaterländische Front), which eventually combines Christian-Social Party and Heimatblock, becoming only legal party; Austrian Nazis (DNSAP) and Socialist Schutzbund are banned
	29 July: Schuschnigg appointed chancellor	25 July: Dollfuss assassinated in a failed Nazi coup; Schuschnigg becomes chancellor
1935	Hermine Schuschnigg dies in a car accident	Heimwehr dissolved
1936	Austro-German Agreement, which acknowledges Austria's sovereignty but includes concession to release those responsible for the July 1934 coup and inclusion of Nazi-sympathizers Edmund Glaes-Horstenau and Guido Schmidt in cabinet	March: Hitler occupies Rhineland May: Mussolini's forces take Ethiopia; Italian East Africa established; rapprochement with Hitler
1938	12 February: meeting with Hitler in Berchtesgarden; coerced into further concessions of amnesty for all imprisoned Nazis and inclusion of Nazi sympathizer Arthur Seyss-Inquart in government. Failed attempt at rapprochement with leftists 24 February: rousing speech before Austrian Federal Diet, ending in "Red-White-Red [colours of Austrian flag] until we are dead!"	

(*Continued*)

(Continued)

	Schuschnigg's Life	Events in Austria or Affecting Austria
	9 March: announces plebiscite to be held on 13 March on the question: "Are you for a free, German, independent and social, Christian and united Austria, for peace and work, for the equality of all those who affirm their support for the people and fatherland?"	
	11 March: German troops invade Austria	11 March: German troops invade Austria
	12 March: Schuschnigg forced to abdicate in favour of Seyss-Inquart and placed under house arrest at his official residence under SA and (from 26 March) SS guard	
	28 May: transferred to Gestapo headquarters at Hotel Metropol and kept in solitary confinement	
	1 June: marries Vera Czernin by proxy	
	20 October: death of father	
		14 October: German troops occupy Sudetenland
		9/10 November: Kristallnacht
1939		March: Bohemia and Moravia become a German protectorate
		22 May: Hitler and Mussolini sign "Pact of Steel" (213)
		August: Hitler's non-aggression pact with Stalin
		1 September: Germany invades Poland; France and England declare war on Germany (205, 241)
	29 October: transferred to Gestapo headquarters at Wittelsbach Palais in Munich; continued solitary confinement, but weekly visits from Vera	

	Schuschnigg's Life	Events in Austria or Affecting Austria
1940		April: Germany invades Denmark, Norway
		May: Germany invades France (**231**), Luxembourg, Netherlands, Belgium
		10 July: Battle of Britain begins (**249, 252**)
		27 September: Axis pact Germany-Italy-Japan
		October: Eastern front expands with Germany invading Romania, Italy invading Greece
1941	23 March: birth of daughter Maria Dolores Elisabeth ("Sissy")	Fighting in North Africa expands (**230, 231, 233, 234, 236**)
		22 June: Germany attacks Soviet Union (Operation Barbarossa)
		November: Romania, Hungary join Axis
	8/9 December: transferred to Sachsenhausen concentration camp; assigned a house in the VIP section and permitted to live there with his wife and child	7 December, Japanese attack on Pearl Harbor, USA enters war (**233**)
1942		August: Battle of Stalingrad begins; German air raids on England continue; first American air raids in Europe
		8 November: Operation Torch, Americans invade North Africa
1943		February: Battle of Stalingrad ends with Soviet victory (**229, 231, 234**)
		May: Italy and Germany surrender in North Africa (**241**)
		Allied air raids on Germany (**234, 236, 240–52**); July: Allies land in Italy (**238, 239, 241–5, 249, 251**)
1944		Soviets advance into Poland (**253**)
		6 June: Allies land in Normandy (**251**)
		20 July: failed assassination attempt on Hitler (**253–5**)
		August 25: Paris liberated (**254**), Vienna bombarded (**255**)
		December: Battle of the Bulge; Belgium, Holland liberated (**255**)

(*Continued*)

(Continued)

	Schuschnigg's Life	Events in Austria or Affecting Austria
1945	Elite prisoners' evacuation begins; 5 February: transferred to Flossenbürg concentration camp	Russian advances in East Europe (**255, 257, 258**), reach Czechoslovakia (**260**)
	8 April: transferred to Dachau concentration camp	13 April: Vienna captured
	27–30 April: on the move toward Tyrol; 1 May: arrival at Hotel Pragser, Wildsee; Gestapo guards hand over VIP prisoners to Austrian army	27 April: Austria declares independence from Germany 28 April: Mussolini's execution; 30 April: Hitler's suicide
	4 May: VIP prisoners liberated by American troops	8 May: VE Day, end of WWII in Europe
	10 May: VIPs transported via Verona to Naples/Capri	
1946	Schuschnigg emigrates to US; accepts position teaching political science at Saint Louis University, Missouri.	

Notes

Introduction

1 See Ernst Klee, Willi Dresser, and Volker Riess, eds., *The Good Old Days: The Holocaust as Seen by Its Perpetrators and Bystanders* (New York, 1991); https://www.jewishgen.org/ForgottenCamps/Camps/SachsenhausenEng.html.

2 Primo Levi, *Survival in Auschwitz: The Nazi Assault on Humanity* (New York, 1961), 47.

3 The captives themselves were aware of their status as hostages. See, for example, Leon Blum, *Le dernier mois* (Paris, 1995), a speech he gave on 14 May 1945: "Je constituais une valeur d'échange" (14); Irmingard Prinzessin von Bayern, *Jugend-Erinnerungen, 1923–1950* (St. Ottilien, 2000), 306, referring to VIP prisoners, "meistens politische Personen, die besonders wertvolle Geiseln darstellten" (mostly politicians, who were particularly valuable hostages); see also Hans Otto Eglau, *Fritz Thyssen: Hitlers Gönner* (Berlin, 2003), noting that their status was ambiguous, but that all signs pointed to the fact that they were considered potential hostages: "Dass [Himmler] angesichts der drohenden militärischen Niederlage seine Geiseln als Faustpfand bei möglichen Verhandlungen mit den Westalliierten einsetzen wollte, ist zwar nicht zweifelsfrei erwiesen. Doch wie er seine Gefangenen vor der heranrückenden Front rechtzeitig in Sicherheit brachte ... deutet auf solche Überlegungen hin" (251).

4 The French politician Paul Reynaud, who was interned in one of the houses for a time, described it as in "good taste, modern, and comfortable" (cited in Koop, *In Hitler's Hand*, 143). The only comparable living quarters were in the Falkenhof, where Leon Blum was interned, but that house was technically not part of a concentration camp. It was

located at the edge of Buchenwald, that is, outside its precincts; it had, in fact, been accessible to the public until 1943 as a model farm where hawks were reared. See Hans-Rudolf Meier et al., *Buchenwald-Spuren: Verflechtungen des Konzentrationslagers mit Weimar und Umgebung*, 206–8, published online at https://www.metallsicherungsanlagen.de /stellenausschreibung/zeitgeschichte-standort/. See also Blum, *Le dernier mois*, 317.

5 Lawrence Langer, *Holocaust Testimonies: The Ruins of Memory* (New Haven, 1993), 41.

6 See below, p. 18.

7 See below, pp. 133 ff. and 146 ff.

8 Bruno Latour, "Why Has Critique Run Out of Steam? From Matters of Fact to Matters of Concern," *Critical Inquiry* 30 (2004): 231.

9 Levi, 22; Schuschnigg in *Austrian Requiem*, 58.

10 Victor Frankl, *From Death Camp to Existentialism* (Boston, 1959); Bruno Bettelheim, *The Informed Heart* (New York, 1960). Bettelheim's claims to a degree in psychology have been debunked, but his analysis of his concentration camp experience is as valid as ever; for a critical examination of his work, see, for example, Paul Marcus, *Autonomy in the Extreme Situation: Bruno Bettelheim, the Nazi Concentration Camps and the Mass Society* (Westport, CT, 1999), and Michaela Wolf, ed., *Interpreting in Nazi Concentration Camps* (New York, 2016), 27–9.

11 See, for example, the section on "Elites" in the comprehensive survey of Nikolaus Wachsmann, *KL: A History of the Nazi Concentration Camps* (New York, 2015), 509–12; the chapters "Classes and Classification" and "The Aristocracy" in Wolfgang Sofsky, *The Order of Terror: The Concentration Camp* (Princeton, 1997), 117–19, 145–52; the chapter "The Categories of Prisoners" in Eugen Kogon, *The Theory and Practice of Hell: The German Concentration Camps and the System behind Them* (New York, 1975), 33–42, and the list of classes of prisoners in Manuela Hrdlicka, *Alltag im KZ: Das Lager Sachsenhausen bei Berlin* (Opladen, 1991).

12 As pointed out by Frank Pingel, "Social Life in an Unsocial Environment," in Jane Caplan and Nikolaus Wachsmann, eds., *Concentration Camps in Nazi Germany: The New Histories* (London, 2010), 58–81, and by Wolf, 25–6, who argue for an extension of research to include cultural and social experiences. The argument that these aspects have been neglected is also made by Gilly Carr and Harold Mytum, eds., *Cultural Heritage and Prisoners of War: Creativity behind Barbed Wires* (New York, 2012), although they are dealing with prisoners of war during WWI and WWII rather than inmates of German concentration

camps: "Traditionally, studies of POWs have focused on treatment, ...
administrative structures and censorship ... methods of initial capture
and escape" (2).

13 See Eglau, commenting that Thyssen kept to the facts: "Strictly speaking,
his account of four years of imprisonment is reduced to a dry list of the
individual phases of his captivity. Hardly a word about his life among
mentally disturbed people, a life unworthy of human dignity, the daily
dread of torture, and the growing fear for his life" (252). Unless indicated
otherwise all translations from the German are mine.

14 See Renata Laqueur, *Schreiben im KZ: Tagebücher 1940–45* (Bremen, 1992),
31. She notes that some prisoners wrote to escape the hell in which they
were living. "Wer schrieb, fühlte sich frei" [Those who wrote, felt free].

15 Rudolf Wunderlich, *Die Aufzeichnungen des KZ-Häftlings Rudolf
Wunderlich*, ed. Joachim S. Hohmann and Guenther Wieland (Frankfurt,
1997), 8: "in der Stunde der Abrechnung der Justiz als Zeuge zur
Verfügug zu stehen"; see also Emil Ackermann, *Niemand and nichts ist
vergessen. Ehemalige Häftlinge aus verschiedenen Ländern berichten über das
KZ Sachsenhausen* (Berlin, 1984), 7.

16 Margaret-Anne Hutton, *Testimony from the Nazi Camp:. French Women's
Voices* (London, 2005), quoting Maisie Renault and Primo Levi (11,
13); John Lenz, *Christ in Dachau or Christ Victorious* (Vienna, 1960), vii;
similarly Ernst Wiechert quoting an unnamed survivor, who assured
him, "I want to write it down, not to accuse, condemn, scream, and call
on the order of the whole world. I just want to write down what I saw"
(*Sämtliche Werke* [Vienna, 1957], vol. 10, 617–18).

17 Arnold Weiss-Rüthel, *Nacht und Nebel: Ein Sachsenhausen-Buch*
(Berlin, 1949), 90–1; Harry Naujoks, *Mein Leben im KZ Sachsenhausen*
(Cologne, 1987), 8, 297, 300 ("kein falsches Bild geben: nur ein Teil der
Häftlinge wurde erreicht ... viele besassen auch gar nicht die Kraft
hinzukommen"); similarly Eugen Kogon, speaking about cultural events
at Buchenwald, acknowledged that prisoners "drew strength from
the few hours of illusions" (129), but only a minority had the energy
to attend the performances. He downplayed the significance of these
events, noting that they served the purposes of the Nazi authorities to
demonstrate to official visitors that all was well and "to enhance the
show that was put on [for them]" (129).

18 Christoph Daxelmüller, "Kulturelle Formen und Aktivitäten als Teil der
Überlebens – und Vernichtungsstrategie in den Konzentrationslagern,"
in Christoph Dieckmann et al., eds., *Das nationalsozialistische
Konzentrationslager* (Göttingen, 1998), vol. 2, 983–1005.

19 Directed by Christoph Daxelmüller at the Institut für Volkskunde
    at the University of Regensburg. Cultural aspects are also
    prominently included in Maja Suderland, *Inside Concentration Camps:
    Social Life at the Extremes* (Cambridge, 2013); Helga Embacher,
    "Frauen in Konzentrations- und Vernichtungslagern – weibliche
    Überlebensstrategien in Extremsituationen," in Robert Streibel and Hans
    Schafranek, eds., *Strategie des Überlebens: Häftlingsgesellschaften im KZ
    und Gulag* (Vienna, 1996), 145–67; Marguerite Rumpf, *"Pantoffeln gebe ich
    Dir mit auf den Weg": Schenken in den Konzentrationslagern Ravensbrück,
    Dachau, Sachsenhausen und Buchenwald* (Würzburg, 2017); Gerhard
    Botz, *Binnenstruktur, Alltagsverhalten und Überlebenschancen in Nazi-
    Konzentrationlagern* (Vienna, 1996).
20 Hrdlicka emphasizes that cultural activities – clandestine or tolerated
    by the authorities – were at any rate a regular and permanent part of
    life in concentration camps ("regelmässiger und fester Bestandteil des
    Alltagsleben im Lager [Sachsenhausen]" (77). Weiss-Rüthel noted that it
    took a certain courage to organize and attend cultural events because the
    authorities tried to thwart anything that fostered community spirit, for
    example, by confiscating instruments or banning performances from time
    to time (89).
21 Daxelmüller cites Jadwiga Apostol-Staniszewska: "Es [i.e., cultural
    pursuit] verlange zudem ethisches Niveau, damit man bei allen
    Versuchen, uns zu Tieren zu machen, nicht das verlor, was da heist
    Menschsein [Cultural pursuit requires a certain ethical level, so that in
    spite of all attempts to turn us into animals, we didn't lose what it means
    to be human]" (999), and Pelagia Lewinska-Tepicht: "Meine Strategie
    des Überlebenskampfes hatte viel mit meinem eigenen, durchdachten
    Wertsystem zu tun. Meine wichtigste Handlungsmaxime war der
    Gedanke, mich nicht zum Tier erniedrigen zu lassen [My strategy in the
    struggle to survive had much to do with my own considered system
    of values. My most important maxim in acting was the thought of not
    letting myself be lowered to the level of an animal]" (999). See also Ellen
    S. Fine, "Literature as Resistance: Survival in the Camps," in *Holocaust
    and Genocide Studies* 1 (1986): 79–89.
22 Wolfgang Benz and Barbara Distel, eds., *Der Ort des Terrors: Geschichte der
    nazionalsozialistischen Konzentrationslager* (Munich, 2006) vol. 3, 31–2.
23 Griselda Pollock and Max Silverman, eds., *Concentrationary Memories,
    Totalitarian Terror and Cultural Resistance* (New York, 2014), 16.
24 Michael Rothberg, "Trauma, Memory, Holocaust," in Dmitri Nikulin, ed.,
    Memory: A History (New York, 2015), 283.

25 Benz, 17.
26 Irmingard of Bayern: "Stacheldrahtzäune und Mauern mit Wachtürmen und starke Scheinwerfer umgrenzten das ganze Gelände und erleuchteten die Mauern [barbed wire fences and walls with watchtowers and strong lights surrounded the whole area and lit up the walls]" (305).
27 Cited by Eglau, 250. The concern seems paranoid. All that was visible from outside the camp were the peaked roofs of the houses. See illustration 44 in Binder, *Sofort Vernichten* (see below, note 32).
28 Kurt von Schuschnigg, *Austrian Requiem* (New York, 1946), in the following cited as "NY" and page number to distinguish it from the German-language edition (Zurich, 1946), cited as "Z" followed by the page number. The passage quoted here is NY 223. The differences between the two editions are discussed below, pp. 22 ff.
29 "Noon Tide," in Henry Phillips, *German Lyrics* (Philadelphia, 1892), 34. Schuschnigg comments: "It is the country of which the German poet Theodore Fontane sings … which to its inhabitants … appears beautiful because it is their home, but which to all others who have the misfortune of coming here is a punishment in itself" (NY 223).
30 NY 224.
31 Diary entry of 20 October 1943 (NY 244).
32 Dieter Binder and Heinrich Schuschnigg, eds., *Sofort Vernichten: Die vertraulichen Briefe Kurt und Vera von Schuschniggs 1938–1945* (Vienna, 1997), in the following cited by "Letter" and number of letter. The passage quoted is in Letter 131.
33 BR Bayern, 20 March 2011, in a program entitled "Die dunklen Jahre Wittelsbachs," by Thomas Mugenthaler; see also Erwein von Aretin, *Wittelsbacher im KZ* (Munich, n.d.) based on the diaries of Crown Prince Rupprecht of Bavaria.
34 Irmingard of Bavaria, 308.
35 Letter 131.
36 See below, pp. 54–5.
37 NY 266. On Breitscheid, see also below, pp. 23–4.
38 Kurt von Schuschnigg Jr, *When Hitler Took Austria: A Memoir of Heroic Faith by the Chancellor's Son* (San Francisco, 2012), in the following cited as *When Hitler Took Austria*. The passage in question is on pp. 136–7.
39 NY 266.
40 Ibid.
41 Eglau, 248–51.
42 The four houses in which the VIP prisoners stayed were bombed and "burned to the ground," as Schuschnigg reports to his brother in a letter

of 8 November 1946 (unpublished letter 75 in Institut für Zeitgeschichte [IFZG], inv. 954).

43 See Benz, 66–7.

44 Quoted in Alfred D. Low, *The Anschluss Movement, 1931–1938, and the Great Powers* (New York, 1985), 162.

45 Kurt von Schuschnigg, *My Austria* (New York, 1938), 25–7.

46 Ibid., 24.

47 Z 322–3.

48 Ibid.

49 Low, 87n12.

50 Ibid., 94–6.

51 Evan Burr Bukey, *Hitler's Austria: Popular Sentiment in the Nazi Era, 1938–1945* (Chapel Hill, 2000), 11.

52 NY 189–90.

53 In her foreword to Schuschnigg's *My Austria* (the English translation of *Dreimal Österreich*, New York, 1938; in England the translation of the book appeared under the title *Farewell Austria*, London, 1938), pp. vi–vii.

54 *Political Science Quarterly* 53 no. 3 (1938): 439; for the title variants see preceding note.

55 Hermine Schuschnigg, née Masera (1906–35).

56 Vera Schuschnigg (née Czernin von Chudenitz, 1904–59) had known Schuschnigg socially for some years, when she was still married to Leopold Count Fugger. She divorced the count in 1936 and obtained an annulment from the church in 1937.

57 Z 336.

58 *When Hitler Took Austria*, 95.

59 NY 69–73.

60 Cited by Anton Hopfgartner, *Kurt Schuschnigg: Ein Mann gegen Hitler* (Graz, 1989), 136. Schuschnigg himself declared that his party was "trying to fashion an authoritarian, but not a totalitarian, state" (Z 263). In the English edition this reads: "It is true that we were an authoritarian state. But according to our German neighbors we had made a cardinal and fatal mistake in our choice. We should have followed their example and established a totalitarian system. But we did not" (NY 140–1).

61 Modern assessments of Schuschnigg's term as chancellor vary. See Gerhard Botz, "Corporate State and Enhanced Authoritarian Dictatorship: The Austria of Dollfuss and Schuschnigg," in Antonio Costa Pinto, ed., *Corporatism and Fascism: The Corporatist Wave in Europe* (New York, 2017), 14467. Botz agrees that Schuschnigg's government was "not totalitarian" and is "best described as strong authoritarian [rule]"

(167). Compare Helmut Wohnout, "A Chancellorial Dictatorship with a 'Corporative' Pretext: The Austrian Constitution between 1934 and 1938," in Günter Bischof, Anton Pelinka, and Alexander Lassner, eds., *The Dollfuss/Schuschnigg Era in Austria: A Reassessment* (New Brunswick, NJ, 2003), 143–62; see also Julie Thorpe, *Pan-Germanism and the Austrofascist State, 1933–38* (Manchester, 2011), who looks at different regime models of fascism and discusses authoritarianism in Austria as a means used by Conservatives to ward off the radicalism of Marxists and Nazis.

62 NY 186.

63 Schuschnigg himself declined "to play the game of what would have happened if the so-called Austro-Marxists had co-operated with the so-called Austro-fascists, and what has been lost because they failed to do so" (NY 205).

64 NY 17. On the accuracy of this quote, see Schuschnigg's statement that the conversation was "written down from memory; it covers only the essential – or at least the significant – passages" (NY 12). The report of Reinhard Spitzy, secretary of foreign minister Ribbentrop, by contrast, states that Schuschnigg made a bad impression when he arrived at Berchtesgaden. He was "pale, bleary-eyed and unshaven." At the dinner which followed the private meeting between the two men, "Hitler was civil and polite throughout ... whereas Schuschnigg sat there silently brooding lost in his own thoughts." In the same context, however, Spitzy acknowledged that "when it came to stage management Hitler, the actor, was simply unsurpassable." Reinhard Spitzy, *How We Squandered the Reich* (Wilby Hall, 1997), 174–5.

65 NY 56. Thirty years later, however, he acknowledged that "symbolic resistance on 11 March 1938 would have stood Austria in good stead" and clearly established that the government and a majority of the people rejected the Anschluss; see Schuschnigg, *The Brutal Takeover* (London 1971), 277.

66 NY 191.

67 *Dreimal Österreich* (1938), an analysis of Austrian politics in the 1920s and 1930s, had been accepted for publication by Thomas-Verlag Jakob Heger at the time of Schuschnigg's arrest and appeared a few months later in Vienna. See above, notes 46, 47.

68 Wolfgang Szepansky, *Dennoch ging ich diesen Weg* (Berlin, 2000), composed poems in his mind because he "did not always have pencil and paper to write them down. And whatever was found by the guards, disappeared" (169).

69 Primo Levi, *The Drowned and the Saved* (New York, 1988), 18–19.

70 See below, p. 68. The block in Sachsenhausen contained a total of 80 cells, each furnished with a cot, table, and chair. The inmates shared a washroom with two toilets and two shower stalls. See Thomas Cushing, "Stalins Sohn fühlte sich verstossen," *Der Spiegel* 13 (1968): 92–5, and Sigismund Payne-Best's description in *The Venlo Incident* (London, 1950), 53–4 and illustration. But some cells were better equipped than others. Payne-Best was allowed to use a regular toilet, whereas most of his fellow prisoners were forced to use a pail. His cell was small and sparsely furnished, but he reports catching a glimpse of another, larger cell which contained an easy chair and a case full of books (48, 91). For other special arrangements, including the conversion of castles into prisons, see Koop, 31–9.

71 Isa Vermehren, *Reise durch den letzten Akt. Ravensbrück, Buchenwald, Dachau: Eine Frau berichtet* (Hamburg, 1979; first edition 1946), 122; Payne-Best, *The Venlo Incident*, 45; Levi, *Survival in Auschwitz*, 116.

72 Zuzana Justman, "My Terezín Diary: And what I did not write about," *New Yorker*, 16 September 2019, 43–9. The quote is on p. 44.

73 Odd Nansen, *From Day to Day: One Man's Diary of Survival in Nazi Concentration Camps* (Nashville, 2016), 447. Similarly, Renata Laqueur, interned in Belsen-Bergen, mused what would become of her diary and what would be the consequences if it were discovered: "Was wohl aus meinem Tagebuch wird? Was passiert, wenn sie es finden?" (30).

74 NY ix.

75 William Shirer, *Berlin Diary: The Journal of a Foreign Correspondent* (New York, 1942), vi; Weiss-Rüthel, 18.

76 Letter 135.

77 "Collective Memory: The Two Cultures," *Sociological Theory* 17 no. 3 (1999): 333–8. The quote is on p. 341.

78 "Auster" was the alias under which Schuschnigg was listed in the camp records. The French edition was published by SFELT in 1947 under the title *Requiem: Les mémoires du chancelier d'Autriche, 1938–1945*.

79 Schuschnigg himself had originally planned to bring out the German edition with Bermann-Fischer in New York (see unpublished letters in the IFZG, inv. 954, nos. 69, 70, 73) and at one point was also in negotiations with the Arche-Verlag in Zurich (no. 54).

80 Verosta (1909–98) held a position in Schuschnigg's ministry of foreign affairs, but was suspended from his post 1938–45 on account of his political views. After the war he taught at the University of Vienna. He strongly advocated the interpretation of Austria as a victim of Hitler in his book *Die internationale Stellung Österreichs 1938–1947* (Vienna, 1947) and was awarded the Preis der Stadt Wien für Geisteswissenschaften in 1978.

81 "des bald nach seinem Erscheinen (1946) vergriffenen Buches" (Z 5).
   Oddly, the editors of the posthumous edition of Schuschnigg's letters
   (see above, note 32) cite only the Zurich edition of the *Requiem* and omit
   any mention of the more recent Austrian edition. See Letter 67, n. 280:
   "Erstausgabe Zürich 1946."

82 There are also slight discrepancies in the subtitles. The 1978 edition drops
   the original division into four parts. It does retain the division into two
   books, but only in the table of contents, not in the text itself.

83 "The following conversation [with Hitler], which was somewhat unilateral,
   I have written down from memory; it covers only the essential – or at least
   the significant – passages" (NY 12). "It is worthwhile to record [my talks
   with Mussolini] here as literally as my memory permits" (NY 109).

84 See, for example, Hutton's discussion of Charlotte Delbo's critical
   approach, pp. 210–19.

85 Z 17. The sentence is eliminated from the English edition! For a
   comparison of the German and English editions see below, pp. 22 ff.

86 Z 405. "Ein Teil des Geschriebenen wurde jeweils nach der Niederschrift zur
   Durchsicht der Gestapo abgeliefert ... Der grössere Teil der Niederschrift
   blieb allerdings bis zum Schluss mein Geheimnis" (Z16–17).

87 "Die einzele Abschnitte ..., soweit es sich nicht um Tagebuchblätter handelt,
   sind einzelne, nachträglich gereihte Niederschriften, die fast durchwegs
   in der Wiener Metropolzeit, also in absoluter Abgeschlossenheit von
   der Aussenwelt entstanden ... vielleicht dass es sich mir noch mehr um
   Erklärung denn um Verteidigung gehandelt hat" (Z 316).

88 Z 5.

89 For Anton Hopfgartner's book, see above, note 60.

90 Manuscript 734 in the Österreichische Staatsarchiv. The front page bears
   the inscription "Aufzeichnungen, die für meinen Buben bestimmt sind.
   Niedergeschrieben in den Monaten September–November 1938" [Notes
   meant for my boy. Written in the months September–November 1938].
   The pages correspond to pp. 154–298 of the published book.

91 Hopfgartner, 261. Schuschnigg acknowledges this in the English version of
   his book: "Since a certain amount of time elapsed between the writing of the
   book and its publication some passages may seem outdated ... [but] as far as
   factual accounts are concerned, I can vouch for its strict accuracy" (NY ix).

92 Putnam's copyright to the English translation is acknowledged by
   Gollancz. The texts of the New York and London editions are identical.
   Gollancz, however, added a curious proviso on the inside of the cover:
   "Important Note. This APOLOGIA is published ... as an historical
   document, and not in the least because the publishers agree with the
   point of view of the writer."

93 Franz von Hildebrand was active in Marseille and organized the
   emigration of the Breitscheids, which was frustrated at the last moment.
   He was the son of Dietrich von Hildebrand (1889–1977), the founder of
   the magazine *Der Christliche Ständestaat*.
94 Now in the Sterling Library at Yale University (Schuschnigg Collection
   346). The list of changes is arranged under the titles "Kürzungen" (cuts)
   and "Einschaltungen und Ergänzungen" (inserts and additions). The archivist
   Nancy Lyon kindly informed me that the typescript was donated to the library
   by Edwin Beinecke in 1958, and had been given to him, at least according
   to his recollection, "by one of the editors of the *New York Herald Tribune*."
95 NY ix.
96 NY 5, 9. Compare the German text at Z 35.
97 Z 25: "Hitler ist ein Phänomen. Unsinning, solches zu leugnen … Hitler hat
   magische Gewalt auf die Menschen; er zieht sie entweder mit magnetischer
   Kraft an sich und lässt sie nicht mehr los aus dem Banne, oder er stösst
   sie vom ersten Moment an ebenso heftig ab … [Die Letzteren] sahen den
   Abgrund and wussten, dass es hier kein Hinüber gab. Ich gehörte zu ihnen."
98 Z 21.
99 Z 318–19.
100 Quoted by Hutton, 212. See also Peter Kuon, "L'écrit reste. L'écrit est
    une trace, tandis que les paroles s'envolent": On the Hermeneutics of
    Holocaust Survivor Memories," in Wolf, 149–60. The words quoted in
    the title about memories being merely a "trace" were spoken by Roger
    Gouffault, a Communist incarcerated at Mauthausen.
101 *Sofort Vernichten: Die vertraulichen Briefe Kurt und Vera von Schuschniggs,
    1938–1945* (Vienna, 1997), 50. In the following, Schuschnigg's letters are
    cited by the numbers assigned to them in this edition. Additional letters
    were deposited by Heinrich Schuschnigg in the IFZG at the University
    of Vienna, inv. 954. These include 8 letters from 1945/6, as well as a
    transcript of a radio broadcast of 3 October 1945, which contain material
    relevant to this study.
102 Letter 66.
103 Letter 41 of June 1941.
104 Frankl, 1. This structure is also suggested by Terrence Des Pres, *The
    Survivor: An Anatomy of Life in Death Camps* (Oxford, 1980), who shows
    prisoners moving from initial shock to adjustment, from dream/illusion
    state to facing reality. Their survival depends on "a set of activities
    evolved through time in successful response to crisis" (192–3).
105 Frankl, 6–21.
106 Ibid., 33–56.
107 Suderland, 8, 107.

1 In Isolation: Living under the Enemy's Eye

1 Nansen, 551.
2 Diary entry of 1 July 1938 (Z 133); Letter 38: "Sometimes it almost seems to me as if I had remained in the world by mistake – detached from everything that is not family – and could only look on."
3 Schuschnigg in his diary entry of 9 June 1938 (Z 129); "praise be to God" does not appear in the English translation at NY 79.
4 Diary entry of 6 September 1938 (NY 141); Naujoks commented that prisoners soon "learned to read between the lines" (45).
5 NY 66; compare *When Hitler Took Austria*, 107.
6 Z 145. This description is curtailed in the English text, which says nothing about Schuschnigg's relief. It reads: "After Himmler's visit, my room was furnished with additional pieces, among them a small radio. It is still rather modest but much better than before" (NY 85).
7 Hopfgartner, 237 (Bundesarchiv Koblenz, RSHA. R/58 403, fol. 70).
8 NY 66.
9 NY 77–8, Z 147, 146.
10 Z 136; not in English edition. Compare with Payne-Best, who mocked his captors by playing the happy prisoner: "Sitting on my stool I practiced a cheerful grin ... this seemed to annoy [my Gestapo visitors]" (*The Venlo Incident*, 55).
11 Victor Klemperer, *The Language of the Third Reich: LTI, Lingua Tertii Imperii. A Philologist's Notebook* (London, 2006), 9; Albert Christel, *Apokalypse unserer Tage: Erinnerungen an das KZ Sachsenhausen* (Frankfurt, 1987), 75. The importance of keeping aware of oneself and one's surroundings is also stressed by Bruno Bettelheim; see Marcus, 103.
12 See, for example, Lisa Guenther, *Solitary Confinement: Social Death and Its Afterlives* (Minneapolis, 2013), xxi, xxvi.
13 NY 82, 78.
14 NY 86; more expansive in Z 146.
15 NY 76. Wolf notes that "national, social, and ethnic stereotypes were rampant among the prisoners ... they reflected predominant principal moral concepts of societies at the time" (36).
16 Except for "ceremony," these similes appear only in the German text, which describes the harassment involving bed-making and toilet-cleaning at greater length (Z 130–1): *Spässchen, Ritual, Akt, Premiere, Serienaufführungen, Zeremoniell*. Interestingly the words "ceremony" and "performance" (*Vorstellung*) also appear in Odd Nansen's diary to describe the cruel treatment of prisoners (446, 496).
17 NY 75, Z 137; the last anecdote is omitted in the English edition.

18 Z 138; omitted in the English edition.

19 Ibid.; also omitted in the English edition.

20 NY 78.

21 Z 357; omitted in the English edition.

22 NY 77, Z 132.

23 NY 85–6; Austrian police had replaced the vicious SS guards in September 1938 (NY 81).

24 Bundesarchiv Berlin R/365 (report of the Stapo Vienna, 21 February 1939).

25 Z 143–4.

26 NY 75, 77, 74.

27 Z 146; omitted in the English edition.

28 Z 139; omitted in the English edition.

29 Z 150; omitted in the English edition.

30 Z 377; omitted in the English edition.

31 She lived there for almost two years, including the time of her pregnancy, and returned to the boarding house with her newborn daughter after two weeks in the hospital. The baby was born on 23 March 1941.

32 *The Venlo Incident*, 62, 71, 99.

33 In his typewritten statement, pp. 5–6, which is in the files of the Great Britain Foreign Office. Unregistered Papers FO 1093–339. See also *The Venlo Incident*, p. 37.

34 Naujoks, 42: "kein Platz für Anbiederung oder gar Unterwerfung"; Szepansky, 169: "Man musste sich selbst zusprechen"; Weiss-Rüthel, 90, 113 ("Unbeugsamkeit und Furchtlosigkeit [durch die] der Lagerleitung ein gewisser Respekt abgetrotzt werden konnte").

35 *When Hitler Took Austria*, 111.

36 Letter 10; Koop, 99.

37 Frankl, 18; Vermehren, 20; Joseph Joos, *Leben auf Widerruf. Begegnungen und Beobachtungen im K.Z. Dachau 1941–1945* (Olten, 1946), 47; Nansen, 455.

38 Letters 10, 20, 22.

39 Letter 48; see also her interview with the American consul on 10 August 1938, when she described his physical condition as poor and states "that he is utterly crushed" (memorandum: https://history.state.gov /historicaldocuments/frus1938v01/d489).

40 The Gestapo also thought he was suicidal (see Koop, 97). Frankl notes that "the thought of suicide was entertained by nearly everyone" (16).

41 He also regretted that he had not died in the car accident that killed his wife. It would have been a "good and honourable end to my life" (Z 330).

42 NY 205–6.

43 Z 356.
44 "Das nicht mehr Sprechen können herrscht wie eine Armut im ganzen Lager ... der Mangel an Erkenntnisfähigheit, des Ich -bewusstseins" (93).
45 Irmingard of Bavaria, 309.
46 NY 68, Z 340.
47 Z 133, NY 79, 211.
48 *When Hitler Took Austria*, 97; six minutes are mentioned in Z 133 and 147, 1 July 1938; eight minutes in NY 78 and 88, four to eight minutes in Z 378.
49 NY 78; see Fabian von Schlabrendorff, *They Almost Killed Hitler* (New York, 1947), 124; Schlabrendorff was in a similar situation as Schuschnigg, in solitary confinement in Berlin. He saw his fellow prisoners only when they washed up in the morning. They were not allowed to talk, "but a look or a quickly spoken word was often enough to secure an understanding" (124). However, they had practical reasons for wanting to communicate, i.e., to assure that their testimony at interrogations tallied.
50 NY 211.
51 Frankl, 37; Henri Michel, *Oranien-Sachsenhausen: KZ-Erinnerungen und Hungermarsch in die Freiheit eines politischen Gefangenen* (Eupen, 1985), 249, in a diary entry of 10 August 1941; Vermehren, 90.
52 *When Hitler Took Austria*, 112.
53 Z 148, NY 85; Fey von Hassell, *Niemals sich beugen: Erinnerungen einer Sondergefangenen der SS* (Munich, 1987), 115.
54 See Cristina Siccardi, *Mafalda di Savoia: Dalla reggia al lager di Buchenwald* (Milan, 1999), 257.
55 NY 219. His question eerily matches the mood in Bertold Brecht's poem "The Wheel Change" of 1953: "I sit by the side of the road. / The driver changes the wheel. / I do not like where I'm coming from. / I do not like where I'm going to. /Why then do I wait for the wheel change / With impatience?"
56 Payne-Best in *The Venlo Incident*, 202; Blum, 65; Hassell, 185; *When Hitler Took Austria*, 112.
57 NY 207; compare Joseph Joos' letter to his daughters, worrying about the effects of his long separation from them (244): "I often think how – being separated from you – I can advise you in your efforts to develop intellectually, that is, how I could somehow catch up on being a father."
58 See Z 400.
59 During the phone call Schuschnigg was kept "under heavy guard" and "the Gestapo made a transcript of the conversation" (NY 63).
60 *When Hitler Took Austria*, 94.

61 R.K. Sheridon, *Kurt von Schuschnigg: A Tribute* (London, 1942), 289–90.
62 *When Hitler Took Austria*, 10, 12.
63 Ibid., 76, 80, 82.
64 Ibid., 107.
65 Letter 2, December 1938.
66 *When Hitler Took Austria*, 110.
67 Ibid., 112.
68 Letter 54.
69 *When Hitler Took Austria*, 118, 121. See Schuschnigg's comment that they "tried to send him somewhere where the Nazi influence was felt as little as possible … It was rather expensive but … he is in good hands" (NY 227).
70 Letters 32, 5, 7.
71 *When Hitler Took Austria*, 129.
72 Ibid., 116, 117, 120.
73 Ibid., 123. But Vera's letter to Hermann Wopfner seems to suggest that there had been difficulties earlier on. Because of Kurt's problems in school, she writes, "I would like to get the boy into a military academy. Seven new schools have been founded on the initiative of the army. He urgently needs discipline, but it is questionable whether I will succeed. I always come up against difficulties, but in my opinion it would be the best solution for him" (Letter 34, February 1941).
74 In the German edition only, Z 406; the Latin quotation is from Pliny, *Naturalis Historia*, 35.
75 NY 219, Z 400.
76 However, he inserted a summary: "For the sake of continuity I shall report the few happenings in an otherwise uneventful year of waiting" (NY 220).
77 In the summary, NY 220.
78 NY 221.

2 The Sachsenhausen Household: Living *en famille*

1 Letters 56, 58.
2 Letter 73.
3 Weiss-Rüthel, 95; Nansen, 402, 421, 445, 486; Z 397.
4 Schlussbericht, Geheime Staatspolizei – Staatspolizeistelle Wien IVA3 – B. No. 1721/43g.
5 It is ironic that men regarded as unreliable by the SS were drafted into the army. In fact, in the last months of the war, even political prisoners in concentration camps were released to join the army (see Weiss-Rüthel, 175).

6 Letter 61.
7 Letter 74.
8 Letter 108; the explanation of the cryptic remark in the letter comes from a commentary supplied by Artur (see Hopfgartner, 243).
9 Letter 123.
10 Letter 39.
11 "I hope my worn typewriter ribbon doesn't make it too hard for you to read this. We are saving everything because there is next to no chance of getting replacements" (Letter 87). "Please excuse my using a pencil, but the pen is on strike, and the typewriter, or rather the ribbon, suffers from pallor!" (Letter 92).
12 Letters 65, 59.
13 Letters 41, 58.
14 Radio program broadcast by BR Bayern, 20 March 2011 (see above, Introduction, note 33) of interview with Franz von Bayern, who was with his parents (Albrecht and Marie) and sisters (Marie Charlotte and Marie Gabriele) in Sachsenhausen.
15 Letter 58, NY 227.
16 Letter 74 of May 1942, NY 227.
17 On the illnesses of her children, see Letters 12, 16, 20; on her mother's death, Letter 32; on her own illness, Letter 81.
18 Z 335.
19 Letter 82.
20 *When Hitler Took Austria*, 126.
21 Letter 54.
22 *When Hitler Took Austria*, 128.
23 Letter 45.
24 Compare Z 410 with NY 226.
25 Letter 82.
26 *When Hitler Took Austria*, 156.
27 Ibid., 125.
28 Ibid., 141.
29 Indeed, Schuschnigg's cousin, Olga Hekajllo, was arrested and killed for this offence. See Letter 39, note 97.
30 *When Hitler Took Austria*, 135–6.
31 Letters 54, 36.
32 Letters 82, 72, 45, 58, 88.
33 Letter 52. Adalbert Stifter (1805–68), Austrian poet and novelist. Kurt confused him with the fourteenth-century Austrian duke Rudolf IV, called "Stifter."

34 Letter 59, Christmas 1941; Franz Grillparzer (1791–1872), Austrian playwright.

35 Letter 74; *When Hitler Took Austria*, 130–4.

36 Letter 82. Karl Schönherr (1867–1943), author of plays on religious and political themes in peasant lives; Johann Nestroy (1801–62), Austrian playwright and actor; Ferdinand Raimund (1790–1836), Austrian playwright; Carlo Goldoni (1707–93), Italian playwright and librettist. For Grillparzer's *Ahnfrau* see above, p. 61. Schuschnigg also gave some thought to books for his little daughter. He would have to reread fairy tales, he wrote (Letter 66), and also mentions Christoph Schmidt's Bible stories for children.

37 *When Hitler Took Austria*, 148, Letter 73.

38 Letter 94.

39 Letter 100; see also Letter 97.

40 Letter 106; *When Hitler Took Austria*, 149.

41 Ibid., 158–9.

42 Letter 119. In the summer of 1944, he was assigned as a cadet engineer to the cruiser Prince Eugen, stationed at Gdansk.

43 *When Hitler Took Austria*, 134, referring to the summer of 1942.

44 Z 475.

45 *When Hitler Took Austria*, 178–200. See Letters 130, 131.

46 Letters 56, 57.

47 Letter 58.

48 In February 1942; Letter 64.

49 Letters 63, 64.

50 Letter 82, May 1942. At least I assume that this was a new maid, since it is unlikely that the "gem" changed into a *Trampel* (oaf) within the space of two months.

51 Letter 88, November 1942.

52 Letter 86; Nansen reports in his diary that as a prisoner he was paid 3 marks for carving toys. His pay "vanished" instantly, being exchanged for beer and cigarettes (455).

53 Eglau, 241.

54 Hassell, 108–9.

55 Siccardi, 257. Mafalda was fatally wounded in an air raid and on her deathbed left her watch to Maria. For Blum's servant, see Blum, *Le dernier mois*, 33.

56 Letters 59, 119.

57 They were temporarily without radio. Schuschnigg reports a week later (Letter 69) that "H" (unidentified) brought them a radio.

58 Letter 67.

59 *The Venlo Incident*, 95–6.

60 Letters 49, 50, 107; 42, 74.

61 Letter 88 and diary entry for 6 December 1942 (NY 232).

62 The sending and receiving of mail was regulated in obsessive detail. In Sachsenhausen, prisoners were allowed only two letters a month, a maximum of four pages with 15 lines on each page. They were of course subject to censorship. Illegible or confusing letters were destroyed. See Hrdlicka, 75; Weiss-Rüthel, 93, quotes the regulations.

63 Weiss-Rüthel, 142; Nansen, 443.

64 Frankl, 38; Nansen, 457; Kupfer-Koberwitz quoted by Laqueur, 55; Payne-Best, *The Venlo Incident*, 100.

65 Joos, 54. Thomas Cushing, p. 92.

66 Siccardi, 258; for the crèche and board games, see above, pp. 54–5; Vermehren, 20; Naujoks, 296.

67 Letters 74, 77, 83.

68 Schuschnigg in Letter 52; Nansen, 443; see also Henri Michel's letter of 10 December 1940: "Es geht mir weiter gut [I continue to be well]," 248.

69 Hassell, 166, 137; Schlabrendoff, 148; Cushing, 94.

70 Nansen, 414 and 440; Laqueur, 13; Joos, 235; by contrast, Arnold Weiss-Rüthel refused to weep, but was looking forward to the "day when I would once again be allowed to weep" (57).

71 Vermehren, 164; compare Christel, 95: Theft was considered one of the most serious crimes (*schwerwiegendste Lagerdelikte*), but this sense of solidarity only characterized cell blocks whose inmates were united by their national or political background.

72 Joos, 48.

3 The Comfort of Religion

1 Frankl, 33, Vermehren, 24; Schlabrendorff, 132; Hebermann quoted by Laqueur p. 128. The term *Katakombengemeinschaft* (catacomb-community) was used by Pastor Werner Koch. See also Benz, 62, and Thomas Rahe, "Die Bedeutung von Religion und Religiosität in den nationalsozialistischen Konzentrationslagern," in Herbert Ulrich et al., eds., *Die nationalsozialistischen Konzentrationslager: Entwicklung und Struktur*, vol. 2 (Göttingen, 1998), 1016–18, about secret masses being said. For the blowing of the shofar, see "An Improbable Relic of Auschwitz: A Shofar That Defied the Nazis," by Ralph Blumenthal in the *New York Times*, 21 September 2019. These practices have sometimes been viewed

as a form of resistance, but Rahe cautions: "Should it be seen as resistance (which ignores the spiritual/moral side) or as continuation of tradition and a means of overcoming the horror and inhumanity, then it ignores the background of death and despair" (Rahe, 1006).

2 Letters 54, 15.

3 "Religiöses aus dem KZ: Über Möglichkeiten der Religionsausübung in Gefängnis und KZ," *Schweizerische Kirchenzeitung* 114 (1946): 26–9, 36–7. The passages quoted are on pp. 36 and 27 respectively.

4 See Vera's interview with the American Consul in Vienna, 10 August 1938: "He [Schuschnigg] has always been extremely devout and had derived great inner strength from his faith" (memorandum https://history.state.gov/historicaldocuments/frus1938v01/d489).

5 Z 341–2.

6 Michel, 104.

7 Z 342; compare 330; similarly, Thomas Rahe cites Zacheusz Pawlak, recounting his reaction to the death of a 14-year-old boy: "My previously firm faith in God died together with my friend … From there on I no longer prayed" (1017).

8 Weiss-Rüthel, 49.

9 Z 345, 319.

10 *Schweizerische Zeitung,* 114 (1946): 28; Z 357.

11 Letters 9, 11.

12 Michel, 252.

13 Frankl, 56; Letters 73, 100, 25; Z 330.

14 Z 319–21, 369, 344–5; Frankl, 36–7; Nansen, 509; Vermehren, 90.

15 Z 369; compare Joseph Joos on Socrates: "How much ethics was pre-shaped before the full truth emerged with Christ?" (250).

16 Z 369; Letter 68.

17 Letters 64, 58.

18 Letter 68; Z 440, *Schweizerische Zeitung,* 114 (1946): 36–7.

19 NY 250; *When Hitler Took Austria,* 155, *Schweizerische Zeitung,* 114 (1946): 36; see also NY 250. Compare Henri Michel on receiving the viaticum, 109, Franz of Bavaria receiving first communion at Sachsenhausen (Radio program broadcast by BR Bayern, 20 March 2011: "Die dunklen Jahre Wittelbachs").

20 Letter 108. The pun on the name of the Austrian Cardinal Innitzer (Unnitzer sounds like "unnützer," the German for "useless") refers to the fact that he did not resist the Nazis. Friedrich Stockinger, who is credited with this pun, was minister of trade and commerce 1933–6; president of the administrative board of the Austrian National Rail System 1936–8. He emigrated to Canada in 1938.

21 Z 334.
22 NY 289; *Schweizerische Zeitung*, 114 (1946): 37; Letter 135a.
23 Ackermann, 24, 71, 73.

4 The Consolation of Books

1 Heinrich Christian Meier, *Der Weg ins Sein* (Hamburg, 1966), 62. The poem is entitled "The Reader."
2 Jerrold Seigel, *Modernity and Bourgeois Life* (New York, 2012), 453.
3 Pierre Pourdieu, "The Forms of Capital," in James Richardson, ed., *Handbook of Research for the Sociology of Education* (New York, 1986), 241–58.
4 See Pamela Pillbeam's statistics in *The Middle Classes in Europe* (London, 1990), 195–7, and the analysis of the concept of the *Bildungsbürger* in Bernd Widdig's *Culture and Inflation in Weimar Germany* (Berkeley, 2001), 178–95.
5 Seigel, 472.
6 NY 215; Joos, 250; see also Laqueur, 67: "Ohne Bücher bin ich krank [without books I am ailing]."
7 NY 215, Z 364.
8 Torsten Seela, *Bücher und Bibliotheken in nationalsozialistischen Konzentrationslagern* (Munich, 1992), 112; Daxelmüller, 988; Paul Neurath, *The Society of Terror: Inside the Dachau and Buchenwald Concentration Camps* (London, 2005), 224.
9 Daxelmüller, 989.
10 Walter Gross, *2000 Tage Dachau* (Munich, n.d.), 176.
11 Szepansky, 185; Seela, 38–9.
12 Langer, 45.
13 "Bildung aus dem Widerspruch [culture out of rebellion]," (Seela, 106); religious literature in particular is "a priori eine Widerstandshandlung [principally an action of resistance]" (111).
14 Regulation quoted by Seela, 24.
15 Joos, 103; similarly Kogon, 131.
16 Seela, 27.
17 Weiss-Rüthel, however, relates that the actor Edgar Bennert, who was the librarian at Sachsenhausen, eventually admitted him to the library at night, so that he could finally "slake his thirst for books." For this privilege, he did not mind "sacrificing a few hours of sleep" (90).
18 Seela, 25.
19 Szepansky, 164.

20 Neurath, 162.

21 Seela, 47, 65, 33; Weiss-Rüthel, 89–90.

22 Naujoks, 175; Kogon, 130.

23 Letter 42.

24 Letter 67. Some of this may have found its way into the German version of Schuschnigg's *Requiem*, which contains thoughts about the multi-nation state, for example, Z 154–66.

25 Letter 20.

26 Letter 41.

27 Z 431, missing in the English version, perhaps because it would not ring a bell with American readers.

28 Letters 73, 67. Compare the experience of Weiss-Rüthel, who had to give up his position as editor and stopped writing when his publisher told him that the risk he posed to the company on account of his opposition to the regime was no longer acceptable (15).

29 Letters 85, 74a, 116, 118, 61, 42.

30 Z 457, 462.

31 Letter 116.

32 Letters 67, 59, 116, 42.

33 Letter 85.

34 Ibid.

35 That is, the *Propyläen-Kunstgeschichte*.

36 Letters 66, 64.

37 Letter 61; Z 23–5, 425, 432.

38 Z 232, 157. Neither reference appears in the English edition.

39 NY 245.

40 Z 432, 474.

41 Z 369, 348.

42 Z 369, 320, 344, 365.

43 Letters 74a, 58.

44 Letters 116, 45, 66, 67; Z 413–14.

45 The Dachau library even had books that had been banned by the Nazis. See Seela's observation that the number of liberal books that did not fit the Nazi pattern were not an indication of a degree of tolerance, but rather attested to the "poor education and low level of understanding among the SS people who controlled the influx" (27).

46 Z 353, 368; Letter 41; Z 408, 478, 365.

47 Letter 118. The reference is to the Homer translations by Johann Heinrich Voss (1751–1826), which remained the German-language standard translation into the twentieth century.

48 Z 470, 461, 440.
49 NY 274; compare Primo Levi reciting a passage from Dante to a receptive
    fellow prisoner and commenting that "it was doing me good" (*Survival in
    Auschwitz*, 103).
50 Letters 52, 66 (see also Z 67); Z 179.
51 Bauernfeld (d. 1890) was a liberal thinker and wrote plays as well as
    a satire on the government. His *Die Republik der Tiere* (The Republic of
    Animals) is comparable to Orwell's *Animal Farm*. His criticism of the
    government led to his dismissal from his position as a civil servant.
52 Z 408–10, 178.
53 Letter 60.
54 Letter 88.
55 Knut Hamsun (1859–1952), Norwegian author, Nobel Prize winner, Nazi
    sympathizer, but apparently popular with Nazi prisoners. Daxelmüller
    (990) quotes a letter from Rudolf Wunderlich to his wife: "Für die kurze
    Freizeit helfen die Bücher; ich habe gleich wieder mal zu einem Hamsun
    gegriffen und zwar 'Nach Jahr und Tag' [The books are helpful to pass
    the short leisure time. So I reached for Hamsun, namely his 'Nach Jahr
    und Tag']"; Ossietzky also read Hamsun (see Seela, 114).
56 Probably Jakob Schaffner (1875–1944). In the years of the Weimar
    Republic, he was considered one of the most important Swiss writers. As
    a supporter of the Nazis he was discredited, however. His work was no
    longer discussed after 1945 and fell into oblivion.
57 Sven von Hedin (1865–1952), Swedish travel writer. His reports on his
    visits to the front lines of the central powers in World War I attracted
    attention on account of their Germanophile bias. His attitude toward the
    Nazis was ambiguous. He accepted awards from them, but at the same
    time refused to remove criticism of the regime from his book *Deutschland
    und der Weltfrieden* and was active in helping Norwegian activists.
58 Letter 39.
59 Raoul Aslan (1886–1958), member of the repertory company at the
    Vienna Burgtheater from 1920, director of the Burgtheater 1945–8.
60 Letters 42, 73. Hans Baptist Freiherr von Hammerstein-Equord (1881–
    1947), minister of the interior in 1936, then national commissioner
    for the advancement of culture in the ministry of education. He was
    forced to retire after the Anschluss and was arrested 20 July 1944. He
    was incarcerated at the Mauthausen concentration camp and, like
    Schuschnigg, was liberated by the Allies.
61 Z 410.
62 Z 410, 394, 450, 173, 233 (repeated 394), 469, 407.

63 Letter 130; Z 451 (compare NY 247).

64 Szepansky, 186; for other plays being performed at Sachsenhausen (scenes from *Faust*, *Peer Gynt*, *Le Misanthrope*) see Weiss-Rüthel, 146.

65 Z 470; Letters 131, 45.

66 Letter 130; Z 160, 431.

67 Z 177–8, 418–19.

68 Joos, 240–2. Kogon mentions Plato's *Dialogues*, Galsworthy's *Swan Song*, and the authors Heine, Klabund, and Mehring – the last three only to show that authors forbidden by the Nazis were available to prisoners, apparently because confiscated private libraries ended up in the libraries of concentration camps without being checked (131). See also above, note 45.

69 NY 282. See Rumpf, 24–5, on the significance of gift-giving among prisoners.

70 Seela, 36, 4.

5 Music to His Ears

1 *When Hitler Took Austria*, 135; Letter 74.

2 Wunderlich, 123. A printer by trade, Wunderlich escaped in 1944 and hid out until the end of the war; see also Szepansky, 167; Naujoks, 89, 97.

3 Letters 59, 64, 67, 69; Z 361–2. On Lehár see below, note 24.

4 At his post, that is. Artur had been drafted in 1940. At home in Berlin, the family made do without a radio to avoid having their conversations tracked through an implanted listening device. See above, p. 51.

5 Letter 38; opera by Albert Lortzing (1802–51).

6 Letter 38.

7 Letters 74, 42. Franz Schubert (1797–1828) and Franz Liszt (1811–86) are used as examples of classical (rather than popular) composers being featured on radio programs.

8 Z 393.

9 Ackermann, 82, 84–5; Nansen, 477, 440; Wunderlich, 82; Michel, 79, 84–7; Vermehren, 97; but see Christel, 72, and Weiss-Rüthel, 96. On enforced singing to exhaust prisoners already fatigued by work; similarly Szepansky, 188: "Die SS misbrauchte das Singen, um uns zu schikanieren [The SS abused singing to harass us]." By contrast, singing on their own initiative brought relief. At Christmas the sense of nostalgia was unbearable, but the mood changed when someone suggested singing songs, Szepansky relates (187).

10 Joos, 62.

11 Letter 42.

12 Letter 45. He is referring to the popular tenor Leo Slezak (1873–1946).
13 Letter 42. He is referring to the *Ring der Nibelungen* (*Rheingold, Walküre,
Siegfried, Götterdämmerung*), by Richard Wagner (1813–83). Alma Mahler
(1879–1964), Viennese composer, editor, and socialite, was married
successively to three prominent Austrians: the composer Gustav Mahler,
the architect Walter Gropius, and the author Franz Werfel.
14 Letter 42.
15 Wilhelm Furtwängler (1886–1954), conductor; director of the Berlin
Philharmonic 1922–45, 1947–54, and conductor for life from 1952;
conductor at the Bayreuth Festival 1936.
16 Operas by Richard Wagner.
17 Letter 42; Arturo Toscanini (1867–1957), Italian conductor, director of
Milan's La Scala 1921–9.
18 Gioachino Rossini (1792–1868), Italian composer.
19 Christoph Willibald Gluck (1714–87), German composer.
20 Operetta by Johann Strauss Jr (1825–99).
21 Franz Rehrl (1890–1947), governor of Salzburg 1922–38.
22 Letter 43.
23 Johann Strauss Sr (1804–49) and Johann Strauss Jr (1825–99), iconic
Austrian composers; they were in fact of Jewish parentage, but the
Nazis concealed this fact. See Hanns Jäger-Sunstenau, *Johann Strauss, der
Walzerkönig und seine Dynastie* (Vienna, 1965), 86–7.
24 Franz Lehár (1870–1948), Austro-Hungarian composer of operettas,
former conductor of military orchestras. His most popular works were
*Die lustige Witwe, Der Graf von Luxemburg, Zigeunerliebe, Das Land des
Lächelns*. Lehár's wife was Jewish, but protected by the Nazis as an
Ehrenaryerin (honorary Aryan or Aryan by marriage).
25 Hans Knappertsbusch (1888–1965), German conductor.
26 Paul Felix Weingartner von Münzberg (1863–1942), Austrian pianist,
composer, and conductor.
27 Opera by Richard Wagner.
28 Richard Strauss (1864–1949), German composer and conductor.
29 Letter 39.
30 Opera by Christoph Willibald Gluck (1714–87).
31 Letter 39. The cattiness of Schuschnigg's observations is, however,
matched by his brother's comments added to the letter. Anday "got on
people's nerves with her constant complaints of being persecuted for
being a Jew," Artur reported. When he saw her at the Berlin Opera in
1939, she told him that her difficulties were based on misinformation.
"What, me a Jew?!" she said reportedly. She did at any rate continue to

perform in Germany. Artur heard her sing at the Munich Opera in 1941. After 1945 he met her repeatedly at private functions in Vienna, and on one such occasion she told him in confidence that she "was a quarter Jewish" (Binder, 122, note 117).

32 Adele Kern (1907–80), a lyric soprano at the Vienna State Opera.
33 Lotte Lehmann (1888–1976) was a soprano at the Vienna State Opera 1916–38; she emigrated to the USA in 1937.
34 NY 144, Z 396–7 (shortened in the English version), NY 236, 247.
35 NY 181.
36 Z 179; Letters 66, 90.
37 Karl Millöcker (1842–99), composer of operettas.
38 Paraphrasing a popular hit by Paul Lincke; Letter 130.
39 Claude Debussy (1862–1918), French composer
40 Letter 42. Johannes Brahms (1833–97), composer.
41 NY 211, Z 225–6.
42 Letters 95, 127.
43 Letter 42. He is referring to the composers Orlando di Lasso (1532–94) and Giovanni Pierluigi da Palestrina (1525–94).
44 Letter 39.
45 Z 394.

6 The Use of Wit

1 Frankl, 42; Ackermann, 36; Hassell, 142; Friedrich Hermann Hettler, *Josef Müller ("Ochsensepp"): Mann des Widerstands und erster CS Vorsitzender* (Munich, 1991), 182. Müller was a Catholic who, like Schuschnigg, had been educated at a Jesuit school; he met Schuschnigg on the evacuation trek in 1945. Schuschnigg mentions him in Z 501; see also Nansen, 28, 432.
2 Noel Carroll, *Humour: A Very Short Introduction* (Oxford, 2018), 8, 38, 77; Herbert Lefcourt, *Humor: The Psychology of Living Buoyantly* (New York, 2001), 104, 112, 137.
3 Ackermann, 146.
4 See, for example, Szepansky who recounts a deliberately cryptic conversation he had with his brother, who was allowed to visit him. "I asked, 'Will the soldiers improve the chances of victory?' ... He understood my meaning, [i.e., victory] over the Fascists ... and replied, 'We are doing what we can'" (177).
5 Z 137.
6 *Time Magazine*, 12 May 1938.
7 Letters 38, 72.

8 Letters 52, 96; diary entry of 10 July 1942; Z 410 (only in the German edition); Letters 91, 72.

9 Letter 64; Z 403; Payne-Best, *The Venlo Incident*, 28; Nansen, 403.

10 Letter 86. See the attempt of Paul Neurath, a prisoner in Dachau and Buchenwald, to characterize the differences between Prussians and Austrians. According to Neurath (230–1), Prussian tradition fostered "zeal, ambition, and Spartan virtues, a rigidity and behavior which forbade the display of feelings and emotions" and a high sense of duty ("preussisches Pflichtbewusstsein"). Austrian tradition, by contrast, fostered "sentimentality, *Gemütlichkeit*, compassion, and sympathy for all that lives, with little concern about national labels ... They did their duty as well as any Prussian, yet they ... considered this the obligation of every honest man." It should be noted that Neurath was a native of Austria! But Joos (a German) likewise believed that Austrian prisoners benefited "from the optimism which characterizes this warm-hearted (*gemütswarme*) and music-loving nation" (107). Indeed, Schuschnigg himself differentiates between German/Prussian and Austrian in a similar manner: "To think like an Austrian means to level differences, to liaise, to connect"; Prussians "stoke the fire, exaggerate, sharpen, and tear apart." In his view, Prussians were self-righteous, hectoring, authoritarian, unable to see the other side, whereas Austrians "look at themselves ironically, are modest and easily embarrassed, sensitive ... avoid crises ... consider the other side to the point of showing a lack of principles ... and reject authority" (Z 26).

11 Irmingard of Bavaria, 307; Eglau, 249; Siccardi, 257; Letter 64.

12 Letter 96.

13 Ibid.

14 Ibid.

15 Letters 52, 69; compare Payne-Best's experience and the availability of illicit radios in other camps, above, p. 39.

16 Letter 106.

17 Letters 38, 66.

18 Letters 64, 95.

19 Letter 72.

20 Ibid.

21 Weiss-Rüthel joked about the special prisoners being called *Ehrenhäftlinge*, "honorary prisoners": "It couldn't be ascertained whether they regarded their arrest an honour or the Gestapo considered it an honour to have arrested them" (51).

22 Letter 106; NY 80.

23 NY 68, 220.
24 Letter 66.
25 https://www.mein-oesterreich.info/persoenlichkeiten/bobby.htm.
26 Letter 66.

7 Cherishing Memories

1 See Steven Rose, *The Making of Memory* (London, 2003), 33; Stephan Feuchtwang, who studied cases of Holocaust survivors, in his "Loss, Transmissions, Recognitions, Authorisations," in Susannah Radstone and Katharine Hodgkins, eds., *Regimes of Memory* (London, 2003), 76–90.
2 Ackermann, 12, 17, 27.
3 Z 142.
4 See Dorthe Berntsen and David C. Rubin, eds., *Understanding Autobiographical Memory* (Cambridge, 2012), 194.
5 Z 356.
6 Letters 36, 39 (*sich Ausstöhnen*).
7 Daniel Alkon, *Memory's Voice* (New York, 1992), 11; Frankl, 38.
8 For the relationship between memories and "fantasy as a weapon" in the fight for emotional survival see Laqueur, 103. The quoted expression is from Floris Bertold Bakels, a Dutch resistance fighter interned at Dachau.
9 Z 212, Letter 52; compare Lars Breuer, *Kommunikative Erinnerung in Deutschland und Polen: Täter- und Opferbilder in Gesprächen über den zweiten Weltkrieg* (Wiesbaden, 2015). Breuer says that memory is a social and communicative process which renders the past present ("ein sozialer und kommunikativer Prozess der Vergegenwärtigung," 13); similarly Jeffrey Olick, "Collective Memory: The Two Cultures," in *Sociological Theory* 17, no. 3 (1999): 333–48 on the past being remade for present purposes (341).
10 Z 358–60.
11 Z 125, 136, 214.
12 Letters 73, 64; NY 69, 85.
13 Letters 38, 89, 36.
14 Michel, 259, 79, 249, 254, 258, 249; Joos, 240, 242; Nansen, 450, 470, 475, 403.
15 Letter 87; compare Letter 14, written by Vera.
16 Letter 83.
17 Letters 74, 97.
18 Letters 74, 117, 118, 30, 87; see also Vera's Letter 11.
19 Letters 89, 58.
20 Z 332; Letters 42, 45, and Vera in Letter 16; compare Primo Levi on his reminiscences, which were "profoundly sweet and sad" (*Survival in Auschwitz*, 106).

21 Alkon, 12.

22 Letters 29, 35, 107, 133, 56.

23 Letters 35, 11.

24 Philippe Tortell, Mark Turin, and Margot Young, eds., *Memory* (Vancouver, 2018), 34.

25 Letter 73. For the corporal punishment administered to Kurt, see above, p. 45.

26 Letter 108.

27 Letter 52. Miss Maria Cazin, an elderly lady from Hannover living in Merano, according to a comment by Artur Schuschnigg, had been "touchingly kind to [his brother] Kurt who was detained in southern Tyrol as a prisoner of war in 1919 before being released. She visited us repeatedly in Innsbruck" (Binder, 166, note 224).

28 Letters 52, 45.

29 Letters 52, 58, 60, 61.

30 Letters 42, 44, 41. The specialist consulted was Prof. Dr. Karl Fellinger, grad. Dr. med. 1929, habilitated 1937; from 1931 to 1940 he worked in the Second Medical Clinic in the Allemeine Krankenhaus in Vienna. In 1945 he was chief physician in the Poliklinik in Vienna, from 1946 to 1975 chief physician in the Second Medical Clinic, in 1964/5 rector at the University of Vienna.

31 Letter 44.

32 Letter 44; *When Hitler Took Austria*, 151; Vera in Letter 1.

33 Letter 93.

34 Schuschnigg's doubt about America's ability to serve as a carrier and protector of culture is not new. It was already reflected in a cartoon (*Simplicissimus* 24 [12 November 1919]) showing a well-dressed American with a pork barrel and a bedraggled German offering a painting in exchange.

35 Letters 73, 118, 130. The reference is to Bruno Grimschitz, ed., *Deutsche Bildnisse von Runge bis Menzel* (Vienna, 1941). "Kaiserschmarren" is a kind of omelet with raisins and vanilla sugar, a traditional Austrian dish.

36 Letter 130.

37 Z 439–40.

38 Unpublished transcript in IFZG, inv. 954, no. 68.

8 Schuschnigg's Political Reminiscences

1 Ackermann, 71; Weiss-Rüthel, 21.

2 NY 95.

3 Langer, xi–xii; see Rosanne Kennedy, "Memory, History and the Law: Testimony and Collective Memory in Holocaust and Stolen Generation Trials," in Joan Tumblety, ed., *Memory and History: Understanding Memory as Source and Subject* (London, 2013), 57: "The decision either to privilege the past by reconstructing 'what the event was' for the society in which it occurred, or to examine the effects of past events in the present, is one of the fault lines between historians and memory scholars today."

4 NY viii, 296.

5 Paul Ricoeur, *Memory, History, Forgetting* (Chicago, 2006), 176.

6 Langer, 7; see Charlotte Delbo, *Auschwitz and After* (New Haven, 1995), 237: "I was unable to get reaccustomed to myself … a self which had become so detached from me."

7 Z 360–2.

8 Langer, 189, 37.

9 Z 446, 351.

10 Unpublished transcript of a broadcast aired by Radio Vatican, 3 October 1945, in IFZG, inv. 954, no. 68.

11 Needless to say, it is not always possible to draw a clear line between obfuscation and self-deception, but while Schuschnigg deals with guilt through a religiously tinted confession and encourages others to examine their political conscience, equivocation is a more common strategy in political memoirs. Thus Kurt Waldheim makes a token reference to "the frailty of memory" in his autobiography, *In the Eye of the Storm: A Memoir* (Bethesda, 1986, p. x), and obfuscates his wartime record with the well-worn excuse that he was merely doing his duty as a soldier. See Eli M. Rosenbaum, *Betrayal: The Untold Story of the Kurt Waldheim Investigation and Cover-Up* (New York, 1993). Albert Speer's memoir *Inside the Third Reich: Memoirs* (New York, 1970), by contrast, displays a "slick honesty whose aim is to disarm," as one reviewer notes (Chimamanda Ngozi Adichie, "Rereading Albert Speer's *Inside the Third Reich*," *New Yorker*, 1 August 2017). Using the opposite approach, Pierre Daye, a Belgian collaborator, staunchly denies any guilt: "Je ne me refuserais pas … à répondre de mes actes. Ma conduit n'a rien eu de caché" (unpublished *Memoirs*, 1208).

12 Z 330.

13 Letter 39.

14 NY 85. It is surprising that, being held in isolation, he was aware of what was being said about him in the outside world. Vera may have been his source, or he was given the "bad news" by the authorities, as a means of unsettling him. See p. 131 above for the delivery of an abusive letter to him in Sachsenhausen.

15 Z 105.
16 NY vii, viii, x.
17 Z 154–5.
18 Z 316. These remarks, which sound like an editorial comment on
    the final version of the manuscript, are dated "Concentration Camp,
    January 1944"!
19 NY 128.
20 Z 411, not in the English text.
21 Z 118, 445.
22 Z 445, 349, 357.
23 Z 299–300, NY 192.
24 Z 383, omitted in the English-language edition.
25 Z 301, NY192–4.
26 Z 455, 218, see 469: "the Geradlinigkeit einer festfundierten und
    unwandelbaren Überzeugung [the straight line of a well-founded and
    unchanging conviction]."
27 NY 190.
28 Z 200, NY 102.
29 Z 218, 261–2.
30 Z 469. "Let the will stand in place of a reason" is a legal principle; the
    expression goes back to Juvenal.
31 Z 454, 469.
32 Z 166. "Aus meinem Kriegserlebnis war mir der Treueinhalt des Begriffes
    Österreich erwachsen" (Z 151).
33 Meaning "cut up."
34 "Nicht mehr als Machtfaktor, vielmehr als kultureller Kristallisationskern
    einer neuen möglichen Entwicklung … als völkerverbindende Brücke"
    (Z 448–9).
35 Z 451.
36 Z 352–4.
37 Z 475, 389.
38 Z 467.
39 Z 469, 472–3. None of these observations are found in the English version.
    Indeed, the sententious tone is hardly compatible with the rest of his diary
    entries.
40 Z 313, not in English.
41 Z 435–6, not in the English version.
42 NY 213–14.
43 Z 510, NY 296.
44 NY 270.

45 Z 487; Schuschnigg, *The Brutal Takeover*, 18.
46 Blum, 64.
47 Z 118, 175.
48 Nicholas Chare, "Symbol Re-formation: Concentrationary Meaning in Charlotte Delbo's *Auschwitz and After*," in Pollack and Silverman, *Concentrationary Memories*, 105.
49 As Langer puts it, speaking of the suffering of Jewish victims: "This is the ailing subtext of their testimonies, wailing beneath the convalescent murmur of their surface lives ... When the subtext of their story echoes for us too as a communal wound, then we will have begun to hear their legacy of unheroic memory and grasp the meaning for our time" (205).

Conclusion

1 Michel, 152.
2 Letter 130 of December 1944.
3 Bukey, 15.
4 Botz, "Corporate State," p. 145. See also Ilse Reiter-Zatloukal in Reiter-Zatloukal et al., eds., *Österreich 1933–1938: Interdisziplinäre Annäherungen an das Dollfuss-/Schuschnigg-Regime* (Vienna, 2012): "Konsens über die Befürwortung des Anschlusses im März 1938 an das Deutsche Reich sowie über die Mitverantwortung am nationalsozialistischen Terrorregime durch beträchtliche Teile der österreichischen Bevölkerung ... fehlt sowohl auf gesellschaftlicher wie politischer Ebene" (7); Emmerich Talos, *Sozialpolitik im Austrofaschismus* (Vienna, 2005): "Unstrittig ist, dass ... [Dollfuss und] Schuschnigg gegen NS-Terror und nationalsozialistischen Expansionismus Widerstand geleistet haben" (412). Their only aim was "die Aufrechterhaltung einer Diktatur."
5 See, for example, Wohnout, 143–62; Gerhard Botz, "'Corporatist State,'" 144–67. The term "half fascism" is used by Hopfgartner, 110.
6 Sofsky, 116.
7 For a survey of assessments of Schuschnigg by historians in the 1930s and 1940s see Florian Wenninger, "Austrian Missions – Das Problem der politischen Äquidistanz der Forschung am Beispiel Austrofaschismus," in Reiter-Zatloukal et al., 257–69.
8 Unpublished letters in IFZG, inv. 954, nos. 72, 75. I have found no further information on the journalist Kaiser-Blüh.

9 Schuschnigg, *The Brutal Takeover*, 23; unpublished letter of 4 December 1945 in IFZG inv. 954, no. 70; for the American position on prewar politicians see Oliver Rathkolb, "'Elimination of Austro-Fascists from Posts of Influence': US-Nachkriegsplanungen für eine umfassende Entfaschisierung," in Ilse Reiter-Zatloukal et al., 273–84.

10 Unpublished letter of 6 February 1946, IFZG inv. 954, no. 71; Schuschnigg, *The Brutal Takeover*, 23.

Bibliography

Ackermann, Emil. *Niemand and nichts ist vergessen: Ehemalige Häftlinge aus verschiedenen Ländern berichten über das KZ Sachsenhausen*. Berlin, 1984.

Adichie, Chamamanda Ngozi. "Rereading Albert Speer's Inside the Third Reich." *New Yorker*, 1 August 2017.

Alkon, Daniel. *Memory's Voice*. New York, 1992.

Aretin, Erwein von. *Wittelsbacher im KZ*. Munich, n.d.

Bankier, David, and Don Michman, eds. *Holocaust Historiography in Context. Emergence, Challenges, Polemics, and Achievements*. Jerusalem, 2008.

Benz, Wolfgang, and Barbara Distel, eds. *Der Ort des Terrors: Geschichte der nationalsozialistischen Konzentrationslager*, vol. 3. Munich, 2006.

Bernard, Jean. *Pfarrerblock 25487: Ein Bericht*. Ed. Charles Reinert and Gebhart Stillfried. Munich, 1962.

Berntsen, Dorthe, and David C. Rubin, eds. *Understanding Autobiographical Memory*. Cambridge, 2012.

Bettelheim, Bruno. *The Informed Heart*. New York, 1960.

Binder, Dieter, and Heinrich Schuschnigg, eds. *Sofort Vernichten: Die vertraulichen Briefe Kurt und Vera von Schuschniggs 1938–1945*. Vienna, 1997.

Bischof, Günter, Anton Pelinka, and Alexander Lassner, eds. *The Dollfuss/Schuschnigg Era in Austria: A Reassessment*. New Brunswick, NJ, 2003.

Blum, Leon. *Le dernier mois*. Paris, 1995.

Botz, Gerhard. *Binnenstruktur, Alltagsverhalten und Überlebenschancen in Nazi-Konzentrationslagern*. Vienna, 1996.

– "'Corporate State and Enhanced Authoritarian Dictatorship: The Austria of Dollfuss and Schuschnigg." In Antonio Costa Pinto, ed., *Corporatism and Fascism: The Corporatist Wave in Europe*, 144–67. New York, 2017.

Breuer, Lars. *Kommunikative Erinnerungen in Deutschland und Polen: Täter- und Opferbilder in Gesprächen über den zweiten Weltkrieg*. Wiesbaden, 2015.

Bukey, Evan Burr. *Hitler's Austria: Popular Sentiment in the Nazi Era, 1938–1945.* Chapel Hill, 2000.

Caplan, Jane, and Nikolaus Wachsmann, eds. *Concentration Camps in Nazi Germany: The New Histories.* London, 2010.

Carr, Gilly, and Harold Mytum, eds. *Cultural Heritage and Prisoners of War: Creativity behind Barbed Wires.* New York, 2012.

Carroll, Noel. *Humour: A Very Short Introduction.* Oxford, 2014.

Chare, Nicholas. "Symbol Re-formation: Concentrationary Meaning in Charlotte Delbo's *Auschwitz and After.*" In Pollock, Griselda and Max Silverman, eds., *Concentrationary Memories: Totalitarian Terror and Cultural Resistance,* 104–14. London, 2014.

Christel, Albert. *Apokalypse unserer Tage: Erinnerungen an das KZ Sachsenhausen,* ed. Manfred Ruppel and Lothar Wolfstetter. Frankfurt, 1987.

Cohen, Elie. *Human Behaviour in the Concentration Camp.* Westport, CT, 1984; first edition, London, 1953.

Cushing, Thomas. "Stalins Sohn fühlte sich verstossen" *Der Spiegel* 13 (1968): 92–5.

Daxelmüller, Christoph. "Kulturelle Formen und Aktivitäten als Teil der Überlebens – und Vernichtungsstrategie in den Konzentrationslagern." In Christoph Dieckmann, Ulrich Herbert, and Karin Orth, eds., *Das nationalsozialistische Konzentrationslager,* vol. 2, 983–1005. Göttingen, 1998.

Daye, Pierre. Unpublished memoirs. (I used the copy in the Hoover Institution Library, Stanford.)

Delbo, Charlotte. *Auschwitz and After.* New Haven, 1995.

Des Pres, Terrence. *The Survivor: An Anatomy of Life in Death Camps.* Oxford, 1980.

Dieckmann, Christoph, Ulrich Herbert, and Karin Orth, eds. *Das nationalsozialistische Konzentrationslager,* vol. 2. Göttingen, 1998.

Drobisch, Klaus. *System der NS-Konzentrationslager 1933–1939.* Berlin, 1993.

Eglau, Hans Otto. *Fritz Thyssen: Hitlers Gönner und Geisel.* Berlin, 2003.

Embacher, Helga. "Frauen in Konzentrations- und Vernichtungslagern – weibliche Überlebensstrategien in Extremsituationen." In Robert Streibel and Hans Schafranek, eds., *Strategie des Überlebens: Häftlingsgesellschaften im KZ und Gulag,* 145–67. Vienna, 1996.

Feinstein, Margaret Myers. *Holocaust Survivors in Postwar Germany, 1945–1957.* Cambridge, MA, 2010.

Feuchtwang, Stephan. "Loss, Transmissions, Recognitions, Authorisations." In Susannah Radstone and Katharine Hodgkins, eds., *Regimes of Memory,* 76–90. London, 2003.

Fine, Ellen. "Literature as Resistance: Survival in the Camps." *Holocaust and Genocide Studies* 1 (1986): 79–89.

Frankl, Victor. *From Death Camp to Existentialism*. Boston, 1959.

Goeschel, Christian, and Nikolaus Wachsmann. *The Nazi Concentration Camps, 1933–1939: A Documentary History*. Lincoln, NE, 2012.

Goldberg, Martin. "Holocaust Autobiography." In James Goodwin, ed., *Autobiography: The Self-Made Text*, 156–64. New York, 1993.

Gross, Walter. *2000 Tage Dachau*. Munich, n.d.

Guenther, Lisa. *Solitary Confinement: Social Death and Its Afterlives*. Minneapolis, 2013.

Hackett, David. *The Buchenwald Report*. Oxford, 1995.

Hassell, Fey von. *Niemals sich beugen. Erinnerungen einer Sondergefangenen der SS*. Munich, 1987.

Hebermann, Nanda. *The Blessed Abyss: Inmate # 6582 in Ravensbrück Concentration Camp for Women*. Detroit, 2000.

Hettler, Friedrich Hermann. *Josef Müller ("Ochsensepp"): Mann des Widerstands und erster CS Vorsitzender*. Munich, 1991.

Hochedlinger, Michael, Martin Krenn, and Simon Peter Terzer, eds. *Verzeichnis der Familienarchive und persönlichen Schriftnachlässen zur österreichichen Geschichte*. Vienna, 2018.

Hopfgartner, Anton. *Kurt Schuschnigg: Ein Mann gegen Hitler*. Graz, 1989.

Hrdlicka, Manuela. *Alltag im KZ: Das Lager Sachsenhausen bei Berlin*. Opladen, 1991.

Hughes, Judith. *Witnessing the Holocaust: Literary Testimonies*. London, 2018.

Hutton, Margaret-Anne. *Testimony from the Nazi Camps: French Women's Voices*. London, 2005.

Irmingard Prinzessin von Bayern. *Jugend-Erinnerungen 1923–1950*. St. Ottilien, 2000.

Joos, Joseph. *Leben auf Widerruf. Begegnungen und Beobachtungen im K.Z. Dachau 1941–1945*. Olten, 1946.

Justman, Zuzana. "My Terezín Diary: And What I Did Not Write About." *New Yorker*, 16 September 2019.

Kennedy, Rosanne. "Memory, History and the Law: Testimony and Collective Memory in Holocaust and Stolen Generation Trials." In Joan Tumblety, ed., *Memory and History: Understanding Memory as Source and Subject*, 58–68. London, 2013.

Kitchen, Martin. *The Coming of Austro-Fascism*. New York, 2016; first ed. 1980.

Klee, Ernst, Willi Dresser, and Volker Riess, eds. *The Good Old Days: The Holocaust as Seen by Its Perpetrators and Bystanders*. New York, 1991.

Klemperer, Victor. *The Language of the Third Reich: LTI, Lingua Tertii Imperii. A Philologist's Notebook*. London, 2006.

Kogon, Eugen. *The Theory and Practice of Hell: The German Concentration Camps and the System behind Them.* New York, 2006; first published 1946.

Koop, Volker. *In Hitler's Hand: Sonder- und Ehrenhäftlinge der SS.* Weimar, 2010.

Kuon, Peter. "L'écrit reste. L'écrit est une trace, tandis que les paroles s'envolent": On the Hermeneutics of Holocaust Survivor Memories." In Michaela Wolf, ed., *Interpreting in Nazi Concentration Camps,* 149–60. New York, 2016.

Langer, Lawrence. *Holocaust Testimonies: The Ruins of Memory.* New Haven, 1993.

Laqueur, Renata. *Schreiben im KZ. Tagebücher 1940–45.* Bremen, 1992.

Latour, Bruno. "Why Has Critique Run Out of Steam? From Matters of Fact to Matters of Concern." *Critical Inquiry* 30 (2004): 225–48.

Lefcourt, Herbert. *Humor: The Psychology of Living Buoyantly.* New York, 2001.

Lenz, John. *Christ in Dachau or Christ Victorious.* Vienna, 1960.

Levi, Primo. *The Drowned and the Saved.* New York, 1988.

– *Survival in Auschwitz: The Nazi Assault on Humanity.* New York, 1961.

Liebling, Alison, and Maruna Shadd, eds. *The Effects of Imprisonment.* Portland, Oregon, 2005.

Low, Alfred. *The Anschluss Movement, 1931–1938 and the Great Powers.* New York, 1985.

Marcus, Paul. *Autonomy in the Extreme Situation: Bruno Bettelheim, the Nazi Concentration Camps and the Mass Society.* Westport, CT, 1999.

McConkey, James. *The Making of Memory.* New York, 1996.

Michel, Henri. *Oranien-Sachsenhausen: KZ-Erinnerungen und Hungermarsch in die Freiheit eines politischen Gefangenen.* Eupen, 1985.

Morsch, Günter, and Astrid Ley, eds. *Sachsenhausen Concentration Camp, 1936–1945: Events and Developments.* Berlin, 2008.

Nansen, Odd. *From Day to Day: One Man's Diary of Survival in Nazi Concentration Camps.* Nashville, 2016.

Naujoks, Harry. *Mein Leben im KZ Sachsenhausen.* Cologne, 1987.

Neurath, Paul. *The Society of Terror: Inside the Dachau and Buchenwald Concentration Camps.* London, 2005.

Niemöller, Martin. *Exile in the Fatherland: Martin Niemöller's Letters from Moabit Prison.* Grand Rapids, MI, 1986.

Nikulin, Dmitri, ed. *Memory: A History.* New York, 2015.

Olick, Jeffrey. "Collective Memory: The Two Cultures." *Sociological Theory* 17, no. 3 (1999): 333–48.

Pätzold, Kurt. "Häftlingsgesellschaft." In Wolfgang Benz and Barbara Distel, eds. *Der Ort des Terrors: Geschichte der nationalsozialistischen Konzentrationslager,* vol. 3, 110–25. Munich, 2006.

Payne-Best, Sigismund. *The Venlo Incident.* London, 1950.

– *War Crimes: Account by Sigismund Payne Best of Imprisonment in Sachsenhausen Concentration Camp.* Published by Great Britain Foreign Office. Unregistered Papers Fo. 1093.

Petropoulos, Jonathan. *The Princes of Hessen in Nazi Germany.* New York, 2006.

Pillbeam, Pamela. *The Middle Classes in Europe, 1789–1914: France, Germany, Italy and Russia.* London, 1990.

Pingel, Frank "Social Life in an Unsocial Environment." In Jane Caplan and Nikolaus Wachsmann, eds., *Concentration Camps in Nazi Germany: The New Histories,* 58–81. London, 2010.

Pinto, Antonio Costa, ed. *Corporatism and Fascism: The Corporatist Wave in Europe.* New York, 2017.

Pollock, Griselda, and Max Silverman, eds. *Concentrationary Memories, Totalitarian Terror and Cultural Resistance.* New York, 2014.

Pourdieu, Pierre. "The Forms of Capital." In James Richardson, ed., *Handbook of Research for the Sociology of Education,* 241–58. New York, 1986.

Radstone, Susannah, and Katharine Hodgkins, eds. *Regimes of Memory.* London, 2003.

Rahe, Thomas. "Die Bedeutung von Religion und Religiosität in den nationalsozialistischen Konzentrationslagern." In Ulrich Herbert, Karin Orth, and Christoph Dieckmann, eds., *Die nationalsozialistischen Konzentrationslager: Entwicklung und Struktur,* vol. 2, 1006–22. Göttingen, 1998.

Rathkolb, Oliver. "Elimination of Austro-Fascists from Posts of Influence: US-Nachkriegsplanungen für eine umfassende Entfaschisierung." In Ilse Reiter-Zatloukal, Christiane Rothländer, and Pia Schölnberger, eds., *Österreich 1933–1938: Interdisziplinäre Annäherungen an das Dollfuss-/Schuschnigg-Regime,* 273–84. Vienna, 2012.

Reiter-Zatloukal, Ilse, Christiane Rothländer, and Pia Schölnberger, eds. *Österreich 1933–1938: Interdisziplinäre Annäherungen an das Dollfuss-/Schuschnigg-Regime.* Vienna, 2012.

Ricoeur, Paul. *Memory, History, Forgetting.* Chicago, 2006.

Rose, Steven. *The Making of Memory.* London, 2003.

Rosenbaum, Eli. *Betrayal: The Untold Story of the Kurt Waldheim Investigation and Cover-Up.* New York, 1993.

Rosenfeld, Alvin. *A Double Dying: Reflections on Holocaust Literature.* Bloomington, 1980.

Rothberg, Michael. "Trauma, Memory, Holocaust." In Dmitri Nikulin, ed., *Memory: A History,* 280–91. New York, 2015.

Rozett, Robert. *Approaching the Holocaust: Texts and Contexts.* London, 2005.

Rumpf, Marguerite. *"Pantoffeln gebe ich Dir mit auf den Weg"*: *Schenken in den Konzentrationslagern Ravensbrück, Dachau, Sachsenhausen und Buchenwald*. Würzburg, 2017.

Sachs, Harvey. "Salzburg, Hitler, and Toscanini." *Grand Street* 6 no. 1 (1986): 183–98.

Schlabrendorff, Fabian von. *They Almost Killed Hitler*. New York, 1947.

Schuschnigg, Kurt. *The Brutal Takeover: The Austrian Ex-chancellor's Account of the Anschluss of Austria by Hitler*. London, 1971.

– *Dreimal Österreich*. Vienna, 1938.

– *My Austria*. New York, 1938.

– "Religiöses aus dem KZ: Über Möglichkeiten der Religionsausübung in Gefängnis und KZ." *Schweizerische Kirchenzeitung* 114 (1946): 26–9, 36–7.

– *Ein Requiem in Rot-Weiss-Rot: Aufzeichnungen des Häftlings Dr. Auster*. Zurich, 1946; new edition Vienna, 1978, under the title *Ein Requiem in Rot-Weiss-Rot*; English edition New York, 1946, under the title *Austrian Requiem*.

– *Sofort Vernichten: Die vertraulichen Briefe Kurt und Vera von Schuschniggs 1938–1945*. Ed. Dieter Binder and Heinrich Schuschnigg. Vienna, 1997.

– Unpublished letters in IFZG, University of Vienna, inv. 954.

Schuschnigg, Kurt, Jr. *When Hitler Took Austria: A Memory of Heroic Faith by the Chancellor's Son*. San Francisco, 2008.

Seela, Torsten. *Bücher und Bibliotheken in nationalsozialistischen Konzentrationslagern*. Munich, 1992.

Sheridon, R.K. *Kurt von Schuschnigg: A Tribute*. London, 1942.

Seigel, Jerrold. *Modernity and Bourgeois Life: Society, Politics, and Culture in England, France and Germany since 1750*. New York, 2012.

Shirer, William. *Berlin Diary: The Journal of a Foreign Correspondent*. New York, 1942.

Siccardi, Cristina. *Mafalda di Savoia: Dalla reggia al lager di Buchenwald*. Milan, 1999.

Sofsky, Wolfgang. *The Order of Terror: The Concentration Camp*. Princeton, 1997.

Speer, Albert. *Inside the Third Reich: Memoirs*. New York, 1970.

Spitzy, Reinhard. *How We Squandered the Reich*. Wilby Hall, 1997; first published in German 1986.

Stier, Oren Baruch, and Shawn Landres, eds. *Religion, Violence, Memory, and Place*. Bloomington, IN, 2006.

Stone, Dan. *The Holocaust and Historical Methodology*. New York, 2012.

– *The Holocaust, Fascism, and Memoir: Essays in the History of Ideas*. London, 2013.

Streibel, Robert, and Hans Schafranek, eds. *Strategie des Überlebens: Häftlingsgesellschaften im KZ und Gulag*. Vienna, 1996.

Suderland, Maja. *Inside Concentration Camps: Social Life at the Extremes*. Cambridge, 2013.

Szepansky, Wolfgang. *Dennoch ging ich diesen Weg*. Berlin, 1985.

Talos, Emmerich. *Sozialpolitik im Austrofaschismus*. Vienna, 2005.

Thorpe, Julie. *Pan-Germanism and the Austrofascist State, 1933–1938*. Manchester, 2011.

Tortell, Philippe, Mark Turin, and Margot Young, eds. *Memory*. Vancouver, 2018.

Vermehren, Isa. *Reise durch den letzten Akt. Ravensbrück, Buchenwald, Dachau: Eine Frau berichtet*. Hamburg, 1979; first edition 1949.

Verosta, Stephan. *Die internationale Stellung Österreichs 1938–1947*. Vienna, 1947.

Wachsmann, Nikolaus. *KL: A History of the Nazi Concentration Camps*. New York, 2015.

Waldheim, Kurt. *In the Eye of the Storm: A Memoir*. Bethesda, 1986.

Wall, Tom. *Dachau to Dolomites: The Irishmen, Himmler's Special Prisoners and the End of World War II*. Newbridge, 2019.

Weiss-Rüthel, Arnold. *Nacht und Nebel: Ein Sachsenhausen-Buch*. Berlin, 1949.

Wenninger, Florian. "Austrian Missions – Das Problem der politischen Äquidistanz der Forschung am Beispiel Austrofaschismus." In Ilse Reiter-Zatloukal et al., eds., *Österreich 1933–1938: Interdisziplinäre Annäherungen an das Dollfuss-/Schuschnigg-Regime*, 257–69. Vienna, 2012.

Widdig, Bernd. *Culture and Inflation in Weimar Germany*. Berkeley, 2001.

Wiechert, Ernst. *Sämtliche Werke*, vol. 10. Vienna, 1957.

Willmitzer, Christa, and Peter Willmitzer. *Deckname "Betti Gerber": Vom Widerstand in Neuhausen zur KZ-Gedenkstätte Dachau. Otto Kohlhofer 1915–1988*. Munich, 2006.

Wohnout, Helmut. "A Chancellorial Dictatorship with a 'Corporative' Pretext: The Austrian Constitution between 1934 and 1938. In Günter Bischof, Anton Pelinka, and Alexander Lassner, eds., *The Dollfuss/Schuschnigg Era in Austria: A Reassessment*. New Brunswick, NJ, 2003.

Wolf, Michaela, ed. *Interpreting in Nazi Concentration Camps*. New York, 2016.

Wunderlich, Rudolf. *Die Aufzeichnungen des KZ-Häftlings Rudolf Wunderlich*. Ed. Joachim S. Hohmann and Günther Wieland. Frankfurt, 1997.

Media

Interview with Heinrich Schuschnigg, nephew of Kurt Schuschnigg, by Konrad Kramar in *Der Kurier*, 19 April 2018.

Interview with members of the Wittelbacher family in a radio program broadcast by BR Bayern, 20 March 2011. "Die dunklen Jahre Wittelbachs," by Thomas Muggenthaler with Franz von Bayern and his sisters Marie Charlotte and Marie Gabriele.

Documentary *Wir, Geiseln der SS,* written by Christian Frey, produced by
Reinhardt Beetz, 2015.

Websites

http://www.mythoselser.de/niederdorf.htm: Die Befreiung der Sippenhäftlinge
in Südtirol.

https://history.state.gov/historicaldocuments/frus1938v01/d489:
Memorandum of the American Consul General J.C. Wiley in Vienna 1938
re information received from Vera Schuschnigg on August 10 1938.

Rudolf Meier et al. *Buchenwald-Spuren: Verflechtungen des Konzentrationslagers mit
Weimar und Umgebung,* findings of a seminar published online at https://
www.metallsicherungsanlagen.de/stellenausschreibung/zeitgeschichte
-standort/.

https://www.jewishgen.org/ForgottenCamps/Camps/SachsenhausenEng.html.

Index